Learning iOS
Design

Addison-Wesley Learning Series

LEARNING JavaScript
A Hands-On Guide to the Fundamentals of Modern JavaScript

TIM WRIGHT

LEARNING OBJECTIVE-C 2.0
A Hands-on Guide to Objective-C for Mac and iOS Developers

SECOND EDITION

ROBERT CLAIR

LEARNING Cocos2D
Hands-On Guide to Building iOS Games with Cocos2D, Box2D, and Chipmunk

ROD STROUGO
RAY WENDERLICH

LEARNING ANDROID GAME PROGRAMMING
A Hands-On Guide to Building Your First Android Game

RICK ROGERS

✦Addison-Wesley

Visit **informit.com/learningseries** for a complete list of available publications.

The **Addison-Wesley Learning Series** is a collection of hands-on programming guides that help you quickly learn a new technology or language so you can apply what you've learned right away.

Each title comes with sample code for the application or applications built in the text. This code is fully annotated and can be reused in your own projects with no strings attached. Many chapters end with a series of exercises to encourage you to reexamine what you have just learned, and to tweak or adjust the code as a way of learning.

Titles in this series take a simple approach: they get you going right away and leave you with the ability to walk off and build your own application and apply the language or technology to whatever you are working on.

✦Addison-Wesley   **informIT** the trusted technology learning source | Safari Books Online

Learning iOS Design

A Hands-On Guide for Programmers and Designers

William Van Hecke

✦Addison-Wesley

Upper Saddle River, NJ • Boston • Indianapolis • San Francisco
New York • Toronto • Montreal • London • Munich • Paris • Madrid
Capetown • Sydney • Tokyo • Singapore • Mexico City

Many of the designations used by manufacturers and sellers to distinguish their products are claimed as trademarks. Where those designations appear in this book, and the publisher was aware of a trademark claim, the designations have been printed with initial capital letters or in all capitals.

The author and publisher have taken care in the preparation of this book, but make no expressed or implied warranty of any kind and assume no responsibility for errors or omissions. No liability is assumed for incidental or consequential damages in connection with or arising out of the use of the information or programs contained herein.

The publisher offers excellent discounts on this book when ordered in quantity for bulk purchases or special sales, which may include electronic versions and/or custom covers and content particular to your business, training goals, marketing focus, and branding interests. For more information, please contact:

U.S. Corporate and Government Sales
(800) 382-3419
corpsales@pearsontechgroup.com

For sales outside the United States, please contact:

International Sales
international@pearsoned.com

Visit us on the Web: informit.com/aw

Library of Congress Cataloging-in-Publication Data

Van Hecke, William.
   Learning iOS design : a hands-on guide for programmers and designers / William Van Hecke.
        pages cm
   Includes index.
   ISBN-13: 978-0-321-88749-8 (pbk. : alk. paper)
   ISBN-10: 0-321-88749-2 (pbk. : alk.paper)
  1. iOS (Electronic resource) 2. Application software—Development. 3. iPad (Computer)—Programming. 4. iPhone (Smartphone)—Programming. I. Title.
   QA76.774.I67V36 2013
   004.167—dc23

                                        2013010043

ISBN-13: 978-0-321-88749-8
ISBN-10:   0-321-88749-2
Text printed in the United States on recycled paper at RR Donnelley in Crawfordsville, Indiana.
First printing, June 2013

Editor-in-Chief
Mark L. Taub

Senior Acquisitions Editor
Trina MacDonald

Development Editor
Sheri Cain

Managing Editor
John Fuller

Full-Service Production Manager
Julie B. Nahil

Project Editor
Anna Popick

Copy Editor
Betsy Hardinger

Indexer
Jack Lewis

Proofreader
Anna Popick

Technical Reviewers
Jon Bell
Jim Correia
Lukas Mathis

Editorial Assistant
Olivia Basegio

Cover Designer
Chuti Prasertsith

Compositor
Rob Mauhar

❖

To Buzz and CeeCee; Touichi and Risako

❖

Contents at a Glance

Contents

xvi   Contents

Foreword

When Apple introduced Mac OS X, Mac users' feelings were ambivalent. Sure, this looked like a fantastic operating system, but a huge part of what made the Mac unique was its software. Photoshop, Illustrator, Claris Works, MacPaint—these were the reasons we used Macs. And with Mac OS X, all of these applications effectively stopped working. There were few native applications for Mac OS X, and fewer still that weren't horrible.

There was, however, one company that consistently developed fantastic software for Mac OS X right from the start. And they kept doing it. For the last decade, The Omni Group has been a sure bet for quality products. Applications like OmniGraffle combine ease of use and sheer power in a way that is unique, yet feels completely natural. On the one hand, these applications are incredibly accessible. It takes very little to create fantastic output. On the other hand, they have great depth. Recently, the Omni Group has expanded their reach to iOS, and they've done something almost nobody else outside of Apple has achieved: they've brought their applications to the iPad in a way that makes them feel native to these portable touchscreen devices, but doesn't diminish their power and depth.

I'm probably not the only designer who has more than once looked at applications like OmniOutliner, OmniGraffle, or the somewhat exorbitantly named OmniGraph-Sketcher and wondered to themselves: How do they do it? How do these people consistently create software that seems to effortlessly present incredibly powerful features in a way that is easily accessible, and a pleasure to use? And even more puzzling, how do they manage to achieve this feat on iOS, a platform famous for its abundance of shallow, poorly designed, one-trick-pony, cash-grab apps?

Well, today's your lucky day, because you're holding the answer to this question in your hands. My friend Bill, who wrote this book, happens to be Omni's User Experience Lead. And he's lifting his kilt, just for you.

I first consciously heard of Bill when he became Internet-famous for talking about Omni's 1:1 replicas of iPads made from wood, cardboard, Plexiglas, and 3-D-printed parts. Who would want to make 1:1 replicas of iPads? Well, Apple had announced the iPad, but had not yet started shipping it. Having already started designing apps for the iPad, Bill's team needed to get an idea for how these apps would feel on an actual device. At this point, less dedicated people would just postpone the whole thing for a few months. But not Bill's team. They went ahead and made their own iPads.

Most UX designers eventually manage to come up with a design that works well. It's this kind of relentless dedication to detail, this kind of work ethic, though, that is the difference between a designer who can come up with a good design, and one who will come up with a mind-blowingly awesome design.

But there's something else that makes Bill unique among his peers. Any designer will tell you that their goal is to make the product they're working on beautiful and easy to use and efficient and pleasant. But Bill goes one step further. His goal isn't just to make apps user-friendly, but to touch the user's soul, to help people make more beautiful things, be more successful, and be happier. In one of his presentations, he recounts how one man converted his classic VW Beetle into an electric car with the help of OmniGraffle. To Bill, that's the ultimate goal. Software design isn't just about making an application easy to use, it's about making the application have a positive impact on people's lives. It's about helping people be better.

This book contains everything you need to know to create awesome, life-altering applications, just like Omni's. While it's targeted at iOS designers, you're going to learn a lot from reading this book regardless of the platform you design for. I pride myself on knowing a lot about design, but when reading this book, I probably didn't encounter a single page that didn't offer at least one interesting idea, new concept, or clever design technique. From learning how to make your application more forgiving to a section on how pricing influences how people perceive your app (yep, its price is part of the app's design), you're in for a treat.

Even better, this book doesn't just offer invaluable content that will forever change the way you design applications, it's also written in a way that prevents you from putting it down. So grab a hot cup of cocoa, put on your favorite music, and settle down into your most comfortable chair, my friend, because you'll be sitting here, staring at this book, for quite a while.

Enjoy it.

—Lukas Mathis, ignorethecode.net; author of *Designed for Use: Create Usable Interfaces for Applications and the Web* (Pragmatic Bookshelf, 2011)
   March 2013

Preface

Hello

It took a while for the world to notice, but design really matters.

A perfect story of the power of design can be found by traveling back to April 2007 to eavesdrop on a chat with Microsoft CEO Steve Ballmer. Apple's Steve Jobs had announced the iPhone that January, and everyone had had a good while to process the announcement and decide what they thought of it. Ballmer, in an interview with *USA Today,* opined on the iPhone's chances to make a dent in the well-populated smartphone market: "There's no chance that the iPhone is going to get any significant market share. No chance."

I'm not normally one to indulge in schadenfreude, but the wrongness of that prediction is too illuminating to ignore. iPhone went on to become an icon that redefined the public's concept of what a mobile phone is, and nearly every "smartphone" on the market takes inspiration from it. Its sibling, iPad, finally popularized the stagnant tablet concept and is on its way to replacing the traditional desktop or notebook computer for millions. iPhone and iPad each own about half of the market share of their respective markets. The App Store model has redefined the way people buy software and has paid out more than $7 billion to third-party developers. As of the beginning of 2013, nearly half a billion iOS devices have been sold.

Why? How did iOS become so successful? What did Ballmer and the rest of the early-2007 iPhone scoffers miss? Ask any authority who followed the story closely to pick one word to describe Apple's advantage, and they'll say *design*. (Some cynics might say *marketing*, but they're wrong.)

iOS is arguably the first technology platform to truly put design first. Instead of the puffed-up and bulleted feature lists, the contortions to accommodate legacy systems, the assumptions about how a phone was supposed to look or behave, and the obsession with being the first to the market, iPhone prioritized beauty, responsiveness, and fun. (And anything that Apple couldn't get just right was omitted until they could.) This view of design is about creating happiness, about cultivating a relationship with the user, about imagining the most positive *user experience* possible and then doing whatever it takes to produce that imagined outcome.

You could almost say that iPhone refused to compromise on its user experience. But as this book argues, all designs are compromises. Surely, countless tradeoffs and tough decisions were made in the process of bringing iOS into being. But what's important is that wherever possible, those compromises erred on the side of paying attention to detail, abandoning conventional wisdom, and putting in more work to make users happier.

Not solely because of Apple and iOS, but in large part, the world is learning that design counts. It's getting harder to compete without good design. It's harder to find good designers than it is to find good engineers (and that itself is pretty hard). Well-designed software really can improve people's lives, help them be more productive, and yes, make them happy. This book aims to give you the practices, examples, and advice you need to make it happen yourself.

You're a Designer

Design is deciding how a thing should be. In every act of design, that decision-making is done to accommodate constraints and to satisfy the needs of some audience or "user." The needs are paramount, because an artifact that doesn't do anything useful for anyone is more a piece of art than a design. And the constraints are your friends, because they narrow the space of possibilities, making your job much more approachable. Almost everything you think about and do as a designer can be narrowed down to these concepts: How are you serving the needs of the user? How are you working within the constraints?

Everything artificial was designed by someone. Most of the time you don't think about the people who decided how the things around us should be: the height of a chair's seat, the shape of a battery charger, the hem of a blanket. That blissful ignorance is the goal of many designers. If people don't think about the design of an object, the designer has probably done a fantastic job. More than two thousand years ago, Ovid said it like this: *Si latet, ars prodest.* If the art is concealed, it succeeds. That's one to print and hang on your wall.

If you've ever made something, then you're a designer. Ever built a couch fort? Arranged some flowers in a vase? Sketched a map for someone? Whether or not you thought very much about it, whether or not you followed well-researched principles, you designed that thing. That's design, with a lowercase *d.* You could take that approach to designing an iOS app, but the result isn't likely to be compelling. Books like this one aim to help you do Design with a capital *D.* That means absorbing and imagining as much as you can about how things could be better. It means making the smartest, most informed decisions possible about the needs and constraints involved. And it almost always means creating plans, sketches, and models along the way to a final product. The good news is that you can get there from here, one step at a time, always experimenting and learning as you go.

Meet the Book

This book introduces and explores the topic of designing iOS apps, even if you don't consider yourself a designer (yet). Even if you've never taken an art or design course, if you consider yourself to have more of an engineering or analytical mind than a creative one, or if you're mystified by what actually goes on in the process of design, you're very welcome here.

At conferences, I've presented the topic of design to a largely engineering-minded audience. Lots of programmers know that they should care about design, but the practice of design seems from the outside to be mysterious or even arbitrary, leaving them disillusioned or apathetic about it. But after some demystification and conversation, some folks have told me that they finally get why design is important and how they can think about it systematically.

This book presents the art and science of design in an accessible, sensible way.

Part I: Turning Ideas into Software steps through the phases of design, turning a vague idea for an app into a fully fleshed-out design. It goes from outlines to sketches to wireframes to mockups and prototypes. Each step of the way, you'll find advice about how to think carefully, critically, and cleverly about your project. Each chapter concludes with exercises conceived to encourage you in planning the design of your own app. Part I includes the following seven chapters.

- **Chapter 1: The Outlines**—This is all about planning, writing things down, and making sense of your app idea. You'll learn about the ways you can use structured thinking and writing to figure out what your app is about and stay on track throughout the project.

- **Chapter 2: The Sketches**—Sketching is the central activity of design. It's all about getting ideas out there and seeing where they lead. You can never know the merits of an idea until it's on a page, a whiteboard, or a screen. This chapter will help you sketch with the right blend of adventurousness and discipline.

- **Chapter 3: Getting Familiar with iOS**—Understanding the constraints of the platform is crucial. iOS offers a versatile kit for building interfaces and experiences; you should know it well enough to decide when to take advantage of it and when to diverge from it.

- **Chapter 4: The Wireframes**—Eventually you need to turn your sketches into precise, screen-by-screen definitions of how the app should be organized. A wireframe is a document that specifies layout and navigation without getting bogged down in pixel-perfect styling just yet.

- **Chapter 5: The Mockups**—It's not the only concern of design by far, but it matters what your application looks like on the surface. In this chapter you'll break out the graphics apps and learn how to assemble beautiful assets into a convincing, pleasant whole.

- **Chapter 6: The Prototypes**—Sometimes a static drawing of an interface is not enough. You need to know how it behaves. This chapter is all about simulating and testing the interactions that make up your app.

- **Chapter 7: Going Cross-Platform**—Plenty of apps exist not as completely standalone experiences, but as parts of a multiplatform suite. This chapter explores the concerns you'll need to deal with if you want to build the same app for more than one device. It uses an app that appears on iPhone, iPad, and Mac as a case study to illustrate how a single idea can wear three different interfaces.

Part II: Principles presents universal principles that apply to any design and that you should follow if you want to craft an effective app that people will appreciate and even love. To make sure your app works on every level, each chapter in this part is based on one of the three levels of cognition identified by psychologist Donald Norman. Many of these principles are applicable to all software design, but here they're tailored to the strengths and challenges of iOS. The exercises for each chapter present sample situations to help you learn how to apply each principle.

- **Chapter 8: The Graceful Interface**—This chapter examines the visceral level of cognition, which relates to the way people feel from instant to instant as they interact with software. It deals with things like touch input, timing, and feel. Most of the concerns here are subconscious. Users may not notice them, but they subtly affect how pleasant the software is to use.

- **Chapter 9: The Gracious Interface**—Here you'll learn about concerns at the behavioral level of cognition. That means how users make decisions moment to moment and how the app communicates possibilities and status. The chapter also discusses how the app can encourage a sense of adventure so that users feel welcome and safe as they explore its possibilities.

- **Chapter 10: The Whole Experience**—The biggest, vaguest, most intangible, and most important level of cognition is the reflective level. This chapter explains how people feel about your app in the long run: whether they rate it well, whether they recommend it to friends, whether they respect you as a developer, and whether they'd buy from you again. Happiness is the ultimate goal.

Part III: Finding Equilibrium is meant to function as a reference, inspiration, and exploratory guide to the various decision points you may encounter in designing an app. It embraces the concept that all designs are compromises and that many decisions have no single correct answer. This means that many answers to the same design problem can coexist, and every design, no matter how unfashionable or unsophisticated it seems, has something to teach (a fact that many critics seem to forget). You can look at each chapter's opposed approaches as a sort of slider control, with a continuum of answers between the extremes at either end. For each challenge, a smart designer like you should seek an answer that works best for your app's unique philosophy. Over time you may find yourself preferring one side of a given slider over the other. Maybe you like to err on the side of focused rather than versatile. Or perhaps you'd rather seek the Aristotelian golden mean, straight down the middle. That's great. That's what it means to have a style. Each type of decision is illustrated by examples of different solutions to the same problem, depending on the angle you prefer. The exercises encourage you to find your own favorite solution for a situation that may have several possible answers.

- **Chapter 11: Focused and Versatile**—One of the biggest decisions you need to make about your app is its scope. Do you want to do one thing flawlessly, or many things competently? What's feasible depends on the resources available and your ability to be aggressive about defining what you expect of the project.

- **Chapter 12: Quiet and Forthcoming**—When most people talk about a design being "simple," what they usually mean is that it's in good order and presents an understandable amount of information and control at once. In contrast, designs feel empowering when they simultaneously present as much as possible. This chapter describes how to control the apparent simplicity of your app from screen to screen, depending on the emotion you prefer to evoke.

- **Chapter 13: Friction and Guidance**—Part of the job of a software designer is to make many things possible, but also to gently guide people through an experience. This chapter is about the ways an interface puts down grooves that encourage a user to move this way or that way next, or slow down before taking the next step.

- **Chapter 14: Consistency and Specialization**—Differentiating yourself from the rest of the apps out there is both an advantage and a risk. When you think of well-designed apps, the examples that come readily to mind are the ones that break from convention and get away with it. But respecting the established guidelines is usually the wiser path. This chapter will help you decide when to stick to the script and when to diverge.

- **Chapter 15: Rich and Plain**—The visual styling of an app is the most conspicuous outward manifestation of its design. Independent of its functionality, your app can look extravagant or subdued, lifelike or digital. This chapter will help you tune the depth, color, and realism of your interface to set its tone and personality.

Meet the Web Site

The web site for this book is **http://learningiosdesign.com**. There, you will find resources such as the Photoshop and OmniGraffle source files for the examples given throughout the book. You can also offer feedback about the book and find updates of its content.

You and Your Team

You can follow this book as you work on your own app idea, especially by working through the practices described in Part I. Even if you don't yet have an app project, or if your app already exists and you want to revise it for a new version, you should be able to benefit from the book. Parts II and III are compatible with dipping into for inspiration or advice.

From time to time, the book may talk as if you are a designer working with a software engineer or a team of engineers. That of course doesn't need to be the case. Maybe you're one of that noble species, the lone programmer/designer hybrid. Maybe you're a product manager looking to understand design better. It doesn't really matter; whenever this book mentions "your engineers," it's fine if that means you!

Art/Science Duality

Design is full of what are called "wicked problems": they're difficult to define, they're impossible to come up with definitive answers to, and they're never finished. That's likely to spook some people, but it's also what makes design so much *fun*. You never know what you're going to get. There's always some way to improve on your work. Everything is a matter of taste, and yet some answers are unequivocally better than others. There's no recipe, and yet there are morsels of wisdom and inspiration to be found everywhere.

Design is an art. And it's a science. And it's neither. Steve Jobs liked to say that what Apple does falls "at the intersection of technology and liberal arts." You may find your team arguing about how to make a decision. One side is showing numbers; usability test metrics clearly indicate that design *A* is more efficient than design *B*. The other side is arguing that based on aesthetics, design *A* just doesn't *feel* right. Who wins? Maybe it's one of those two options; maybe it's a third, new option. Figuring it out is part of the thrill of design.

You could take a completely scientific approach, refusing to budge on anything until you've run a statistically significant study. You could also take a completely artistic approach, following your muse and composing your personal magnum opus in app form. But you won't get very far with either one alone—data and heart both matter.

Inspiration Is Everywhere

This book can give you specific advice on specific topics and situations that occur often in the work of designing apps for iOS. But your growth as a designer depends, more than anything else, on your willingness to absorb inspiration from around you. Pay attention to all kinds of design: graphics, interiors, architecture, games, anything. Read widely: psychology, art, history, biology, everything. The most seemingly irrelevant knowledge may end up informing your work as a designer someday, in some oblique way. If you do nothing else, use lots of well-regarded apps and think about what makes them successful. The more you examine and ponder great work of all kinds, the better you'll get at it yourself.

Again, growing as a designer is a lifelong journey, but here is a necessarily short list of reading material to get you started. Some of these books are mentioned again in the chapters where they're especially relevant.

- *Universal Principles of Design* by William Lidwell, Kritina Holden, and Jill Butler—A delightful collection of 125 concepts that apply to all categories of design. Very compatible with flipping through for quick inspiration.

- *The Elements of Typographic Style* by Robert Bringhurst—One of the most carefully built, wisdom-packed books of all time. Yes, Bringhurst will make you knowledgeable about type, but he will also inspire you with his methodical, tasteful approach to design in general.

- *Visual Explanations: Images and Quantities, Evidence and Narrative* by Edward Tufte—Or any of his four main books, really. Tufte tends to lean toward information design for print, but the principles he espouses should be useful to anyone who has any interest in making things understandable and beautiful.

- *Designing Interactions* by Bill Moggridge—This book is a collection of captivating interviews (included on DVD) from original Macintosh software lead Bill Atkinson to legendary game designer Will Wright.

- *Sketching User Experiences: Getting the Design Right and the Right Design* by Bill Buxton—Much of the reverence that technology designers have for the practice of sketching can be credited to Buxton. Sketching is good for your brain and good for your work.

- *The Design of Everyday Things* by Donald Norman—A classic that has stood the test of time. This book pioneered the dissatisfaction with poorly designed experiences and set the stage for a generation of designers to make the world a more agreeable place to live in.

- *Handbook of Usability Testing: How to Plan, Design, and Conduct Effective Tests* by Jeffrey Rubin and Dana Chisnell—If you're interested in the scientific side of design, this is an excellent walkthrough of the procedures and principles of collecting data from a sample of the target audience using your app.

- "The Nature of Design Practice and Implications for Interaction Design Research" by Erik Stolterman—A brief academic paper, chock full of references to other influential papers, about what design really is and how to deal with its complexity.

- *Basic Visual Concepts and Principles: For Artists, Architects and Designers* by Charles Wallschlaeger and Cynthia Busic-Snyder—A solid grounding in perception and the construction of visuals.

- *Revolution in the Valley: The Insanely Great Story of How the Mac Was Made* by Andy Hertzfeld—This book is a treasure trove of firsthand anecdotes about the culture and creativity surrounding the development of the original Macintosh. If it doesn't get you excited about making technology, nothing will.

- *How the Mind Works* by Steven Pinker—A comprehensive tour of what we understand so far about human psychology. Not directly related to software design, but a surprising source of insight into how people think and why design principles work the way they do.

- *Thinking, Fast and Slow* by Daniel Kahneman—An up-to-date psychology book about how people pay attention, judge situations, and make decisions. Another surprisingly enlightening read for science-minded designers.

And here are a couple of things that aren't books.

- "Inventing on Principle"—A one-hour talk by Bret Victor, interaction designer for iPad (among many other impressive accomplishments). Victor has among the most thoughtful and inspirational minds in technology design, and this talk is a fantastic place to start learning from him. This is the sort of talk you'll want to come back to once a year or so.

- Ideo Method Cards—A deck of cards from the legendary product design firm Ideo. Each card describes a "user-centered" practice that can be of use to designers working through an interesting problem. You can casually flip through the deck for ideas, assemble a mini-deck for a given project, or make up your own ways of getting the most out of them.

- Oblique Strategies—A set of cards, each bearing an enigmatic phrase meant to motivate and give direction to a person facing a creative problem. They were originally created by Brian Eno and Peter Schmidt for musicians, but creative people of all kinds have since found them useful for breaking through difficulty. The cards themselves are rare, but plenty of web- and app-based editions are available.

I found these resources helpful. Hopefully some of them will be at home in your own garden of influences and inspirations.

Now…let's make some software.

Acknowledgments

Turns out writing a book is hard! Mountains of thanks go out to all these people for making it possible.

Thanks to Barbara Gavin and Erica Sadun for taking a chance on a shy and inexperienced speaker and inviting me to speak at the Voices That Matter series of conferences, which eventually led to this book project. Thanks to Trina MacDonald at Addison-Wesley for guiding me through the writing process. Thanks to Betsy Hardinger for editing that makes me seem like a much better writer than I am. Monumental thanks to my review board: Lukas Mathis, Jim Correia, and Jon Bell; my trust in their wisdom is the reason I've been able to maintain confidence in this endeavor.

Thanks to all my colleagues at the Omni Group for giving me the chance to make good software and talk to brilliant people all day *as my job*. Every day, I feel as if I'm getting away with something. Thanks to my instructors and classmates at the University of Washington's Human-Centered Design & Engineering professional M.S. program, where I've finally been able to get an academic grounding in the thing I've been doing all this time. Thanks to my dear friends in #rosa for their endless support and encouragement.

Admiration and thanks go to Yasunori Mitsuda, whose Xenogears albums provided the soundtrack that kept me pushing keys. Thanks, too, to the various coffee shops of Seattle, for providing the perfect writing environment.

It seems as if every book's acknowledgments page mentions family members' patience; now I understand why. Copious gratitude and love to my wife, Hiroko, for her steadfast patience and support. Ultimately, everything is thanks to her.

About the Author

Since 2004, **William Van Hecke** has been User Experience Lead at the Omni Group, one of the world's most accomplished and affable Mac and iOS developers. Bill got his start designing software by reverse-engineering his older brother's text adventures in MS Basic on the Macintosh Plus, and then graduated to creating HyperCard games to mail to his cousins on floppy disk.

Bill's primary hobby is hobby-collecting: reading fiction and science; playing bass guitar; appreciating, translating, and developing niche video games; studying the Japanese language; mastering tabletop gaming; and exploring 3-D modeling. You can find Bill on Twitter, prattling on about these topics and more (@fet).

We Want to Hear from You!

As the reader of this book, you are our most important critic and commentator. We value your opinion and want to know what we're doing right, what we could do better, what areas you'd like to see us publish in, and any other words of wisdom you're willing to pass our way.

You can email or write me directly to let us know what you did or didn't like about this book—as well as what we can do to make our books stronger.

Please note that we cannot help you with technical problems related to the topic of this book, and that due to the high volume of mail we receive, we might not be able to reply to every message.

When you write, please be sure to include this book's title and author as well as your name and phone or email address.

Email: trina.macdonald@pearson.com

Mail: Reader Feedback
          Addison-Wesley Learning Series
          800 East 96th Street
          Indianapolis, IN 46240 USA

Reader Services

Visit our web site and register this book at **informit.com/register** for convenient access to any updates, downloads, or errata that might be available for this book.

Part I

Turning Ideas into Software

1

The Outlines

If you want to turn your ideas into software, the first step is to get them out into the open, where you can see them.

It's easy to think you have a mental grasp of everything you need to do throughout the life of a project. But it's even easier to overlook something, to fail to account for all the ramifications of a feature, or otherwise to not fully think through the details. That's fine! Software is complicated. Trying to keep an entire development project in your brain is unrealistic—and unnecessary. Instead, you can craft outlines to get the details written down in a reliable, organized way, freeing your brain to focus on one challenge at a time.

Challenges will come. No matter how thoroughly you think through the project before you get started, you'll find yourself running into unexpected situations and edge cases. That's precisely why being prepared is important: first, you need to work out the big-picture stuff and the common cases. Then you'll have a sensible structure in place to give context to the edge cases and surprises that come along.

Some design challenges are better served by sketching, as you'll see in Chapter 2. But what about ideas that aren't concrete enough to draw? Sometimes you need the grace and power of abstract language, combined with an outline's orderly structure, to figure out where to go next.

The Process: Nonlinear but Orderly

Lots of developers, from hobbyists to seasoned pros, have a habit of following a disorderly (or "organic") development process. The code itself, and the alpha version of the app, *are* the design. Features appear when they become the most interesting thing to work on. No documents exist to describe what the app is now or should be in the future.

In that style of development, it's easy for interface elements to be gradually deposited on the screen like sediment, as new functionality is added. Every time, it seems innocent enough to add just one more little feature, just one more little interface element. Eventually you have an interface design that's characteristic of "mature" desktop applications that have been accumulating features and user interface (UI) elements for decades. For this reason, "mature" often really means "crufty and cumbersome."

The more you can define and outline your app up front, the more easily you can avoid this fate. This book presents the practices of turning ideas into software in a particular order:

- Outline
- Sketch
- Wireframe
- Mockup
- Prototype

But that's only because they need to be presented in *some* order; it doesn't mean you need to follow them in that order. In reality, projects can and do follow a nonlinear and organic process, weaving among those steps via whichever path seems most effective for the design problem at hand—as you can see in Figure 1.1. Even in organizations where the overall software development process is rigid and strict, this sort of frothy, semirandom bouncing around between practices needs to be going on at the lowest levels if you're going to design anything worthwhile.

Writing about Software

You're probably familiar with the classic outline: a hierarchical, indented list of items. It's a fantastic way to keep track of projects, and there are plenty of apps out there for

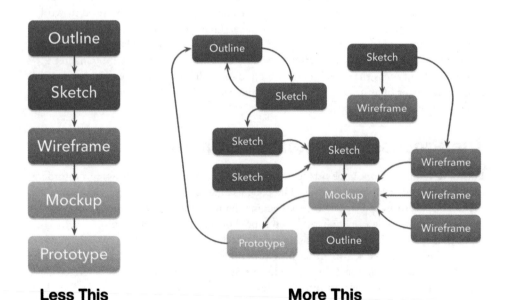

Figure 1.1   The swirling chaos of a software design project

keeping such lists. While reading this chapter, though, think about all the different practices there are for writing about software design and development:

- **Traditional outlines** are great for exploring ideas in your initial mental sweep, constructing requirements documents, and communicating complicated ideas to a team. At any point in a project, if you find yourself up against a complex problem, consider building a traditional outline to make sense of it. Folks with analytical minds often feel that outlines are the most natural way for them to organize information. You'll find a number of excellent outlining applications for Mac and iPad that make it easy.

- **Plain text files** are a nice, simple way of jotting down ideas and things to consider. But it's harder to make text files hierarchical and clearly itemized. They're easy to share, especially if you keep them in sync via a cloud service.

- **Tasks in a to-do application** can keep you on track once you've figured out what needs to be done. They tend to be ephemeral and personal, though, rather than providing a team with a comprehensive and definitive record of everything about a topic.

- **Tickets in a bug-tracking database** make it easier for everyone on a team to see the current understanding of a problem, the discussions that have happened around it, and the proposed solution. But they're not great at giving a big-picture view; you can't rely on bug tracking to help you understand anything bigger than an individual problem.

- **Paper and whiteboards** are perfect for quick, in-person planning on your own or while meeting with someone else. And there is still no easier way to gracefully combine outlining and sketching. Once you're finished with a whiteboard session, you can take a photo for safekeeping, in case you ever wonder, "What were we thinking in that meeting?"

- **Plans in project-management software** are a formal way of keeping track of what needs to be done. For project managers and other boss types, they can be invaluable for keeping an eye on the big picture, but they're not very useful for focusing on the decision-to-decision detail of a tough design problem.

- A **design specification**, or "spec," is a definitive, complete description of a team's plans and intentions for a piece of software. Depending on how formal your organization and your processes are, you might even be required to follow the IEEE 1016 standard for this kind of document.

Most likely, you will find yourself using some combination of these tools to keep track of the various levels of detail in your design project: attaching text files to bug reports, transcribing photos of whiteboard lists into specification outlines, and so on. Which ones you prefer will depend on how much detail you need, whether you're working with a team, and which apps you're comfortable using.

What's important is to put together comprehensive, itemized lists of things that need to be considered for your project, from the grandest goals to the tiniest, hair-splittingest details. Some outlines may be hundreds of items long, such as a write-up of all the components in the architecture of a complex app. Others may be just a handful of highly precise decisions that took hours of agonizing to get just right.

Even if you don't prepare formal specs, it's often invaluable to have a single document (or set of documents), as casual or as formal as you want, to fully describe the team's understanding of what it is they're building. (And it's helpful even if you're not working with a team!) Keep these specs checked in to your version control system just like source code, and keep them up-to-date.

Also keep the designs for—and the discussions about—rejected ideas, because they illustrate why you didn't go with a certain seemingly appealing choice. Rejected ideas keep you from having the same arguments over and over again, and they become part of the "antirequirements" of the app, described later. Treating the software itself as its own spec is a great way to lose track of important work that needs doing, or for people to misunderstand incomplete bits of the software as being intentional and already finalized.

The Mental Sweep

All right, it's time to outline. At the very beginning of a project, it's worthwhile to sweep through your mind for all the features, challenges, ideas, and questions you have. You can get them all out into a flat list and then later organize them into a hierarchy, or you can create the hierarchy as you go. The important part is to make sure you get everything out there. One item that you list might lead to another, and so on, faster than you can keep up. Or you might need to sit and rack your brain for a while to come up with more than a few things.

Here are some suggestions that might knock loose something in your mind as you think about your project:

- General requirements: what is the app for? Who is the audience?
- Antirequirements: what is the app definitely not for? Who isn't part of the audience?
- Initial setup
- Types of data
- Viewing data
- Adding, editing, and deleting data
- Grouping and hierarchy
- Tasks that need to be particularly fast or easy
- Tasks that should probably be supported, but are ancillary to the main purpose
- Import, export, and sharing

- Compatibility with other apps or services
- Preferences

In the end, you should have a list that more or less represents all the initial design problems you'll have to work through, as you currently understand them. Some may turn out not to be necessary, most will turn out to contain many subproblems, and new ones are sure to arise, but at least this first list gives you something to start from.

More Inputs to Outlining

Beyond that mental sweep, there are plenty of sources of input for outlines. When you have a meeting to hammer out details about a feature, an outline is a great way to keep track of all the topics, subtopics, questions, and decisions as you go.

If you have direct access to existing users (because you're working on an existing product) or to members of your target audience, you can gain mountains of invaluable insight from them. After all, you can't be sure to think of everything yourself, and the communication you get from users (support email, reviews, etc.) tends to focus on concrete shortcomings and not on presenting a complete and balanced representation of their needs.

There are a variety of ways to collect insight from the people who'll be using your app. Here are some of the most commonly used ones.

- **Interviews**—This could be a formal process, in which you invite members of your target audience to participate in a structured session that you transcribe and then analyze for data; or it could be as informal as having a few key questions ready when you bump into a user in person at, say, a conference or trade show. If you're good at getting honest answers out of people (something that's easier when they see you as a human being), fifteen minutes of real conversation with a passionate user can be worth more than a whole week of meetings within your organization.

- **Contextual inquiry**—If you're looking to help people do a specific kind of job, this is a fantastic way to get insight into the problems you'll need to deal with. In a contextual inquiry, you visit users as they work, watch them do the work, and get them to explain it to you as thoroughly as possible. If you're interested in this practice, pick up the book *Contextual Design* by Hugh Beyer and Karen Holtzblatt, its pioneers.

- **Competitive analysis**—If you're planning to make something that fits into an existing product space, you definitely have some work to do to see what else is out there. What other apps do the same sort of thing as yours? Why do you think those developers chose the feature sets and made the design decisions they did? What might they know that you don't? And most important, what's so great about your app that someone would want to buy it instead of the other ones out there? Thinking through these questions in a systematic way can give you a much deeper sense of how to differentiate your product and make something truly valuable.

The Ideo Method Cards (described in the Preface) have quite a few more practices you can use to get to the bottom of what your users want and need.

Once you have a product out there in the world being used, outlines and bug databases are good ways to write up user feedback and the results of user research. Even if you read all the emails and tweets about your app and do occasional user testing, you should be fastidious about keeping track of what people tell you that they like and dislike about your app.

When you keep records, you can actually look up whether people tend to complain about how a certain feature works, or whether test participants have trouble with a certain interaction, rather than rely on notoriously selective human memory. But! Always remember that the user feedback you get does not accurately represent the whole of what users think about your app. It represents the subset of experience that could be articulated by the minority of users who had the inclination to write in. You can find much more about the developer-user relationship in Chapter 10, The Whole Experience.

If you've done software development, you're probably familiar with version control systems (like Subversion or Git), which keep a central repository of all the changes the team has made to the source code over time. Version control isn't useful only for code; you can and should keep all your design resources in it, too. Having access to the history of your design thinking is invaluable, and it keeps you from having to track down a lost sketch or design yet another gear icon because you can't find the last one you made.

Version control doesn't have to be intimidating; if you're not the command-line type, you can use a graphical client like the superb Versions, by Black Pixel. (And its visual comparison tool, Kaleidoscope, is great for seeing the differences between versions of a design document.) Another excellent tool is Layer Vault, a web-based versioning system specifically created for designers.

Outlining Requirements

A product requirements document can be a pretty formal thing, used to hold teams accountable for what they eventually ship. An outline is not one of those. If your organization uses them, this initial outline may eventually evolve into an official requirements document. But here it's intended as a tool to help you think, to form an idea of the product in your mind. Nobody outside your design team (very possibly a team of one) needs to see it.

Introducing SnackLog

This book makes extensive use of a hypothetical sample app, SnackLog, a tool for keeping track of purchases that you make throughout the day. Instead of reading a

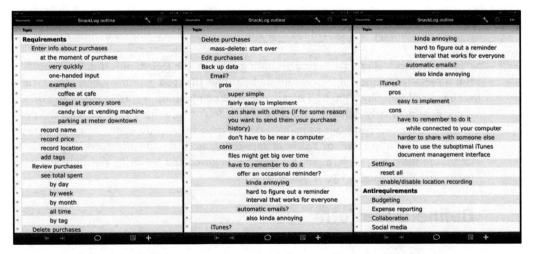

Figure 1.2 Outlining the requirements and antirequirements of SnackLog, our example app

detailed description of the app, though, see how thoroughly you can understand the idea of the app by reading its initial requirements outline, shown in Figure 1.2.

As you may have gathered, the whole point of SnackLog is to easily record casual purchases like coffee and parking, and not to be a full-blown money-management app. The need SnackLog serves is to track small cash purchases you make while you're out and about and stop them from falling through the cracks of your full-fledged budgeting system.

Note that this requirements outline doesn't mention anything about screens, navigation, or the details of how the features work. Instead, it tries to map out *what* the app needs to do; figuring out *how* can come later.

Antirequirements

The App Store lets customers browse all the software available for the platform, all in one place. Being up front about what your app is good at can make all the difference in whether people give it a chance. But it's just as important to differentiate your app from other apps in the store by specifying what it *isn't* for.

There are heaps of expense-report apps for business travelers and money-management apps that aim to balance your entire household budget. SnackLog is neither of those things, and making that clear will help you find your niche and keep you focused as you design. You don't necessarily need to be explicit in your App Store description about what your app doesn't do. But after potential users read your description and see your screenshots, there shouldn't be any doubt in their minds about what your app does. There should be as little chance as possible that people will get the wrong idea about your app and download it when they actually wanted something slightly different.

User feedback is crucial to understanding how people feel about using your app. But some often-requested features might be things that you genuinely don't think fit with your philosophy. Don't go up against your competition feature-for-feature, or implement popularly requested features, if you don't really think they fit with the personality of the app you want to make. Stick to your antirequirements! There is plenty of room in the App Store for a slew of apps that concentrate on alternative approaches to solving the same problem. See Chapter 11, Focused and Versatile, for more about narrowing the features in your product.

Define a Platform

As you think about what your app should be good at and what issues it should avoid, you may find yourself arriving at similar questions time and time again. If you have a good sense of the personality of the app you want to make, you can define a sort of platform—like a political platform—that lists the values, assumptions, and goals at the heart of the app. Then as you make decisions throughout the life of the project, you can refer to that platform to help guide you. For instance, SnackLog might have platform items like these.

- People need to remember what they bought only long enough to put it in their full-fledged budgeting system.
- People make small purchases that usually fit into a short list of categories.
- People tend to make the same small purchases (coffee, snacks, etc.) over and over again.
- If the purchase recording process takes more than 15 seconds, people won't bother with it.
- If people can't easily record a purchase while carrying a hot cup of coffee, they will decide not to use the app rather than put down their drink.

A task-management app might have a platform that included these assertions.

- A to-do list is not a calendar; appointments don't belong in it.
- When planning your to-do lists, you should be able to see all items.
- When working on your to-do lists, you should only see the work that can be done now.
- It should be quick and easy to jot down new to-do items as they come up, without losing your current context.
- View settings shouldn't allow users to easily hide important items from themselves.

If you take a stand on topics like these, you will develop the unique perspective your app offers on the genre. Once you have a platform with some strong assertions that you really believe in, your marketing copy will almost write itself. In fact, you may want to approach platform definition as if you're writing the marketing copy for an app that doesn't yet exist: write the kind of description you'd like your app to have in the App Store before you design it. That helps you think about audiences and goals rather than focus too much on features. The better you define your app's platform, the easier it will be to convince people why it's interesting and special and worth installing.

Listing Ramifications

Note that some of the items in the SnackLog outline are questions. Often, you don't know whether a feature fits until you really think it through. The later phases (sketches, wireframes, mockups, and prototypes) often make the answers clear. But outlines can also help you work through the possible answers (and further questions) that emerge from a major question. Here's an outline exploring the ramifications of two backup options.

- Email?
  - Pros—super simple, fairly easy to implement, can share with others (if for some reason you want to send them your purchase history), don't have to be near a computer
  - Cons—files might get big over time, have to remember to do it (offer an occasional reminder? Kind of annoying. Hard to figure out a reminder interval that works for everyone), automatic emails? (also kind of annoying)
- iTunes?
  - Pros—easy to implement
  - Cons—have to remember to do it (while connected to your computer), harder to share with someone else, have to use the suboptimal iTunes document-management interface

A ramifications outline is a fine way to have a little debate with yourself in order to find all the pros and cons of an idea. After writing up this outline, you might find that email looks like a good option. It isn't perfect, but it looks more appealing than the alternative. For now, that's all you need to know: which direction looks most promising for when you start sketching. If several options look equally promising, you can use sketching to pit them against each other.

iOS and Featurefulness

When considering how featureful an iOS app you want to make, you've got to consider the platform. Part of the magic of iPhone and iPad is that they're aggressive about paring back how much an individual app is expected to do. Because of the platform's touch-based interaction model, relatively limited hardware specs, and intense priority on instant feedback, apps tend to be sleeker and leaner. There is plenty of room for powerful, feature-rich software on iOS, but the typical app is far more streamlined and focused than its desktop equivalent. That focus means you can deliver a precisely tuned experience to your target users without worrying too much about pleasing everyone else.

So for each question you consider, err on the side of omitting features, especially features you can add later. Big, ambitious apps can still be big and ambitious, of course. But they'll be less big and ambitious than if you were creating them for the desktop.

Part III of this book, particularly Chapter 11, goes into great detail about how to decide which features fit into your app and fit onto the iOS platform. When considering whether to include a feature mentioned in your initial outline, you may find useful guidance there.

Reducing Problems

Outlines also come in handy for answering a key design question: are these actually the same thing? A huge part of design is figuring out what the product really is and how all its parts fit together. Can two needs actually be served with a single feature? Is a certain feature trying to do too much, and would it be smoother if it were broken into more than one feature? Much of your personal style as a designer is defined by how aggressive you are in consolidating or dividing elements of your app, so be ready to spend a lot of time thinking about it.

Say you're considering whether to include both tagging and multiple user support in your design for SnackLog. As you organize your outline, you find that they both seem to fit under "categorization." That's a sign they might be candidates for consolidation. Think about what, if anything, makes them different. They both require you to set up and apply labels to purchases. They are both things you might want to filter or search on while browsing purchases. Looking pretty similar so far.

There are a couple of multiuser support features you can rule out, because they don't seem to belong on iOS—for instance, hiding one user's purchases from the other users. iOS devices are generally used by one person. If there are multiple people keeping track of information with one device, they are very likely to be family members and don't mind sharing information. Ultimately, it rarely makes sense to offer explicit multiple-user support in an iOS app. But if people really do want to share SnackLog, they should be able to just create a tag for each person and get most of the functionality of multiuser support. So these two features can be rolled into one.

So you strike down the idea of doing multiuser support, for two reasons. First, it would seem out of place on iOS. Second, you can get most of the way there with tags anyway. In fact, you're not really entirely striking it down; instead, you're rolling the two features together. iOS is full of this kind of feature problem reduction.

Also remember that sometimes what seems like a single feature actually needs to be split out into two or more dedicated features. Take deletion. At first it may seem that deleting all items is only a variation on deleting a single item. So maybe whatever interaction you come up with for them should be presented side by side. (Getting ahead of ourselves into actual interaction design, imagine a trash-can icon that, when you tap it, offers Delete One and Delete All buttons.) That would be kinda terrible. People delete single items all the time, but only rarely would they want to delete their entire purchase history. Both are deletion operations, but you need to design them in very different ways. As you revise your outline, you might move the Delete All feature away from the browsing functions and into a settings area. You might even stop calling it "Delete," and start calling it "Reset," to differentiate the two. Coming up with terminology that matches the way you think about features will help you design them.

Outlining Architecture

Now that you have a good sense of the features you'd like to include, it's time to work out how they fit together in the geography of the app. Here, an architecture outline will help you as you go through sketching and wireframing. This kind of outline helps you organize features into screens and subscreens full of controls. You might develop it during sketching, as you draw various layouts that could serve the features you've decided on. See Figure 1.3 for a simple architecture outline.

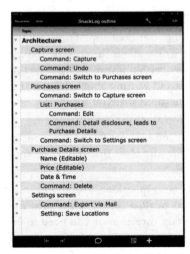

Figure 1.3   A quick outline of SnackLog's simple architecture

Your Outline Is Your To-Do List

As you move on to sketches, wireframes, mockups, and prototypes, refer to your outlines. They serve as checklists for all of the things you need to consider. Did you sketch this feature? Does your wireframe account for that problem? Go through your outlines one item at a time, and make sure you haven't forgotten anything. Developing an app is a huge project with a squillion tiny parts, and you're sure to find things you need to add or change at the last minute. But being thorough up front will help you avoid the worst of it.

Summary

Indented, hierarchical lists aren't the only way to outline ideas, but they're a particularly good one. You can use any kind of well-organized writing to keep track of your project, but try to get down a comprehensive list of everything you need to include in your designs. Outlines of all shapes and sizes can help you sort out complex topics at any stage of designing your app.

Starting with a mental sweep gets all your ideas onto the page. Constructing an initial requirements outline sets you up to attack all the design challenges your project presents. Reducing problems and outlining questions strengthen your requirements outline.

Exercises

1. Now that you've seen an initial requirements outline for a simple app like Snack-Log, try creating one for your own app. Think through all the things the app needs to do, but don't worry about the specific implementation or interaction details. Calling out how certain features should feel (quick, distraction-free, personalized) is fine, but avoid writing about the actual design yet (buttons, colors, navigation). Include questions that you have. Any interesting app idea should summon up at least a few unanswered questions.

2. Examine your outline, and look for features or concepts that might benefit from being reduced. Are there any ideas that should be combined? Are there any ideas that should be split up?

3. Try outlining some of your questions, keeping in mind how your app would fit in with other iPhone or iPad apps. List the pros and cons. Then see whether you're leaning in a certain direction or you need to explore further.

2

The Sketches

Sketching! The central activity of design! As a designer, you need to be able to sketch any and every idea that comes to mind, to get it out of your brain and into a form where everyone can see it. Sometimes it's important for *you* to see the idea, and sometimes it's important for *others* to see it. When you have something to share, something to refer to, and something to start from, only then can the next idea be built on top of it (or diverge from it).

Outlines are a way to use writing to explore design questions, and sketches are a way to use drawing to explore them. Depending on the question, you may need to create an outline, a sketch, or a combination of the two. As you practice both disciplines, you'll get better at knowing which to use. Sometimes you may be able to skip over both and go straight to wireframing; see more about that in Chapter 4, The Wireframes.

Being an effective software designer isn't about having art skills, generating brilliant ideas, or keeping up with the hip design blogs (although that stuff doesn't hurt). It's a lot more about sketching your ideas and the ideas of your team, studying how well they work, and then sketching some more. Your value as a designer doesn't have much to do with the ability to come up with a great idea. But it's vital to develop the ability to recognize the promise of an idea, regardless of where it came from, and then shepherd it forward until its viability becomes apparent.

If you're intrigued by the power of sketching (and you should be), you can't do much better than to pick up the book *Sketching User Experiences* by Bill Buxton. It's an exciting ride through the philosophy and the process of product design through the voice of a guy who recognizes and upholds the primacy of sketching.

Thinking by Drawing

Sketches let you communicate visually with yourself and other members of your team. Even if something seems fairly clear in your mind, go ahead and sketch it out to make sure it still makes sense. It only takes a moment.

Once you have something on paper, on the screen, or on the whiteboard, you have something that people can point to. You and your team can say, What if *this* bit were over *here?* What are the main components of this screen? Of this interaction? Of this experience? Even if you don't nail down the fine details just yet, it's invaluable to know roughly what you plan to include, and roughly where in the product it lives.

The most exciting design ideas tend to come out during the sketching process. Most apps are a huge network of sensible, pragmatic decisions, with a sprinkling of clever and innovative design ideas throughout; both kinds of ideas emerge in sketching. Sometimes it's a sketch that starts at a meeting or a conversation around the coffee machine; other times, it's a lone designer having a one-person "conversation" via the sketchbook.

Design Happens in Conversations

You're in a meeting that has been going on for half an hour. Everyone's talking about your proposal for the design of the Framistan. They're all sure they understand the concept and the ramifications of your proposal. Some of them agree with your ideas. Others don't.

Eventually, to make a point about some detail of it, you doodle the Framistan on the whiteboard. All of a sudden, half of the people in the room sit up: "I didn't know there was a Cancel button!" "Oh, it's just a panel, not a full-screen thing?" "Ah, but what happens when you rotate the iPad?" And so on. Turns out everyone had a slightly different, varyingly vague image of the Framistan. Once they understand what *you* think the Framistan should look like, only then can they constructively add their own ideas.

Starting such meetings with a sketch, and continuing to sketch as you talk, prevents this sort of confusion. As the conversation goes on, the sketch evolves to represent the group's understanding of the idea. Erase stuff, cross stuff out, add stuff, and keep the sketch up-to-date. Have one or two people in charge of drawing, so that the sketch remains coherent as it's updated. If there are competing ideas, sketch them side by side. When you're finished, you can just snap a photo of the whiteboard (or paper or iPad) for emailing out to the group and adding to the design documents.

Wherever you have design conversations, you should have a whiteboard or some other effortless way to sketch. Erase it regularly to encourage people to use it. (See Figure 2.1.)

Of course, you might not be working with a team. You might be a lone designer–developer hybrid. Sketch anyway. Just using your imagination is rarely enough; you need a quick way to have a visual conversation with yourself. You may find that you've been making assumptions that don't make sense. Or that you've forgotten important elements. In the end you'll have a much better idea of the shape of your app, and you'll be far better prepared to start nailing down the specifics.

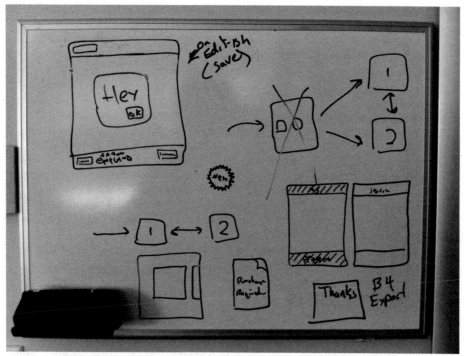

Figure 2.1   The author's own mini-whiteboard after a healthy design conversation with several teammates

Lots of times, you'll get partway through a sketch and then suddenly stop, realizing why the idea behind it is wrong—that's fine. The sooner you sketch something out, the sooner you discover whether it has legs. Aggressive sketching is a great way to pre-emptively cull dead-end ideas.

Even if you already *know* an idea is wrong, sketching it out can help you figure out why, and what might work better. Sketch it wrong on purpose. Maybe some part of your wrong sketch will lead into the next idea and get you a right sketch.

Rubber Ducking

This productivity hack in the programming world also works well for designers. The story goes that some anonymous programmer kept a rubber ducky toy at his desk. Whenever he ran into a seemingly insurmountable problem, he'd turn to the duck and engage it in conversation, explaining the problem as you would to any aquatic bird lacking a firm grasp on the nuances of programming. Invariably, trying to explain the problem to someone—anyone—prompts the problem to become clear and a solution to present itself.

The designer's equivalent to rubber ducking is similar, except that it often includes sketching. When you have a problem without an obvious solution, just try drawing it. Put it into words, step by step, as if to an audience lacking in any knowledge of the project you're working on. You'll be surprised by how often this causes the complications to melt away.

Often a designer ends up accidentally using a teammate as a rubber duck. My teammate Joel will casually saunter into my office to talk over a design problem he's struggling with. Most of the time we end up in a normal back-and-forth conversation. But say it's for a project I haven't worked on lately, so he starts by catching me up with the state of things. Eventually he gets to the problem at hand and tries to put into words what's troubling about it. Meanwhile he's scribbling on my whiteboard. Halfway through a sentence, he gets excited about some idea that has randomly inserted itself into his train of thought. He interrupts himself: "So we can't do the thing with the Edit button... unless...Yeah! Thanks, Bill!" At this point, I haven't said a word, but I helped solve Joel's problem all the same. "Happy to be your rubber duck for today," I say, as he hurries back to his office to work on his new idea.

Tools for Sketching

Anything and everything that allows you to create and update quick, messy drawings is a fair sketching tool. It's easy to get hung up on choosing precisely the right sketchbook—the one that has just the right paper stock, that perfect nonphotocopying grid pattern, and the artisanal leather cover. You can spend a lifetime auditioning pens and pencils, markers, stencils, and other sketching accoutrements. You can install and try out a whole iPad home screen's worth of drawing and sketching apps.

That's fine! People like well-made tools that get the job done and are a pleasure to use. But don't get carried away and become paralyzed by the preciousness of your tools to the point that you aren't actually sketching. Sketches should be quick, rough, and disposable. It can be fun to go back and reminisce about old sketches, but you should be just as happy to get rid of them once they've served their purpose. It's hard to justify sketching out all five of your crazy ideas when your fancy notebook cost you 25¢ per page, and you left your shmancy pens at home anyway for fear they'd get lost.

Paper and whiteboards are the obvious choices and probably still the best. It takes virtually no physical or cognitive effort to get a simple idea from your mind onto the surface. Updating sketches as you go is an important part of sketching; unless you're sketching something simple enough that you can redo it every time you change your mind, make sure you can erase.

Software is getting better at replicating the breezy, casual ease of sketching on paper or a whiteboard, particularly on the iPad. Especially if you pick up a capacitive stylus, made to work on touchscreens, you can go a long way toward replacing your notebook with an app such as the following.

- **Paper** is an increasingly popular sketchbook app with an emphasis on emulating analog materials.
- **Remarks** is a featureful sketching and annotation app with a fast drawing engine and options for syncing.
- **OmniGraffle** is a full-on diagramming and graphics app with vector graphics, layers, and so on, which also includes freehand sketching.
- **Penultimate** is a popular writing and sketching app with "wrist protection," if you tend to want to rest your hand on the screen while you draw.

One major drawback of using the iPad, though, is that even though the latency of iOS is admirably low, it is still not fast enough to feel like real drawing. The strokes on-screen are bound to lag behind your input enough to break the illusion, make you second-guess yourself, and slow you down. Sketching should be fast and easy. If you find yourself spending too many cognitive cycles worrying about whether your input is going to get interpreted properly, or if you have to hit Undo all the time because the stroke didn't come out at just the right angle, or if your handwriting gets mangled to the point of illegibility, consider going analog after all.

Sketches Are Sketchy

Sketches are intentionally rough; they only depict the gist of an idea, rather than an entire, fully formed product plan. The sketchiness itself reminds viewers to pay attention to the concept, not the execution. A good sketch knows it is a sketch and doesn't purport to be a mockup (which looks like a final product) or a prototype (which behaves like a final product).

If you've been worrying about your artistic skills, don't. Sketching isn't drawing. All you need to do is make marks on a page that communicate an idea and get a conversation going. Their aesthetic appeal or tidiness is irrelevant.

Be wary of graphics software that creates too-perfect shapes and text. Those pristinely uniform renderings will slow you down as you try to get things precisely lined up and neatly organized. Save it for the wireframes and the mockups, where precision is the goal. (Some drawing apps, like OmniGraffle, make it easy to turn sketchy-style objects directly into precise, high-fidelity objects when you're ready.)

More importantly, the sketchiness of a sketch makes it unmistakable to people who see it that they're not supposed to be worrying about style, dimensions, precise positions, or any other specifics. That helps you sketch faster without concern about whether you're creating an aesthetically appropriate rendering. And it helps viewers set their expectations for what they're evaluating. That's why it's not merely cute when drawing apps simulate analog tools; a rough style helps communicate the tentative nature of the drawing.

Sketches simply offer a suggestion of a potential way that a thing could be: a proposal for what could exist and how it could relate to other things that could exist.

They say, "Hey. These objects are on this screen, in roughly this arrangement." "From here, you can go there or there or there." "There is no Back button here." They definitely don't say, "This panel has a pale, desaturated green background," or "This button is 32 points tall," or "The label on this table view should be worded in precisely this way."

Because of that sketchiness, though, it can be confusing to come back to a rough sketch later and try to make sense of it. So once you've gotten the idea-testing value out of a sketching session, it can be helpful to write or draw out what you learned from it. Don't necessarily count on the sketch itself to jog your memory.

When to Sketch

Here are the main situations when it makes sense to get sketching.

- **Illustrating architecture outlines**—Initially, you should go through your architecture outline and sketch out every screen in it. Every feature should be visible, every navigation should be accounted for, and every item in the outline should be present in some way in the sketches. Suddenly, your list of notions and ideas is a collection of pictures that you can examine and build upon. Now the sketches and outlines together represent a high-level understanding of what the app is like.

- **Going straight to architecture sketches**—If your app is small enough that its functions are defined by the screens it offers, you might even be able to skip the architecture outline and start out with architecture sketching. This is easiest for widget-type apps (like the built-in Stocks or Notes apps) that present a limited number of screens, with mostly static interfaces and not much navigation.

- **A hybrid approach**—Sometimes, even early on, you already have a pretty good intuitive sense of what the app's main interface should look like. In these cases, if you trust your intuition, you can start by sketching out that screen: editing a typical document in a productivity app, looking at a typical status screen in an informational app, starting a typical lesson in an educational app, and so on. Doing this first sketch will probably give you plenty of material to consider for your outlines. Once you know what the main interface looks like, it'll be easier to list all the other things you need to work on.

Beyond that, you should sketch all the time. Most questions that come up during the course of a project will benefit from a little sketching. The sketches can range from vague to complete, depending on the situation. Two people at a whiteboard, talking about one detail of an interface, might generate several rough scribbles just as part of their conversation. Someone else happening upon the whiteboard afterward probably won't have any idea what the sketches are about; they were just ephemeral communication aids. In contrast, your architecture sketches should be clear enough that you or others can refer to them and get the idea of each screen without much explanation.

Design never follows a predictable path, with the product described in the original outline actually coming into existence exactly as you imagined it. That's fine. Constant revision is part of the process. When you inevitably decide to add or change a feature, go ahead and sketch it out as if it were in your plan from the beginning.

Generally, almost everything about your app should get sketched at least once and will probably end up being sketched quite a few times. If you keep your early sketches, you can come back to them later in the project to marvel at which parts survived unchanged, to revive old ideas that might still have merit, and to laugh at your past self's crazy and naïve notions.

Keeping the Platform in Mind

If you haven't yet, now is the time to read the *iOS Human Interface Guidelines* (HIG) at the Apple developer site. To gain a baseline understanding of what is possible and expected on the platform, you need to internalize the HIG. Even if you've been seriously using and thinking critically about iOS apps for years, there is guaranteed to be something in there you didn't know about. For instance, do you know about the four styles of modal view available, and what each one is good for?

It's well worth your time to familiarize yourself with the basics of what you can do on iOS: table views, navigation controllers, split views, popovers, and so on. If you want to go even further, Chapter 3 in this book expands and comments on the HIG.

Of course, when you're sketching for iPhone or iPad, it's crucial to keep the form factor (the shape of the hardware) in mind. Remember that on iPad, anything you sketch should work in both portrait (vertical) and landscape (horizontal) orientations; on iPhone you can more easily get away with a single-orientation app. Likewise, any screen that takes text input should accommodate both the keyboard and the completion bar that appears above the keyboard in some languages.

You don't have to draw several copies of every idea—one in each combination of orientation and keyboard state—but try not to create anything that relies on the screen being in a certain orientation or that would break down once the keyboard appears. Keep these considerations in mind for now, and be ready to get serious about them in Chapter 3, Getting Familiar with iOS.

Using Precedents

For the most part, your sketches won't be utterly original concepts that you create from whole cloth. When novelists write stories, they don't invent new words and new idioms for every sentence (James Joyce excepted). They take advantage of the innovations of writers who came before them. Most of your sketches don't need to be utterly original; it's more responsible to create new work based on existing precedents. Every design decision you make that echoes another app makes your own app seem more familiar and more at home on iOS.

When you get familiar with the platform, you can use commonly known screens and interactions as motifs that inform your sketches. Instead of having to start from scratch, you can start with an existing experience and then modify it to suit your task. Here are examples:

- A message list in a social app that imitates the Mail message list
- A media picker grid that imitates iBooks or Podcasts
- An audio recording interface that evokes Voice Memos

For more about precedents, motifs, patterns, and shorthands, see Chapter 14, Consistency and Specialization.

Playing Devil's Advocate

Imagine that you disagree with someone on your team about whether a certain feature should be included in your app, or about how a feature should be presented. Sometimes your best rhetorical weapon is your ability to sketch.

Take your preferred idea and the opposing idea, and sketch them both fully. Be honest. Don't intentionally overcomplicate the opposing idea or sabotage its potential just because you don't like it. Sketch both ideas to the best of your ability.

If you're right, then in the end the sketch of your idea should be obviously more appealing than the opposing option. It makes a great visual aid to put them side by side and point out the differences. "Look, if we include this feature, then we need to add this control and that control, and the top screen gets muddled up because we have to split out the different kinds of Framistans..."

If you're wrong, and the opposing idea was not so bad after all, then it's a good thing you sketched it and discovered its potential. Either way, each drawback you find in one of the options strengthens the appeal of the options that don't have that drawback. So sometimes, sketching idea B can make idea A seem more and more like the right way to go.

Sketching Interfaces

The most straightforward sort of sketch is one of a literal interface: you actually draw a roughly iPad- or iPhone-shaped rectangle and fill it with approximate representations of on-screen controls. This helps you see the big-picture concerns about each screen. Each sketch serves to answer a question. A sketch can answer any of the following questions, but probably not all of them at once:

- About how much content will fit comfortably into the space you have
- Which standard elements should appear: a top toolbar, a bottom toolbar, a tab bar, and so on
- What custom controls you need to build

- How controls are grouped
- Which controls get the prime locations at the corners and edges of the screen
- How much room you'll have for content

But a sketch doesn't address these kinds of questions:

- Actual colors, textures, and other styling
- Precise sizes
- Exact wording of labels and explanatory text

The goal in making an interface sketch is to get an initial sense of what a particular screen will feel like. Are there too many buttons in the tab bar? (Apple's HIG sets a limit at five for iPhone tab bars.) Are you missing a way to go back to the previous screen? The sketch need only be as precise as needed to answer the question at hand; the all-inclusive drawing comes in the wireframing phase. Your architecture sketches are more likely to have an exhaustive inventory of the contents of each screen, and other sketches may omit most of the screen contents to focus on a single aspect.

Now look at some interface sketches for SnackLog. Items in the original outlines are taking shape as designs for the first time. In the requirements outline, we knew we wanted very quick, one-handed input of purchases. Now we know how we might achieve that: a photo-taking interface overlaid with a transparent number pad for entering a price (sketched out on the right side in Figure 2.2). This idea was arrived

 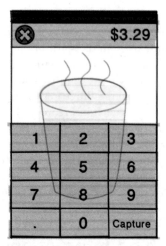

Figure 2.2   Two approaches to SnackLog's purchase capture screen.
On the left, an uninspired approach that would require lots of tapping.
On the right, an efficient approach that combines a photo-taking interface
with a number pad. These images were made with sketching software
for the sake of understandability; when you're sketching actively for
yourself, you can (and should) aim for rougher results (like the
whiteboard in Figure 2.1).

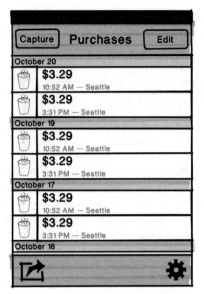

Figure 2.3   A straightforward sketch of a Purchases list screen for
SnackLog. The sample data must have come from someone with a very
consistent coffee habit.

at after trying several ideas, and it was chosen because it does the best job of fulfilling
the requirements in a way that feels like the spirit of the sort of app we want to make.
It's certainly more in the spirit of the app idea than the stodgy sketch of two fields and
a button. It's unique, but it retains a sense of familiarity by echoing the number pad
interfaces that users are familiar with in the iPhone lock screen and the Phone app.

We're keeping the Purchases list separate to make the capture process as smooth as
possible (see its sketch in Figure 2.3). In keeping with the photo-oriented nature of
the design, each purchase is identified by an image rather than a title (unless the user
manually enters one). The overall design follows the precedent of countless table-
view-based iPhone apps (Mail, Contacts, Music, etc.), which present a list of data in
the form of grouped cells arranged vertically. This presentation works well because
it's familiar and easy to implement. There's no need to reinvent the wheel to present a
collection of items ordered by date.

Sketching Interactions

Sometimes you need to illustrate not only what a static screen looks like but also how
people will interact with it. Press this button, get this popover. Tap this table cell, navigate a level deeper. And so on. The experience of moving from one state to another

is at least as important to software design as the individual states are. (And making it explicit is especially important if you're counting on someone else for your engineering work.)

You can use distinctive annotations to indicate what happens from moment to moment as someone follows a specific series of steps in your app. Give each interaction its own frame, as in a storyboard or comic book. Show where each tap or other gesture occurs on each screen. Connect screens with arrows to show the movement from one to the next. When there is a decision point, you can draw a branching path. If you like, draw only the relevant parts of each screen, as long as the rest of the screen is understood to be there. Figure 2.4 shows a sketch of the main interaction in SnackLog.

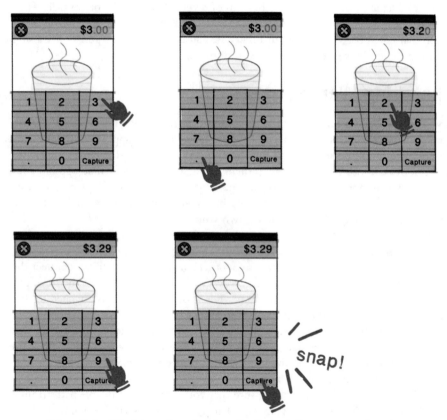

Figure 2.4   This interaction sketch walks through the process of capturing a purchase in SnackLog: launching the app, entering a price, and snapping a photo are the only steps needed. This sketch feels very much in line with the requirements for speed and ease of entry.

Here are a few interactions you might sketch out:

- What happens when you tap (or touch and hold, or drag, or swipe, or double-tap, or tap-then-wait-then-tap) an object on the screen?

- How do you get from the top level to a specific screen in a big hierarchical navigation view?

- When does a contextual menu (the black bubble with available commands) appear on an object?

- How do users create an account on the app's associated web service? (And if they already have an account, how do they connect to it?)

These sketches will help you understand whether an interaction is smooth, whether it makes sense, and whether users will ever think to undertake it. If you need to sketch 14 steps—including scrolling to the bottom of several long screens of controls—in order to illustrate a common or essential task, rethink the interaction. Conversely, if an action that could blow away data or otherwise cause annoyance requires only a single tap, for goodness' sake, require more commitment.

Sketching Workflows

A **workflow sketch** is a map of the various screens in an app and the ways you get from one to another, like a visual, high-level outline of your app. If your app is simple enough, you might be able to map out the entire thing in one diagram. Otherwise, you can break it into chunks and map them one at a time. If your iPad app has a few popovers, for instance, you might draw a map for each one. Some apps have persistent ways, such as tab bars, for quickly jumping between chunks of functionality. For these apps, it makes sense to give each tab its own workflow map.

At their most abstract, workflows can be simple arrangements of boxes and arrows, showing paths through the various screens of your app. If each node represents the controls you use to get from one state to another, though, then you can connect the control to the place it leads to: draw an arrow from the control, out of the screen it's on, and across to the screen it navigates to. The root of the arrow is attached to the control, and the head of the arrow points to an entire screen.

A popular arrangement for iPad apps is **master/detail**—a sidebar on the left that controls what's visible in the main content area on the right. If you're using the master/detail approach, make sure you indicate what appears on the main content area as a user navigates around in the sidebar.

Workflow sketches help you make sure that your app has reasonable paths from one screen to another. You can find pathways that seem unnecessarily demanding: should there really be three screens in between the initial launch and the account setup? You can also find out where you have too many ways to get to the same place: do you need four different pathways to get to Settings, or can you remove the paths from three of them? If the geography of your app seems difficult to explain in flowchart form, that's a sign it will be confusing in practice.

On iOS, the expectation is that people can drop into your app, get quickly to the desired task, get it done, and get out. They don't want to deal with convoluted webs of navigation. In fact, your workflow should expect and accommodate the sudden pressing of the Home button at any time, without any negative effect. Of course, the amount of time people spend depends on the app in question. People tend to spend more time per session in an e-reader app than in a stock ticker. But even in the middle of a long session with your app, users may be switching away to check Twitter, to look things up on Wikipedia, and to drop tasks in their to-do list. Aim for a workflow that's as lean as it can be and provides shortcuts back to the most important screens.

Figure 2.5 shows the casual, exploratory sketching session that resulted in the combined photo and number pad capture screen in SnackLog. It starts out as the uninspired experience already seen in Figure 2.2: tap the Price field to be taken to a text

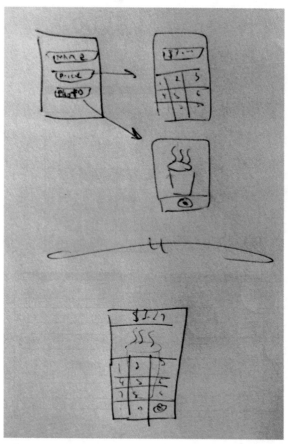

Figure 2.5   A quick workflow sketch to explore and refine the
overall capturing experience in SnackLog

input screen with a number pad, or tap the Take Photo button to be taken to a camera screen.

What's important here? Sketching these screens side by side allowed the designer to recognize the value of combining them. That realization would have been a lot less likely had the designer decided not to put this thought on paper. All it took to reach the central innovation of the app was to doodle a naïve design and then stare at it for a minute. Making yourself follow the wrong design all the way to its logical conclusion is a great way to get unstuck by consciously acknowledging what you *don't* want to do. Put another way, intentionally drawing a wrong design can lead directly to a right design.

Figure 2.6 shows a more refined workflow sketch for the new SnackLog concept. It's a simple app with not many screens at all; other apps might have dozens. The details of the controls are not very important, so they're rendered in a fairly terse way.

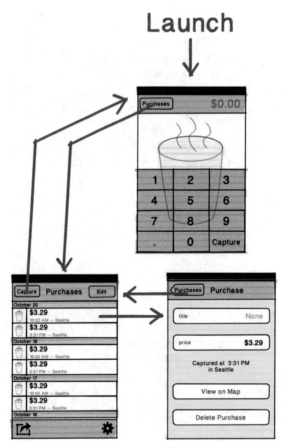

Figure 2.6   The main screens of SnackLog, showing how a user can get between them

Notice that the streamlined design has few screens and little friction between entering the app and getting something recorded. There aren't any shortcuts here, because from any given screen, any other screen is only a couple of taps away. You only need to provide such shortcuts if the only other way to navigate would be an onerous amount of work. Think about the Music app on iPhone, which lets you use the tabs to get to the top level of any of four sections, rather than making you tap Back, Back, Back, Back.

Summary

Sketching is the most versatile tool in your kit as a designer. If you have several ideas for an interface or an interaction, sketch them all and let them fight it out on paper. If you have only one idea, sketch it anyway. The act of drawing it may give you new insights. When you think you have the high-level concept of your app figured out, sketch it. You may find ways to make it leaner, more sensible, or more graceful. The better you get at sketching to communicate with yourself and others, the better a designer you'll be.

Sketches should be rough, quick, and only as detailed as necessary to get their point across. Your app is made out of ideas, and those ideas take shape in your sketches. Not all of your ideas have to be utterly original. Start with the *iOS Human Interface Guidelines* for strong guidance on how a baseline app should look and behave, and then mine the operating system and existing third-party apps for a wealth of motifs and precedents. Then add your own touches and unique usefulness on top.

Exercises

If you've been paying attention to this chapter, your three tasks shouldn't be surprising. It's time to apply the sketching skills you've learned to your own app concept.

1. For each screen listed in your architecture outline, sketch out the interface. If several possibilities come to mind, sketch them side by side and see which one makes the most sense. If only one possibility comes to mind, think harder. If you need to, invent obviously wrong interfaces and sketch them, if only to make sure they're actually wrong after all.

2. Pick the most important interactions in your app, and sketch how they work. What is a typical task someone would use your app for? Draw it screen by screen, and see how much physical and cognitive effort it takes to get through. Compare it to other possible interactions that could do the same job.

3. Draw a workflow map for your entire app. Can you simplify any pathways from screen to screen? Do you need to provide quicker ways to get to important screens?

3

Getting Familiar with iOS

A major part of getting good at designing for iOS is simply coming to understand what the platform has to offer. Much of your design work will consist of choosing from a set of standard navigation schemes and controls. Occasionally you'll need to dream up a custom element, but even your original designs should be in the spirit of the platform.

Although you may see these standard elements and behaviors in the apps you already use every day, you might not realize the reasons Apple and savvy third-party developers use them the way they do. This chapter supplements the *iOS Human Interface Guidelines* with further explanation and advice about the standard choices available. Then I talk about how to create your own custom designs that feel at home on iOS.

After you read this chapter, you'll be ready to start wireframing. While outlining and sketching, you can get away with scrawling a vague blob in the general vicinity of a feature and saying something like, "We'll need to provide some way to turn this setting on and off." When it comes time to wireframe, though, you'd better know your options for a setting that needs a two-way toggle (probably a switch, a segmented control, or a table with checkmarks, depending on the needs of the design).

Navigation: Screen to Screen

Put too simply, the primary challenge of wireframing is figuring out how to fit a list of features onto a series of two-dimensional screens. Part of that challenge is providing navigation between the screens in a way that makes sense and is easy for users. Let's look at some dependable ways to construct a sensible navigation scheme for your app.

Navigation Controller

A **navigation controller** is the most common way to get between screens on iOS (see Figure 3.1 for an example). A **navigation bar** at the top of a screen indicates the current location and contains a back button; rightward-pointing chevrons in the content area offer ways to proceed down the hierarchy. This arrangement allows for any number of branching paths, with a consistent way of getting back up to the top.

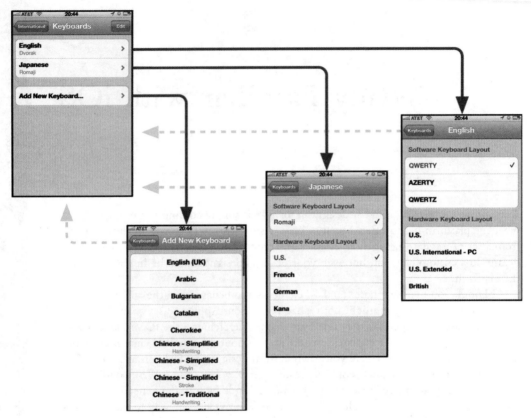

Figure 3.1   The Keyboards branch of the navigation controller hierarchy in the
iPhone Settings app. Tapping a table cell with a chevron takes you to a new screen.
Tapping the back button in the navigation bar takes you back a screen.

The result is a navigation scheme in which a user can scroll vertically on tall screens of
information, and move horizontally to step through the greater hierarchy of screens.
Navigation controllers work well only for a limited number of levels. If your hierarchy
requires users to routinely delve four or five levels deep, you may need to flatten
it out. (Chapter 12, Quiet and Forthcoming, explains how to flatten interface
hierarchies.)

   Navigation controllers are very familiar to iOS users. They trace their heritage all
the way back to 2001, on the original iPod, where selecting a row required spinning a
physical wheel. They're still the most reliable, most predictable way on iOS to present
a treelike hierarchy of information. Users take it for granted that many iOS apps have
a navigation bar at the top of each screen, and that's the first place they look to check
which screen they're on and how to go back a screen. Yes, the navigation controller is
the go-to workhorse for getting around in an iOS app, and it'll seldom do you wrong.

Most navigation controllers use standard table views (described later in this chapter) to list the options on each screen, but that's not the only approach you can try. (See Figure 3.2 for examples of other approaches.) Following are the only strong rules for creating a navigation controller experience.

- Delving down a level should involve tapping an element that either bears a rightward-pointing chevron or otherwise presents an obviously tappable piece of content that the user would want to navigate to.

- There should be a recognizable back button in the upper left, labeled with the name of the screen that it takes you back to (not with the word "Back").

- Moving between screens should use a horizontal slide animation—the content slides leftward for delving down, and rightward for going back up.

As long as you follow those guidelines, the navigation experience should feel comfortable and familiar to users. In that spirit, here are a few ways of presenting options that differ from the ordinary table view.

- A map, where users can tap a pin to open a label and then tap a disclosure button (bearing a chevron) to navigate to a detail screen. The Maps app on iPhone is an obvious example, because a map is a much more appropriate way to display geographical data than a list would be.

- A collection of big, expressive images, especially when there is a strong case for relying on images rather than text to identify your items. This would be an exception to the need for rightward chevrons, because they would unbalance the composition of each icon. Podcasts' cover view is an example; people react more immediately and emotionally to colorful cover images than to a list of titles.

- A grid of carefully laid-out previews of content. For an app that focuses on a specific kind of content, this approach can be far more expressive and inviting

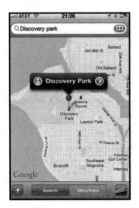  

Figure 3.2   Navigation controllers don't need to use ordinary table views, as shown on these Maps, Clock, and Podcast screens.

than a simple list of titles. Instapaper offers cleanly arranged previews of web articles to help you decide which one to read.

Split View

Only available on iPad, a **split view** offers a way to present navigation and content at the same time, something that helps flatten the navigation hierarchy. Most iPad apps that have a branching hierarchy work well with a split view. The relationship between the two sides is simple: what's selected on the left pane appears in detail on the right pane. Either side can have a navigation controller with ordinary horizontal navigation, but both shouldn't have navigation. (Really, they shouldn't. It has been tried, and the result is a confusing mess.) This means that you have two options for spreading navigation across a split view (see Figure 3.3 for an illustration of these two approaches).

- One is like the Settings app, where the sidebar always portrays the top level, and the content area can navigate. This makes it easier to jump around between lots of top-level items and then delve into detail for items on the right side if necessary.

- The other option is like Mail, where the sidebar can navigate, and the content area always displays details about what's selected on the left. This is a good approach when you have a well-defined, consistent type of content being displayed on the right, such as emails. People can navigate around their mailbox structure, and as soon as they tap an email, the right side updates to show it.

Remember that when you use a split view, you need to decide what happens in portrait orientation: either the split should remain visible, or the sidebar should be

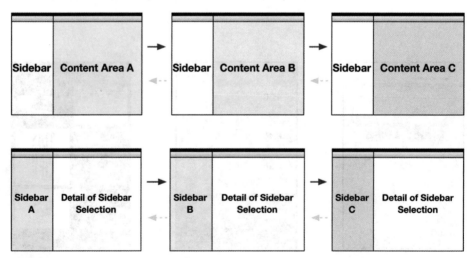

Figure 3.3   At top, Settings-like split view navigation. At bottom, Mail-like split view navigation.

hidden, sliding in when summoned by the button in the upper-left corner. The answer is easy when you use Settings-style navigation as just described: keep the sidebar visible. The back button in the upper-left means you wouldn't have a place to put a sidebar toggle button. (Some apps, such as Facebook, do it anyway. The sidebar is hidden, and it's unavailable at any level other than the top.)

For a Mail-style app, the answer depends on how important it is to keep the sidebar visible at all times versus how likely it is that the user will want to focus on the content area. In Mail, the sidebar is hidden in portrait orientation because users want to focus on a generously sized message area. (See Figure 3.4 for an illustration of these options.)

Tabs

A **tab bar** provides ever-present top-level navigation at the bottom of the screen. It's perfect for an app that needs to provide quick access to a few distinct top-level screens. The quintessential example is the Music app on iPhone: it offers tabs for Artists, Playlists, Audiobooks, and so on. Listeners on the go probably want to quickly jump to a certain category and then quickly navigate to the content they're interested in. The tab bar means that even if they last left the app several levels deep in the Artists hierarchy,

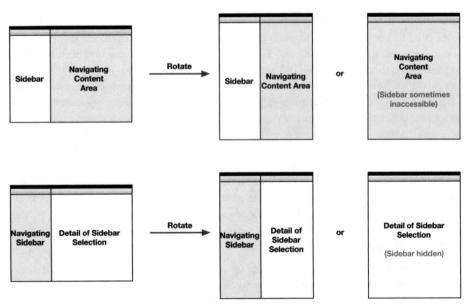

Figure 3.4 Portrait orientation and split views. At top, a navigation controller in the main content area. Hiding the sidebar means the user must navigate all the way to the top level to get the sidebar back; keeping the sidebar is the kinder choice. At bottom, a navigation controller in the sidebar. Hiding the sidebar helps the user focus on the content area; keeping it gives the user easier access to navigation.

they can still immediately tap the Audiobooks tab and start navigating that hierarchy instead. (Or they could even tap the already selected tab to jump to its top level and start over.) If you use a tab bar, it should provide the top-level navigation of the entire app. Tabbed views can contain navigation controllers, but not the other way around.

Deciding to go tabbed is a big choice, because that tab bar will be visible for most or all of the time people are using the app. You can offer only four or five top-level categories at a time. When you have more than five, the burden is on the user to decide which ones she thinks she'll need most often; everything else gets hidden behind the More tab. Even if you have only a few tabs now, this decision can come back to haunt you when you want to add more of them later. Unless your app strongly benefits from the always-there top-level navigation provided by a tab bar, you might want to consider an ordinary navigation controller instead.

Every screen, except for some special screens dedicated to specific tasks (modal views, described shortly), needs to dedicate 49 points of height to that heavy black bar. (And even though you can tint it any color, you should keep it relatively heavy.) The tab bar's size, color, and shiny highlighting effects give it a dominant role in the visual composition of a screen, compared with lesser elements like toolbars. That reinforces the significance of the tab bar's role as the top-level navigation of the whole app, with the power to send users to different branches of hierarchy with only one tap.

Segmented-Controls-as-Tabs

From time to time, you may want to offer a couple of views of the same information, or variants of the same screen. You might be able to offer a switch between those options in the form of a segmented control that behaves like tabs. A proper tab bar controls the whole app, jumping from one top-level section to another, but this light-weight tab style (let's call it segmented-controls-as-tabs) affects only the content or presentation of the current screen. As a result, you can offer two or three personalities for a single screen. If you have a popover to give quick access to more than one set of controls, such a segmented control may be the answer. iWork makes good use of this technique in its inspector popovers.

Don't rely too heavily on this technique. It can feel arbitrary and confusing when a navigation scheme switches back and forth between the horizontal sliding of a navigation controller and the control-swapping of segmented-controls-as-tabs.

Multiple Personalities

Here is a way to gracefully cram a couple of completely distinct interfaces and navigation structures into one app. In response to the tap of a button (usually in an upper corner of the screen), the entire interface transitions to reveal a new interface, sometimes with its own navigation scheme. The most prominent example is iBooks, with its entire store-shopping experience presented on the reverse side of its reading experience, complete with a three-dimensional flip transition between the two. The big, fancy animation makes it feel as if you're taking a major navigational leap—"going to the store"—without having to open a separate app. When you buy a book, it hovers in midair as the app flips back to the bookshelf, thus logically connecting the two sides. It's a fairly rare scheme, and you should use it only when you're certain you need it, but it can be invaluable when you need to include two similar but distinctive interfaces in one app.

Modal View

You can use a **modal view** to handle a specific task that doesn't quite fit into your ordinary navigation hierarchy. While the modal view is open, the normal navigation and functionality of the app are temporarily unavailable; the app is in a specific "mode," hence the name. A classic example is composing a message in the Mail app. This mode is available from anywhere and has nothing to do with where you are in the hierarchy, so it takes you out of the hierarchy momentarily to deal with the task of writing a message. Then it drops you back where you were.

On iPad, you have several choices for presenting modal views (see Figure 3.5), each with its own personality.

- **Full screen**—The iPad screen is pretty big, so a full-screen modal view is a big deal. This option makes sense when users will be spending a lot of time in the mode and it's OK for them to forget about the main app itself in the meantime. A full-screen modal view takes over the whole device, behaving like an app within an app, dedicated to a specific task. Think of things like a web browser built into a Twitter app. You could very well follow a link that someone tweeted and end up spending 45 minutes reading an engrossing article or watching a video; that experience needs to use the whole screen, and not relegate you to a fragment of the screen while the rest of the app peeks out at you in the background.

- **Page sheet**—This is a step down from the full-screen style, in that a page sheet has a constrained width. In portrait orientation, it looks like a full-screen modal view, filling the width of the screen at 768 points wide; but in landscape orientation, it's still only 768 points wide, leaving some of the underlying interface visible but dimmed. The Mail app uses this style for its composition window. The resulting experience is close to the full-screen style. Users can easily spend a lot of time and thought writing an email, so they should be given a quiet, dedicated space to do so. But there is one key difference from the full-screen style: a page sheet keeps the interface from getting too wide. A 1,024-point-wide composition area would result in really long lines of text, a classic blunder of poor typography; the distance the eye needs to travel to go from the end of one line to the beginning of the next is too far, causing reading mistakes and cognitive fatigue. (See more about typography in Chapter 4.)

- **Form sheet**—This is a step down from a page sheet. A form sheet takes up only 540 × 620 points, hovering in the middle of the screen, with the rest of the interface dimmed. This doesn't depart very far from the normal context of the app, so it feels more lightweight. It's useful for tasks that need a bit of space but that you expect to take only a moment, such as entering account credentials for a web service, exporting a document, or changing appwide settings.

- **Current context**—Sometimes you need to present a mode *inside* an existing view, such as a popover or one side of a split view. Perhaps you want to allow access to the sidebar pane while a mode is under way in the content pane. Or you need to break out of the navigation hierarchy of a popover to take care of a special task. You shouldn't need to use this style of modal view very often, but it's good to know you have it for special situations.

- **Popover** (as an alternative to a modal view)—A popover isn't usually a modal view, but you can use it to fulfill the role of one in a lightweight way. When you're considering a modal view, ask yourself whether a popover might do the job better. A popover keeps users much more in context rather than pull them away from what they're working on. (If you need to make a popover feel more modal, you can give it Cancel and Done buttons and disallow tapping away to dismiss it, but this design is falling out of fashion.) So if the task at hand is related to the existing interface on the screen, and doesn't need all the space afforded by a modal view, try a popover instead.

On iPhone, modal views are simpler: they're always full-screen, because anything smaller would be barely worthwhile (although the **partial curl** transition style does leave much of the existing screen in place). Most of the time you should use the straightforward vertical transition, which simply slides the modal view up from the bottom of the screen and then slides it away when the task is finished. Notice that the transition doesn't push the previous screen out of the way, as horizontal navigation does; instead, it merely covers it up, thus promising that it'll still be there when the mode is over. Users recognize and understand that type of transition as being a momentary diversion from normal navigation. Other transitions might leave users guessing about whether they've been transported to some other part of the app. See Chapter 6, The Prototypes, for more about transitions.

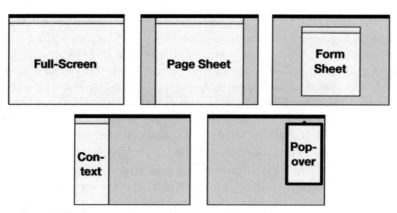

Figure 3.5   Types of modal view. The "current context" type can appear anywhere; in this example it appears in a sidebar. A popover can be modal or nonmodal.

Popover

A popover is a marvelous little iPad-specific element that seems unremarkable at first. It's a little window with a triangular stem pointing at the object that summoned it. But the humble popover contributes great sophistication to the iPad experience, for a few subtle reasons.

- You don't need to manage it like a window on the desktop. It can't be moved, and it's generally only as big as it needs to be.

- It appears at the time and place you need it.

- It disappears as soon as you're finished with it, either because you reached the end of its little workflow or because you decided to stop using it and tapped away.

- It generally keeps you in the context of the surrounding interface so that the interlude of using the popover doesn't interfere too much with the train of thought you had before opening it.

- It assumes that you're editing in-place and that you want your work to be saved, unless you manually cancel or undo it. Simply tapping away from a popover shouldn't discard your charges.

All this combines to make using popovers a lightweight experience. Consequently, interfaces can be designed to be "quieter" than they would be otherwise. Functionality can be easily summoned, used, and then put away for next time, rather than spread out all over the screen all the time so that you can get at it easily. (See Chapter 14 for more about quiet interfaces.)

Another exciting thing about popovers is that they can contain screens and navigation hierarchies all their own, distinct from what's going on in the main app. You can think of a popover as a little iPhone sitting inside the iPad screen, with its own miniature app that deals with one concern of the greater app. Popover navigation can use navigation controllers, segmented-controls-as-tabs, and modal views.

Custom Navigation

So far, we've looked at the standard navigation methods offered out of the box with iOS. If you need to—and if you have the software engineering wherewithal at your disposal—you can create almost any navigation scheme that you dream up. But be careful. Lots of apps with unique needs present their experience in a clever, original way, but not all apps have those unique needs. Applying an unexpectedly distinctive design to a problem that could have been solved with a standard approach can backfire. Think carefully before deciding to use a clever and unique navigation scheme as a primary way of differentiating your app. (See Chapter 14 for advice about unique designs.)

The most important thing to keep in mind when thinking up new navigation schemes is that they should feel spatially consistent. The conventional navigation controller scheme works well in users' minds because they can easily build a map of how it works (often called a **mental model.**) Deeper levels are further to the right, higher levels are off to the left, and modal views slide in from off-screen and then slide away when they're no longer needed. In iBooks, tapping a book on the shelf causes it to zoom toward the viewer and open. The iWork apps present a similar experience by showing a grid of documents that zoom up when you tap on them and zoom back when you're finished editing. GarageBand is more ambitious. It starts with that same document grid but adds a carousel of various instruments, and a tracks overview is revealed by a vertical rotation effect. (See Figure 3.6 for a map of GarageBand's navigation scheme.)

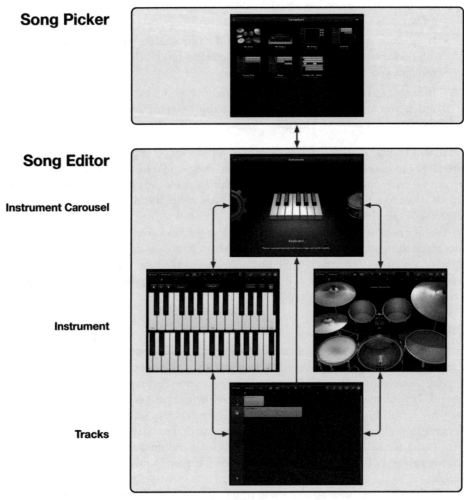

Figure 3.6   GarageBand on iPad has a custom navigation scheme that's complex but consistent.

Even if users never consciously think about the mental map they've made of the app, they'll be put off if that mental map is violated. Use smooth, sensible transitions every time the screen changes, especially when the changes are big ones. The simpler you can make the spatial representation of your navigation, the easier it will be to make it feel stable and consistent to users.

Advice on the Standard Elements

Elements are the building blocks that make up screens: views, controls, alerts, and so on. In wireframing, you just need to find the right elements and put them together on the right screens in the right arrangement. Of course, that is like saying that writing a best-selling novel is only a matter of picking the right words and putting them in the right order. You'll need a lot of wisdom to put together great app designs, but to begin with you should make sure you're familiar with the building blocks at your disposal.

As a rule, you should choose standard elements provided by the OS over building your own. For nearly every need, there's a standard control that does the job reliably and predictably. Standard controls have the benefit of being familiar to users, who of course spend most of their time in other apps. Chapter 14, Consistency and Specialization, goes into more depth about the choice to go standard or custom.

For a basic understanding of the standard elements the platform offers, you should read the *iOS Human Interface Guidelines*. The beginning of the chapter said that, too, and so did Chapter 2. Really, you should read them. That will give you Apple's official baseline position on how these elements are to be used. But for further advice and suggestions about how to put them to use effectively, based on actual Apple and third-party examples, here is a rundown of each individual element.

Bars

These basic screen-spanning bars show content and controls.

- **Status bar**—The only decision you need to make about the status bar is whether to hide it and, on the iPhone, what style it should be. The different states of the status bar mainly affect the immersiveness of the app; the more immersive treatments avoid distracting the user from the content being shown. The standard light status bar blends in with the interface. This works best when there's no immersion necessary, as in communication or productivity apps. On the opposite end of the spectrum are media or entertainment apps, where you'll want to hide the status bar to avoid distracting from the content. But don't hide the bar just to show off how cool and immersive you can be. Users tend to care about the time and their battery level. Only if the immersiveness is more important than that information can you justify hiding the status bar. If you're not hiding the bar, remember to accommodate 20 points at the top of each screen in your wireframes and mockups, and consider what your screens will do when the double-height status bar appears. (See The Worst-Case Height Compression Scenario in Chapter 4.)

- **Navigation bar**—This bar spans the entire top of the screen (on iPhone) or a specific view (on iPad). It's 44 points tall, except in landscape mode on an iPhone; then it's 32. A navigation bar is the primary way people move through the various screens. It sits at the top of the view, framing it with a reminder of where you are and how to go back up a level. Don't confuse the navigation bar with a toolbar. Navigation bars are only about showing a back button, a title, and possibly a single (bordered-style) button for managing content (an Add button, an Edit button, a View button, etc.).

- **Toolbar**—This bar spans the entire screen (on iPhone) or a specific view (on iPad) and serves to contain controls. It's 44 points tall, except in landscape mode on an iPhone; then it's 32. If the navigation controller is the workhorse for moving between screens, the toolbar is the equivalent for choosing commands on screens. A toolbar can contain a limited number of controls, so you'll need to be scrupulous about picking them. On iPhone, you're limited to five 44×44-point buttons. On iPad there isn't a hard limit, but you should do your best not to clutter the bar. Unlike desktop computer users, iOS users aren't accustomed to wading through lots of controls. Instead you should think of ways to consolidate functionality behind a single button, by using popovers, modal views, and action sheets. (See Chapter 14.)

You have two choices of button style in a toolbar: regular and bordered. The bordered style is great for emphasizing that something is a button, when going borderless would make it ambiguous. A button with a text label is the prime example of something that needs an extra bit of emphasis. Another example is when there's non-buttony stuff hanging around in the same bar, and that's why a button in a navigation bar is always bordered; otherwise, it could be construed as being part of the screen title. The HIG advises against using both button styles in the same toolbar, but on iPad such a design isn't a big deal. iWork keeps bordered buttons on the left side of the toolbar, and borderless ones on the right. That's fine; just don't mix the styles willy-nilly. (See Figure 3.7 for the example set by Keynote's toolbar.)

- **Tab bar**—This is a 49-point-tall bar that spans the entire screen and always appears below the content it switches. (The purpose of a tab bar is described in detail earlier in this chapter, in the section called Tabs.) When you're

Figure 3.7 Keynote has similar toolbar configurations on iPad and iPhone. Bordered and unbordered buttons are kept separate for the sake of tidiness.

wireframing for tab bars, remember they're slightly taller than toolbars, and you can put only five tabs into one on iPhone. For a while, it was fashionable to make a custom tab bar that promotes one tab by having it protrude outward from the top of the bar. Instagram made that design famous. But the practice seems to be falling out of favor and doesn't appear in that app anymore. Fads.

Content Views

These are the basic, general-purpose views for presenting content and controls.

- **Popover**—Earlier you learned why popovers are awesome, so here are a few tips for keeping them that way. For the most part, users expect popovers to be 320 points wide, for that iPhone-within-an-iPad feeling. Popovers much wider than that feel awkward hanging off that tiny triangular stem, and a form sheet would probably work better. Make popovers as tall as you need, of course, but no taller.

  When navigating among the screens of a popover, don't worry if you leave empty space (because the popover is too tall for the content) or if scrolling is required (because it is too short). Such minor imperfections are better than making users sit through a resize animation every time they navigate somewhere. So just find a height that works reasonably well for all screens in the popover, and stick to it.

- **Split view**—Remember that the sidebar is always 320 points wide, mimicking the width of an iPhone screen and allowing you to use similar layout strategies for both sidebars and iPhone screens. Normally, the sidebar is always visible in landscape orientation; in portrait view, it is often hidden and needs to be slid in from the side. But thanks to the official Facebook app, it's fashionable to offer a slide-in sidebar that is always hidden until summoned, regardless of the orientation. This design puts more focus on the content area, at the expense of quick access to navigation. The tradeoff is that it's a bit nonstandard and thus is harder to implement and maintain. Weigh that against the importance of emphasizing the content in both orientations.

- **Table view**—Table views are the go-to element for displaying information, editable or otherwise. Table views appear in sidebars, main content areas, popovers, modal views...everywhere. They can be used for navigation (with chevrons or detail disclosure buttons), for selection (with checkmarks), or for data editing (usually using the value styles, described shortly). The name is a bit misleading: you might expect a table to offer multiple columns, but iOS table views are a single column (although each cell can display several bits of information). There are two standard table styles and four standard cell styles to choose from, each with a terribly nondescript name that makes it hard to keep them straight.

- **Text view**—Standard text views are straightforward. They're good when you need to display, or the user needs to enter, lots of text. Of course, "lots" is relative.

- **Web view**—There is about one good reason to use a web view: to load an actual page from the web for tasks like logging in to sites or following a link in the user's content. You formerly had to use web views to display rich text with styling applied to it, because the standard text view was plain-text only; but as of iOS 6, you can put rich text in labels and text views. (Some apps try to put most of their functionality inside the web view, actually running a web app wrapped thinly in an iOS app. For advice on that particular venture, see the hybrid web-app admonishment in Chapter 14.)

Here are the styles of cells you can use in your table views.

- **Plain table**—This table style pushes the content all the way to the edges of the view; an example is the message list in Mail. A plain table is great for presenting a single, homogenous list of items, especially when the list is likely to get long. That's why you see it used for email messages, contact names, music tracks, to-do list items, or any other uniform collection of items that can get arbitrarily long. Even within such homogenous lists, though, there can be subdivision indicators, such as letters of the alphabet. In those cases you can use **section headers,** which float among the rows as little eye-catching milestones without being tappable. And if a sectioned list is likely to be *really* long, you can provide an index along the edge of the screen for quickly jumping to a certain group. The index tends to look silly or awkward if you don't have lots of data or if you use it for sections that aren't strictly ordered in a familiar way such as the alphabet.

- **Grouped table**—This table style keeps the content in self-contained stacks with rounded corners. An example is the Settings app in iPhone. A grouped table works best when you have heterogeneous kinds of information to present on one screen, when the separation of sections is critical, or when you offer controls and labels that don't fit into table cells. Imagine if the Settings app had a single huge plain-style table for all the settings. There would be no strong separation between the kinds of options; there would be no place to put the explanatory labels; and lots of sections would consist of a contrived header and a single item. See Table 3.1 for a comparison of plain and grouped tables.

Table 3.1 **Plain Versus Grouped Table Views**

Plain Table	Grouped Table
It's good for any length of list.	It's best for shorter lists.
It's good for homogenous data.	It works fine with wildly different kinds of data.
Labeled sections help delineate subgroupings like alphabetization.	Groups provide stronger separation than sections.
All sections need to be labeled.	Groups can be labeled or unlabeled.
All sections are expected to hold roughly equivalent kinds of data.	Each group can hold a different kind of data.
It can offer an index for jumping quickly to a section.	A single index doesn't make sense, because there is more than one table on the screen.

- **Default cells**—The default cell style simply presents a text label and, optionally, an image. This style is generally used in navigation to help users identify the information they want to navigate to next. It's used to identify artists in the Music app, people in the Contacts app, and so on. The designers could have used the subtitle style to include plenty of extra data, but in these cases they recognized that almost every time, users want to navigate to the full detail screen. No single piece of information would be most helpful to promote from the detail screen to the cell, so they left the cell simple, encouraging users to delve into the detail screen. After all, taps are cheap, and it costs very little to delve inside and get a dedicated screen of information about the item you're interested in.

- **Subtitle cells**—This cell style includes smaller, gray text below the title to give additional detail about each item. It's useful when you need to let users compare a certain key piece of information between items without having to delve into the individual detail screens. For instance, the app list in the Notifications screen of Settings uses a subtitle to indicate the kinds of notifications set up for each app. Users can see at a glance the answer to their likely question: "Which apps have notifications enabled, and what kinds?" It's a clear case of a piece of information that saves people time and trouble when it's pulled up a level into the cell.

- **Value 1 cells**—Yep, that's the official name of this style. In the Interface Builder component of Xcode, it's called "right detail," which is a bit more descriptive. This style combines a label and a value, usually to allow users to edit the value. The label is bold and left-aligned; the value is grayish-blue and right-aligned. This layout emphasizes the label text, because (at least in left-to-right languages), people find it easier to compare strings of text that are left-aligned; scanning down the beginnings of the labels is easy. You can also offer switches or other small controls in the value area instead of a text string. Value 1 cells are seen in various places throughout the Settings app, accommodating users' need to scan the names of the various options presented there, looking for the one they're interested in. Scanning the values wouldn't help that process very much.

- **Value 2 cells**—Also known as "left detail," this style combines a label with a value that can usually be edited. The text label is deemphasized by its small size and its fainter color, whereas the value is dark and bold. In this layout, it's easy to recognize and compare the values, because they're left-aligned in the middle of the cell. This cell type works well when you have pieces of information that are more recognizable by their values than by their labels, and that's why it is used in the Contacts app on iPhone. Names, phone numbers, addresses, email addresses, and other bits of contact information are pretty recognizable without seeing the label, so you can easily scan the values on the screen and find the one you need. (See Figure 3.8 for a comparison of the various cell styles.)

Figure 3.8   Left to right: default, subtitle, value 1, and value 2 cells.
Each is useful for listing information in a subtly different way.

- **Custom cell styles**—You can put almost anything in a custom table cell. So if
  you need something a bit different (or very different) from the standard choices,
  and you have a good reason for it, you can create your own style. For an example, see the message list in Mail. Each row provides a large, bold sender name, a
  small, regular-weight subject line, a small gray message preview, and a blue time
  indicator. When you dig through your email looking for a specific message, all
  these bits of information are likely to be helpful; none of them could be omitted
  safely. To implement the message list using one of the standard styles would have
  done a disservice to the task of browsing email messages. (See Figure 3.9 for
  some custom table cell styles.)

Alerts

Alerts are an efficient, effortless way to drive your user crazy. For decades on the desktop and on the web, the alert was a way to pester users with whatever the developer
felt like saying, whether the user cared or not. iOS did a lot to reduce the number of
alerts that users have to deal with, reserving them for times when something is seriously amiss and the user needs to be notified or asked for immediate input. Consequently, when an alert appears it usually heralds an important moment. If it instead
says something inane, banal, or cryptic, it waters down (or poisons) the purpose of
alerts and reduces the attention users give them.

Here are some good times to use alerts:

- When the app can't proceed unless users enters their account credentials
- When a background process encounters a problem, such as a sync conflict, that
  needs an immediate decision from the user

Figure 3.9   Left to right: Mail, Podcasts, Tweetbot, and Instapaper.
Custom table cell styles support any layout you can dream up.

The following are some terrible times to use alerts.

- When an operation completes normally. The interface should make this apparent without interrupting the user.
- When something the user just tried to interact with, still visible on the screen, has a problem. In that case, the thing itself should show its status.
- When you want to influence the user's behavior (see Chapter 10).

Look at the animation that a new alert performs when it appears on the screen. It emerges from nothing, fades in, floats perpendicular to the screen toward the user, and then bounces back into place. Almost everything else that happens on an iOS device is connected to something already on the screen, giving it context and meaning. An alert is for those rare cases when something happening behind the scenes, something that normally proceeds without the user's needing to care about it, suddenly needs the user to care about it.

Action Sheets

Action sheets are another humble but heroic player in iOS's quest to make software quieter and more respectful. Action sheets are a stack of buttons that appears in response to an action by the user. Their effect is profound.

On iPhone, action sheets always slide up from the bottom of the screen and always offer a cancel button in addition to their action buttons. On iPad, action sheets might do the same thing in the virtual-iPhone-interface that is a popover, or they might appear in a dedicated popover of their own. If they appear in a popover of their own, there is no cancel button; instead, the rest of the screen serves as a safe place to tap away and cancel the action.

Here's what is cool about using an action sheet.

- It hides several similar actions behind a single button, thus simplifying the interface until the moment of need.
- It doesn't necessarily offer explanatory text, thus making it feel lightweight and reinforcing the fact that it always appears because of the last thing the user did. (You can add explanatory text if you really can't get the situation across with the button labels.)
- It's easy for a user to open, check the available options, and then cancel if none of them is what the user wanted.

An especially thoughtful case is the action sheet that shows a single action button. In old-fashioned interfaces, where an especially consequential action would be accompanied by a fussy dialog box with long explanatory text and buttons for proceeding or canceling, iOS offers a single, clearly labeled confirmation button. If you really intend to proceed, you can move your finger an inch and tap the action button. If not, you just tap away. That's elegant.

Standard Controls

Most controls are fairly straightforward and are well documented in the HIG. Here are some tips for using them.

- **Activity indicator**—This is also known as the **indeterminate progress indicator,** or **spinny.** On iOS, these are much more common than progress bars. If something takes less than a few seconds, you just put up a spinny in a location connected to the work being done, and don't bother the user with guesses about how much time is remaining. An activity indicator should suggest what it's for by an associated text label, by its location on the screen, or both.

- **Date and time picker**—This is also known as the **wheels of time.** Nine times out of ten, this is the right way to get date input from users. Spinning to dates that are even decades away is quick and easy. If multiple fields are visible on the screen, this control helps highlight or otherwise call out the value that the wheels are editing.

- **Detail disclosure button**—Normally, when you need to delve inside an item to see more detail on another screen, you tap a table cell that has a chevron on the right side. A detail disclosure button serves as a backup "delve inside" tap target for times when you can't follow that pattern. You might need to use it in two cases.

  - The item to be delved inside isn't a table cell and thus isn't obviously tappable for more information—for example, the bubble that emerges from a pin on the Maps app for iPhone, or a photo in Messages.

  - The table cell itself has some other function. In the Phone app for iPhone, tapping the cell for a favorite contact starts calling the person, whereas tapping the detail disclosure button delves into a detail screen about the person.

  In that second case, adding a detail disclosure button makes the most sense when both choices are about equally likely and when the shiny blue button doesn't compromise the cleanliness of your visual design. Another option is to split the two functions between normal mode and Edit mode.

- **Info button**—This venerable emblem, which is used on the desktop mainly for editing content details, is supposedly for revealing "configuration details" on iOS. For a while the same icon was used in the iWork apps on iOS to summon the style inspector popovers, but it has been replaced by a more expressive paintbrush icon. Meanwhile, the tools popover, which is closer to "configuration details," is summoned from a *wrench* icon. Many third-party apps that have configuration screens opt instead for a gear icon, because the meaning of the info icon is so muddled.

- **Label**—This is an ordinary little string of text that you can use to...label things. Generally, it's best to match the style and layout of the default labels on a grouped table view.

– To name something, put a bold label immediately (10–12 optical points) above it. Keep it on one line.

– To offer additional explanation about something, put a regular-weight label immediately (10–12 optical points) below it.

– To offer freestanding explanatory text that's not related to a particular element, put some empty space (20–24 optical points) between it and the nearest controls.

You don't need to label everything. A group of obviously color-related controls doesn't need to be called "Colors." The only table on a screen titled "Addresses" doesn't also need to be labeled "Addresses." Make sure you add labels only when they actually communicate something that wouldn't get across otherwise.

- **Network activity indicator**—This activity indicator in the status bar informs the user of communication happening over the network. Users look here to see whether their network connection is being used, especially if they're expecting some stale information on the screen to be updated. This indicator is a subtle hint to keep waiting, because the update is on the way.

- **Page indicator**—This is yet another quietly heroic interface element. Thanks to its presence on the home screen, this simple series of dots is immediately recognizable to most users as an invitation to swipe sideways for more content. It gives you the opportunity to display lots of screen-sized chunks of information without actually requiring navigation from screen to screen. (See Chapter 12 for more praise of pagination.)

- **Picker**—This generalized variant of the wheels of time is used for pop-up menus on web sites but is pretty rarely seen natively. Most times that you would use it, you could instead use a table view; the interactions of scrolling through a table view and of spinning the wheel are almost identical. The main benefit of the picker is that it lets you stay in context, and that's why it works well on the web. (On a web site, you need to stay in context in order to see the identifying information around the pop-up, so you can't just navigate to a dedicated screen for a table view. Nor can you insert an arbitrarily tall table view into a web site that wasn't designed for it.) Another benefit is that it's slightly lighter weight than a table, because the user simply scrolls to update the value; there's no need to tap an item to select it.

- **Progress view**—This is equivalent to the old-fashioned progress bar seen often on the desktop. As mentioned in the description of the activity indicator, most of the time you don't need a progress view. First, most operations should not take so long that you need to show the user how far along they are. Second, people need to see a progress bar only when they have no choice except to wait for the process to complete in order to get something done. Here are good examples of using progress views:

– Waiting for a document to be downloaded from iCloud so that you can work on it

- Waiting for an iMovie project to be exported so that you can send it to someone
- Waiting for an email with heavy attachments to be sent so that you can make sure it succeeds

If the process usually takes less than a few seconds, or if waiting for it doesn't affect the user's ability to get work done, you're probably better off with a spinny activity indicator.

- **Rounded rectangle button**—This is the one general-purpose, standard style of button that you can place in content areas. When you're using buttons in the content area, make sure you use them for *actions*. Don't use them for the following other purposes (as always, unless you have a good reason to).
  - Navigation is usually better handled with table cells bearing chevrons or detail disclosure buttons.
  - Choosing from a number of options is usually better handled by a table view with checkmarks or a segmented control.
  - Toggling a setting on or off is usually better handled by a switch.
- **Search bar and scope bar**—These are handy when a screen shows a number of items and it takes more than a few moments to scroll through them and find one manually. A common trick is to include the search bar at the top of the content area and load the screen so that it's scrolled just out of view. This design lets people scroll to the search bar if they need it but otherwise leaves it tucked away out of sight.
- **Segmented control**—A segmented control is a concise way to offer a very short list of mutually exclusive options. Often, it's a headache to come up with good labels that fit inside the narrow buttons, and you should use a table view with checkmark selection instead. The following are some good uses for segmented controls.
  - Selecting from a handful of options, if you can get your point across with recognizable images or very short text labels. You can even offer a label just above or below the segmented control that updates to reinforce the current choice with a text description.
  - Providing options that show or hide other controls based on the setting. The visual weight (see Chapter 4) and experience weight (see Chapter 13) of the content-area style of segmented control lend it well to this use. Pushing a big segment and watching it highlight in intense blue feels appropriately consequential to the subsequent appearance or disappearance of controls.
  - Switching between views on a screen in the same way tabs do. See Segmented-Controls–as-Tabs earlier in this chapter.

Whatever you do, don't make a segmented control behave like a button. It's for choosing between options, and not for performing actions. And remember that for simple on/off toggles, you have the switch at your disposal; a segmented control with "on" and "off" segments doesn't make a lot of sense.

- **Slider**—This is a great way to provide quick control over a continuous setting when the actual numbers aren't very important. Excellent examples in the operating system are the brightness and volume sliders. Nobody ever thinks, "I could hear better if the volume was at 86% right now" or, "It's getting dark; I should turn the brightness to 39%." Instead, they think, "Quite a bit louder" or, "A little dimmer." That's the sort of thing sliders excel at. People don't know exactly what setting they need beforehand; instead, they need continuous feedback while moving the knob. So make sure users can see or hear the result as they move the slider. It's frustrating having to go somewhere or do something to get the feedback they need.

- **Stepper**—A stepper is good for numerical settings when the number matters but adjustments tend to be within a small range. Poking the plus or minus button until you see the number you want is a cognitively cheap interaction, compared with typing in a number. A setting that was almost always set to 1, 2, or 3, for instance, would work well with a stepper.

- **Switch**—You can put a switch in a table cell to offer a simple on/off toggle. Flipping a switch feels fairly weighty, so you can easily use it for consequential settings or let it show or hide other controls. Make sure that the two opposing settings are easily gleaned from looking at the label. Something like "Automatically download new items" goes well with a switch. A vague title like "Horizontal Layout," where the opposing option is not immediately apparent, is not as good. (That would be better served by a segmented control with the label "Layout" and segments called "Horizontal" and "Vertical.")

- **Text field**—The text field is commonplace on the desktop and the web, but it often feels a bit crusty on iOS, especially if it's just sitting in a content area, lacking any placeholder text. Sometimes, you can offer a better way of entering information, such as picking from a table view. Text input is even more of a pain on a touchscreen than on a physical keyboard, so avoid it when you can. In content areas, a table cell with text input enabled is often more attractive. But when you need text input and you can't use a table cell, then a text field makes sense. (See a comparison between text fields and table cells in Figure 3.10.)

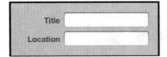

Figure 3.10   Text fields (left) look dated, feel cramped, and are hard to balance. A table cell with text input enabled looks nicer, and using placeholder text instead of a value cell style leaves more room for typing.

Custom Controls

If you work on a sufficiently complex software project for a long enough time, you're bound to run into cases where the standard building blocks don't quite provide the best experience you can imagine. This section isn't about customizing the appearance of standard controls; that's a topic for the mockups phase in Chapter 5. Instead, it's about making controls that behave in a new way.

Most of the time, you can and should base your custom control on a standard one. There's likely to be a standard control that kinda does what you want but that you need to tweak. By carefully adjusting its characteristics to satisfy the interaction you have in mind, you can keep your custom control as close as possible to the spirit of the platform.

Of course, it's possible to create an entirely original control from whole cloth, without basing it on anything that came before. If you and your team can pull this off perfectly, you'll be heralded as UI design heroes. If you execute it anything less than perfectly, however, it'll come off as awkward and painful to use.

Suppose you want to provide a long list of options in a quick, easily browsed way, without taking up a lot of space. These options are easily represented by small square icons, so a big tall table view with labels would be overkill. But a segmented control can't hold all the options you're planning. What kind of custom control could you create to do the job?

Start by looking at the standard controls that offer a way to pick from a list. The picker control's vertical spinning wheels do a good job of offering a lot of options without taking up much space. What if you could adapt the picker concept to a more compact, icon-based set of options? Presenting…the **horizontal mini-picker.** (See Figure 3.11.)

This control can hold any number of options, as long as they're represented by distinctive, square icons. It takes up only as much space as a single table cell row, thanks to its horizontal orientation. And it's immediately familiar, because it takes advantage of an existing control's interaction metaphor. In fact, to typical users, it probably wouldn't be obvious that the control was custom made. For all they know, it's simply a standard control offered by the operating system. That's great! Blending in as a natural part of the platform is a noble goal.

There are plenty of ways a control can give away its custom status. If you miss any of the following considerations, your control is a lot less likely to be perceived as fitting in with the rest of the system.

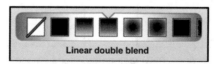

Figure 3.11   A horizontal mini-picker for choosing fill styles in OmniGraffle. It tweaks the concept of a vertical picker for a slightly different purpose.

- How does the control react to various gestures—tap, double-tap, touch and hold, drag/swipe, and the like?

- What happens if you accidentally touch the control and then try to drag your finger away without letting go? (On a standard button, this lets you cancel a mistap.)

- How does the control adapt to different amounts of available space, especially when the orientation of the device changes?

- What does the highlight look like while you're in the middle of tapping the control?

- How does the control work with accessibility features, especially VoiceOver?

Summary

iOS offers a healthy collection of carefully thought-out building blocks that you can use to craft your own navigation hierarchies and screens. Plenty of life-improving apps can be built using only these standard elements and navigation schemes. But if you need to, you can build your own custom navigation and custom controls. Just make sure that anything you create conforms to the spirit of the platform.

Now that you've familiarized yourself with the toolkit available (by reading the HIG and this chapter), you're ready to start building wireframes in earnest.

Exercises

It's time to try out your new knowledge. Give these exercises a shot to solidify your familiarity with the standard iOS elements and your understanding of when to customize beyond them. Do each one a few times, choosing a different example for each iteration, if you like.

1. Think of a single feature in your own app. What screens and elements might you need? Sketch out a couple of approaches using different kinds of controls to see which one feels right.

2. Choose a standard control. Imagine how you could design a custom version of it that serves a slightly different purpose. Can you make it more precise (or less, if that's what is needed), more compact, or more expressive? What purpose would your custom control serve better than any existing standard control?

3. Draw the geography of your app the way GarageBand's is drawn in Figure 3.6. Can you make spatial sense of the navigation scheme you're using?

4

The Wireframes

In the grand hierarchy of pictures of imaginary software, wireframes exist somewhere between sketches and mockups. Their purpose is to nail down the details that sketches leave out: what exactly exists on each screen and how it all fits together—the *geography* of an app. A sketch is casual and usually disposable; you might attach a sketch to a design document as a reminder of the conversation that led to a decision, but the sketch probably doesn't represent a definitive understanding of how the software should end up. Wireframes, on the other hand, document some details of how the app should be built. (See Figure 4.1 for an illustration of the difference.)

 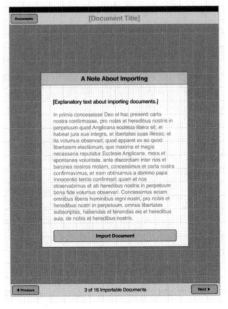

Figure 4.1   A sketch (left) becomes a wireframe, gaining detail about the screen elements and their layout.

The distinction is not always black and white. Some wireframes are kind of sketchy, and some sketches are kind of wireframey. But generally speaking, wireframes have the following unique characteristics as compared with other types of software design images.

- A wireframe includes all the elements that should go on the final screen; a sketch probably omits some.

- A wireframe delineates the type, position, and size of elements to a reasonably final degree; a sketch can drastically distort them.

- A wireframe doesn't specify an exact, pixel-perfect rendering of what elements should look like; that's what mockups are for. Instead, it uses a minimal rendering—usually plain, flat shapes, lines, and text.

- A wireframe may give some indication of the relative visual weight of elements on the screen, usually by differences in shading.

A wireframe may or may not be interactive; if it is, it's also a prototype.

Thinking in Screens

iOS apps are made of **screens.** Sure, they also include animations, audio cues, notifications, and other bits that can't be represented by static screens. And some apps do a lot of work behind the scenes that never becomes visible. But the basic constituent unit of any app, from a user's perspective, is the screen. The login screen, the home screen, the item detail screen, the archive screen, the user info screen, the settings screen, the share screen—these are the places users visit as they journey around your app. Each screen might have a number of states it can be in as well as a number of elements it might display depending on the situation.

Many **interface screens** are bigger than the physical size of the **hardware display** they appear on and can be scrolled or zoomed around. Don't confuse these different types of screens. (In this book, "screen" always means a place in the app, and not the glass on the front of the device.) On iPad, popovers give you a roughly iPhone-sized mini-display within a display, which can move between its own set of screens. All these screens and the states they move through are the skeleton of an app; you need to get them right to get the app right. (By now, it's normal if "screen" no longer looks like a word to you.)

Thanks to outlining, sketching, meeting, arguing, and deep thinking, you've got a good idea of all the screens that need to go into your app, and it's time to plot out precisely what each one should contain and how it should be organized. You need wireframing. Making yourself draw out every button, switch, field, and label will almost certainly raise some questions.

- How are we going to fit all six of these features onto one toolbar?

- Should this feature really be exposed at this point in the app?

- Do we want to present this option up front, or tuck it away somewhere else?
- Is this the right place to diverge from Apple's guidelines and precedents?
- Should these controls really be separate, or can we combine them?
- Oh dear, what have we gotten ourselves into? Is this even the app we should be making?

And so on. That's fine! That is part of the process. You might need to do more sketching or hold discussions to figure out how you want to answer those questions. Part III of this book is all about finding your own answers to those questions that don't have definitive solutions, so you may want to peruse it when you run into one. Get excited: this step—figuring out how you want to answer the questions that come up during wireframing—is when you develop the unique personality of your app.

Thinking in Points

We're used to dealing with pixels when measuring interface elements. And for a couple of years, only two sets of pixel dimensions mattered to iOS designers: the iPhone (at 320×480) and the iPad (at 768×1,024). As of the introduction of the iPhone 4 and the third-generation iPad, you now need to think about both standard and Retina resolutions, for both device families. Thankfully, the Retina resolutions are evenly divisible by the standard ones: one standard pixel split in half, in both dimensions, produces four Retina pixels. So you can simply multiply pixel distances by 2 and carry on.

But for the most part, you shouldn't be thinking in pixels until you get to the mockup stage and start creating production graphics. For wireframes, you should be thinking in points. The **point** comes from typography and publishing, where it has held a variety of values over the centuries but which finally settled at $\frac{1}{72}$ inches, the "PostScript point." The Apple point, though, is a new unit that indicates a resolution-independent distance on the display. On a standard-resolution display, 1 point equals 1 pixel; on a Retina display, 1 point equals 2 pixels. (See Figure 4.2.)

The important thing to remember is that you shouldn't take the presence of more pixels to mean you can increase information density. Retina displays are not for cramming numerous comically tiny elements onto a single screen. Rather, they're for increasing the *fidelity* of the same old identically sized elements. So Retina displays shouldn't even affect your wireframing process. Carry on designing for a screen that's 320×480 or 768×1,024, and enjoy the extra sharpness and fidelity you'll get if it appears on a Retina display.

Optical Measurements

For wireframing, you'll need to use an app that can lay out objects on a canvas, and you'll need to be able to measure their positions and their relationships to each other

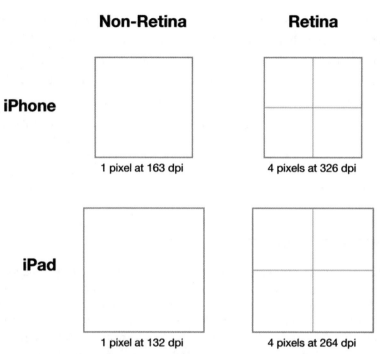

Figure 4.2   The meaning of 1 point on the four iOS displays. The size of a point can vary and can consist of 1 or 4 pixels.

very precisely. But the measurements reported by Xcode and by various graphics apps for a given object are sometimes at odds with each other, and are often at odds with what your eyes actually see. This is because the actual *visual* edges of a given object don't necessarily coincide with the bounds of that object as understood by the app displaying it. Objects have whitespace inside, or shadow effects dangling off of them, or text ascenders and descenders, or other accoutrements that make it hard for the software to know where the theoretical thing, as seen by a human, begins and ends.

Bounds and Optical Edges Are Sometimes Equal

Sometimes, of course, the visual edges of an object *do* correspond with its bounds as understood by the software drawing it. That's the case for a rectangle without any of those accoutrements like extra whitespace or shadows. For those objects, you can rely on the measurements reported by the software.

To plan clean, professional layouts, you need to think optically and measure sizes and distances optically. This often means ignoring what OmniGraffle, Photoshop, Fireworks, and Xcode say about where things are and how big they are. Instead, use the following techniques—and your eyes.

First, you need to know where to measure from. This is getting a bit into mockup territory, because you're going to see examples that include final effects. You aren't supposed to be worrying concretely about production graphics at this point, but you need to know about these techniques while you're wireframing.

Measuring Text Optically

Measuring text horizontally is easy: just look at the left- or rightmost point that's mostly opaque. If there's a faint column of antialiased pixels or a few pixels protruding from a round character shape (like an O), you can ignore them and move on to the heavily filled pixels.

Effectively every typeface—and certainly Helvetica Neue, the standard font on iOS—has its weight vertically delineated by its baseline and its cap height.

- The **baseline** is the horizontal line that the bottoms of most letters sit upon. (The curves of rounded letters go below it just a bit, and the descenders of certain letters protrude down beyond it.)

- The **cap height** is the line that the capital letters reach up to. (Some lowercase letters also reach it.)

These two lines delineate the vertical bounds of text for the purposes of optically aligning and measuring distances between elements. (See Figure 4.3.) Yes, this means that the descent of letters like y and p, and the ascent of letters like Å and Ž, may protrude outside the visual weight of the text and into the margins around it. Generous margins should more than accommodate that. Tons of apps get this wrong, either by including the descent or excluding the cap height in the weight of a text element. You can do better.

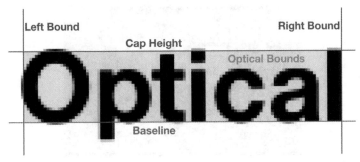

Figure 4.3 Measuring text optically. The shaded area represents the bounds of the text for the purposes of positioning and balance. Rounded shapes and faint antialiasing can protrude slightly.

Measuring Images and Controls Optically

Any control or image should have some sort of contrasting border or edge that defines its optical boundary. (If the edges seem to blur into the surface that the element is resting on, then you have a contrast problem. See Chapter 5 for more about contrast.) The boundary where the dark object transitions to the light background, or vice versa, is the optical boundary of the object. (See Figure 4.4.)

Where to Measure From

Some designers measure from the inside of the boundary; others measure from the outside. Is the edge of a table cell defined by the last white pixel inside, or the last gray pixel of the border? It doesn't matter which you pick, as long as you're consistent.

Techniques for Measuring

When you need an exact pixel measurement, here are some ways you can get it.

- **Zoom in really close**—On your Mac, go to the Accessibility pane of System Preferences and turn on the systemwide zoom. Turn off image smoothing, because you want to see those pixels nice and chunky. Now you can use the keyboard commands or the modified scroll gesture to zoom way the heck in on your designs and count the pixels yourself. Lots of times this is the quickest way to check on very small distances, but it gets tedious and error-prone at around 16 pixels. On iOS, the accessibility zoom always has blurry smoothing applied—you can't turn it off. You can work around that limitation with the app Screenshot Journal, which is intended for designers and developers, so it has a nice, chunky zoom.

Figure 4.4   Measuring controls optically. In this example, the outside of the stroke is considered to define the bounds of the button. Note that the underhighlight for the etched effect is not part of the bounds.

- **Guides and grids**—Any decent diagramming or graphics app should offer manual guides and customizable grids that you can use to draw laser-straight lines across your canvas. These are an excellent way to make sure objects are aligned and spaced evenly.

- **Standalone measurement tools**—Expect to run into lots of situations when you need to get the exact dimensions of an element in the iOS simulator or your wireframes, align two distant objects, or perform some other feat of precision. A standalone screen measurement tool (independent of your graphics app) is invaluable. You aren't likely to do better than the Iconfactory's xScope, a suite of tools for measuring, scrutinizing, and previewing pixels; it works like the guides and grids mentioned earlier, but for your whole screen rather than within a certain app.

- **Ruler objects**—Another option is to prepare precisely sized ruler objects inside your graphics app of choice, and keep them on a layer that you can unhide when you need to check a size or distance. These objects should be ones that you know are the same size optically and are shown in the app's logic—such as a plain, filled rectangle with no outer stroke—so that you can rely on the sizes reported by the app.

Tools for Wireframing

When it comes to sketching tools, you want anything that helps you get ideas out as quickly and roughly as possible. But for wireframes, precision is paramount. Theoretically you could do wireframes on graph paper, if you have an unusually steady hand, a mathematical mind, and a superb eraser. But you're almost certainly best served by a desktop software tool. You should choose something that lets you nudge objects pixel by pixel, measure exact distances, and quickly make adjustments to get your positioning and dimensions just right. This book doesn't rely on a specific piece of software, but among your options are OmniGraffle, Fireworks, Illustrator, Photoshop, Axure, and Balsamiq.

Designing in Xcode

Some designers use Xcode itself for interface design, which has the benefit that you can use the resulting product in the actual app. But it works great only as long as you stick strictly to stock, standard controls and elements. You'll miss out on custom elements, annotations, layers, and the rest of the graphical and logical benefits offered by a proper graphic design app. Once you have the hang of designing in design software, it'll save you much more time and effort than designing in Xcode.

Here are some crucial features to look for in your wireframing tools.

- **Layers**—One of the best skills you can have for building good wireframes is layer management. Be fastidious about keeping related elements together on layers, and name your layers descriptively; an orderly layer structure will serve you well. You can use layer visibility to compare alternative approaches to the same problem. You can also describe several states of a screen on just one canvas; popovers, sheets, alerts, and so on can each live on their own layer for easy showing and hiding. Some apps (like Photoshop) let you save layer comps that remember the visibility of each layer, or (like OmniGraffle) share layers across canvases.

- **Grids**—Get used to using the grid to position objects exactly where you want them. For initial layout, a good grid setting is 44 pixels with 11 subdivisions, resulting in 4-pixel squares. The major grid lines help you see the minimum 44-point-square tap target, and the minor grid lines give you some fine movement, 4 pixels at a time, without getting too fiddly. You may occasionally need to bump the subdivisions to 44 or 22 for a moment to move elements just a pixel or two. Even if you want maximum precision, leave the subdivisions at 1 pixel to prevent yourself from accidentally placing an object between pixel boundaries. A design document showing objects off the pixel grid looks cheap and mushy.

- **Styles**—Over time, you're bound to develop your own tastes and practices for wireframe creation. But it's good to keep in mind that you have options. The term "wireframe" of course comes from the classic outlines-only style of drawing interface elements, which looks precise like a blueprint and cares very little about the eventual appearance of each element. If you want to be a bit more detailed, you can use shading—monochrome or a very limited color palette is best—to indicate the relative visual weight or the semantic grouping of elements. Going in the opposite direction, you could even make your wireframes look intentionally slightly sketchy, just to communicate clearly that they're not finalized. (See Figure 4.5 for some wireframing styles.)

- **Dimension lines**—If you're passing your designs off to be implemented, and especially if you aren't going to have a mockup step between the wireframes and the implementation, it's helpful to include dimension lines between elements to make sizes and distances explicit. Some tools (like OmniGraffle) can even automatically calculate and display the length of a line. Put dimension lines on their own layer so that you can show them when they're needed and hide them otherwise.

- **Templates and stencils**—Whatever your graphics app of choice, you can find prepopulated templates and stencils full of wireframing components for common iOS screens and controls. Assuming that the resources you use are accurate, you can save a lot of time and effort in creating elements that are the correct dimensions. Or you can always create your own internal suite of stencils that fit the way you design so that you don't have to re-create every object every time.

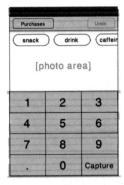   

Figure 4.5   Several wireframing styles. Left to right: slightly sketchy, with the precise dimensions not yet nailed down; bare wires, to avoid suggesting any visual treatments; shaded, for suggesting relative visual weight; color-coded, for easy recognition of groups of elements.

Principles of Layout

Before we get into the specifics of laying out iOS screens, it's helpful to learn (or review) some basic principles. As you lay out each screen, you should be thinking about what the placement and relationships of the elements communicate to users. There's no single canonical process for turning a set of requirements into a "correct" layout. But the principles discussed here will guide you as you experiment with layout possibilities and try to find a balance between the needs and constraints of the design.

Much of this section is based on the rudiments of Gestalt psychology—a theoretical framework that has a lot to say about how human beings perceive things. It's been highly influential in visual design. It tends to show up in art school curricula, and a century after its founding it is even useful for laying out iOS app screens. You could spend a lot of time studying Gestalt theory. If this sort of thing is interesting to you, check the reading list in the Inspiration Is Everywhere section of the Preface.

Unity Is the Goal

The following principles are aimed toward the creation of **unity** in your layout. In a unified design, every component seems to be just where it needs to be. Nothing extraneous is present. Nothing feels uncomfortable or haphazard. Each part makes sense on its own and contributes to a whole that makes sense, too. And if all is well, users don't notice this unity. Unless they're familiar with design and they're looking at the screen with a critical eye, most people don't realize what is pleasant about a layout. They just happily proceed to use it. If pressed, they might be able to say that it seems "clean" or "professional." But if the app falls short of achieving unity, people *will* notice. Customers can spot a disjointed layout from a mile away, and they recognize it as a warning sign that the developer hasn't put enough care and time into polishing the product.

How well an app is laid out is related to, but is not the same as, how well rendered it is graphically. That's another test for your layout to pass, and you'll get to that in Chapter 5, The Mockups. For now, focus on constructing good bones so that you can layer on the appealing styling later.

Read on for the principles. When you carefully consider all of them and get them working harmoniously, you'll achieve unity. Most of the principles probably seem obvious on their own, but it's surprising how easy it is to neglect them if they're not near the front of your consciousness. And it's the combination of them that creates a magical, ineffable sense of good design. If a design seems "off" somehow, it's probably time to run through this list and see which principle is being violated.

Visual Weight

Each element in a layout possesses some amount of **visual weight** relative to the others and to the layout as a whole. This weight affects how readily the element is noticed by the eye, how important it seems, and how it affects the balance of the layout. Visual weight is determined mainly by multiplying the following two attributes.

- **Size**—The bigger an element is, the more visual weight it carries.
- **Background contrast**—The more an element stands out from the background, the more visual weight it carries.

It's easy for a new designer to think that size is the only attribute that contributes to visual weight, neglecting the role of contrast. But the relationship between size and contrast means you can have elements that are different sizes but feel equally weighty, or elements that are the same size but seem to carry different weights. (See Figure 4.6 for an illustration.)

The final contrast depends largely on the visual treatment you end up giving the element in the mockup phase. But you should consider now the amount of contrast you intend to give the element so that you can weigh that against its size. For now, while wireframing, you can indicate contrast roughly by filling objects with three shades of gray to represent light, medium, and dark elements and areas.

For instance, suppose your app has a crucial button that you want to make particularly large for easy tapping. Giving it the same style as all your other buttons, while also making it much bigger, would result in an uncomfortably heavy button. It would far outweigh everything else on the screen. But if during the wireframing phase you indicate that it should be given a low-contrast treatment, you can then plan on styling it accordingly during mockups.

Or you may have a button that you need to keep small, for space reasons or even to minimize accidental taps. To keep it from getting lost among the other elements on the screen, you can increase its contrast with the background. A fine example of this

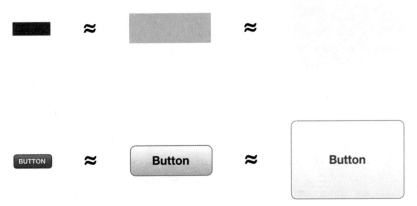

Figure 4.6   Objects of different sizes can have equivalent visual weights, as shown here with abstract wireframe objects (top row) and then again with visual treatments (bottom row).

is the purchase button in the App Store. It's actually smaller than the recommended minimum tap target size, because it's important to avoid accidental taps. But its heavy, high-contrast treatment makes its importance apparent.

Similarity and Distinction

Similar objects seem related, and dissimilar objects seem different. It seems banal to even write down. But there it is, because it's crucial to remember it as you design. When you're weighing your options for which element to use, where to place it, or how to size and orient it, compare it to existing elements on the same screen. Its similarity or dissimilarity to the other elements can tip the scale. Consider what their level of similarity says about the on-screen elements.

If you offer five similarly styled toolbar buttons, for example, a user expects them to be roughly equivalent. It's safe to assume that they are all actions that can be taken on whatever is currently visible in the content area, and that they're about equally likely to be used. Identically styled items listed in a table view are seen as peers—none particularly more important than another.

Any dissimilarities you introduce should have meaning. People tend to look for a reason when something is not like the things around it. The Done or Save button that concludes a modal view tends to be blue. Some apps give a distinctive size or style to a single toolbar button or tab to indicate that it is somehow more important than the rest. The Delete Contact button in the Contacts app lives among flat, white table views, but it's presented in a unique shiny red style to call out its distinct (and destructive) purpose.

Proximity and Distance

Objects that are close together seem related, and objects that are far apart seem different. This fact works along with similarity and distinction to determine how the eye groups things. The closer two things are in space, the more strongly their similarity links them, and vice versa.

When elements have similar purposes or meanings, put them close together. In many cases, such as in grouped table views, you can actually stick them together, sharing a border, with no space or separation between them. Or if you have two elements you need to separate conceptually, try putting some space or some sort of visual separator between them.

The grouped table views in the various screens of the Settings app are the prototypical example of using grouping and separation to associate and disassociate elements. Notice that they bear group labels only when necessary; often, the cells in each group do a fine job of explaining what the group is for. Really, the whole Settings app is a gold mine of admirably clever problem solving through layout.

Alignment

Most objects on a screen should align with something else on the screen. That is, if you draw an imaginary straight line along the edge or center of an object and continue it across the screen, the line should coincide with the edges or centers of other objects rather than miss them. (See Figure 4.7.) Look at any clean design, and you're bound to find that objects are rarely just a bit out of alignment. Either they're perfectly aligned, or they're far enough out of alignment that it's obvious the misalignment is intentional.

Alignment and Interface Layers

There's one major exception to the rule that objects should align, and it has to do with interface layers (which are not necessarily the same as the layers feature in graphics software). The Thinking in Layers section later in this chapter explains how to use interface layers to conceptually separate chunks of your interface. To reinforce the distinction, it's good for objects on different interface layers to be slightly out of alignment with each other. Notice that in Apple apps, the side margins in a navigation bar don't align with the side margins in the content area. The narrower margins in the navigation bar layer subtly suggest that it's a different interface layer that "contains" the content area layer.

Here are some tips for keeping elements aligned.

- **Edge alignment**—Aim to edge-align as many as possible of rectilinear (box-like) objects in your design: buttons, tables, square icons, and so on. For similar

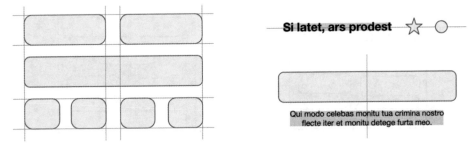

Figure 4.7   Edge alignment and center alignment. Pink lines show alignment; orange areas show the optical bounds of text elements.

objects in close proximity, edge alignment reinforces their relationship. If objects are farther apart, or less similar, then their edge alignment simply looks nice; it doesn't suggest a strong relationship.

- **Center alignment**—For rectilinear objects, this design is weaker and more prone to messiness than edge alignment. But it's excellent for irregular shapes, like blobs of text or bare graphics. For example, borderless toolbar buttons are usually aligned to their vertical center rather than edge-aligned, because each one has its own unique shape. Similarly, text that doesn't live in a box is often center-aligned. The title in a navigation bar is usually centered on the screen horizontally and centered in the bar vertically.

- **Aligning text**—Generally, text wants to align to other text more than it wants to align to boxes. You might at first think that a table view label should be left-aligned with the table border. But it looks much more at peace when it's left-aligned with the text *inside* the table. To vertically align different-sized pieces of text, the traditional approach is to ground them by making them share the same baseline; otherwise, both pieces of text will seem to be floating uncomfortably in space. If the two pieces of text are of very different sizes, though, then center-aligning to the vertical weight works better.

- **The guide test**—This is the quickest, most straightforward way to check the alignment of a layout and then fix it. Put the layout on the canvas of a graphics app that supports manual guides (straight lines that span the whole canvas). For every visual edge you see, add a guide. The edges of aligned objects can share a guide, but misaligned objects get their own guides. When you're finished, the guides express the visual logic of your layout, whether it's neat and sensible or a chaotic mess. From there you can adjust elements and remove guides until you have the most elegant layout that still supports the needs of the design. (See Figure 4.8 for a before-and-after example.)

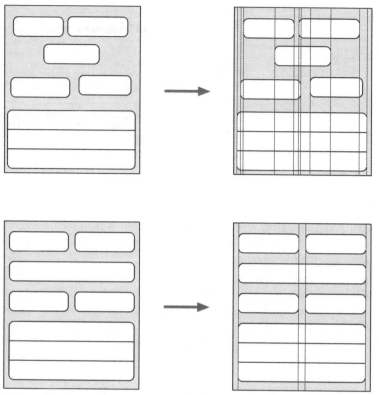

Figure 4.8   Applying the guide test to a particularly heinous layout (top),
and then to a repaired version of the same layout (bottom). Only the
guides for horizontal alignment are shown.

Rhythm

A good sense of **visual rhythm** is usually a cumulative effect of your spacing, alignment, and balance. But you can take an extra measure to ensure that the sizes and distances you choose are harmonious: use a scale. A **scale** is a preset list of measurements for you to rely on rather than choose an arbitrary value every time you need to position or size something. When the same harmonious numbers keep appearing throughout a design, it lends a sense of unity and order. (See Figure 4.9 for scales in use.)

Here are two scales that work well for iOS designs; you can pick one of these or invent your own.

- **Basic scale: 10, 20, 44**—For almost any design, you can get away with using this simplified scale. You use 10 points for a "normal" distance—for separating controls from each other, from labels, and from the edges of the screen or the view that contains them. Use 20 points when you need extra separation, as for groups

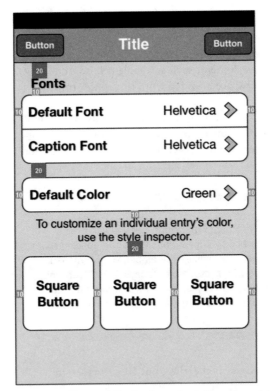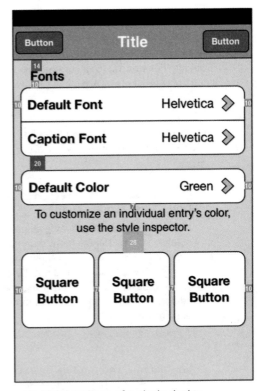

Figure 4.9   Basic-scale (left) and modular-scale (right) variants of a single design

of unrelated controls. Many standard iOS controls (such as table cells and toolbars) are 44 points; if you need much bigger spaces, using multiples of 44 when possible will coordinate well with them. You may need to use some other sizes on an ad hoc basis—for instance, a 52-point-tall table cell for holding a lot of text. That's fine! But don't also create 50- and 54-point-tall cells that will clash with it.

- **Modular scale: 7, 10, 14, 20, 28, 40, 56, 80…**—A modular scale is based on iterated multiplication by some number. In this case it's $\sqrt{2}$, which results in a doubling every two iterations. You can get very involved with choosing a ratio and devising a scheme for how you use each step in the scale; ventures like this are part of the endlessly rewarding pursuit of design. If you enjoy this sort of thing and want to learn more, pick up *The Elements of Typographic Style* by Robert Bringhurst. If not, there's no shame in using the basic scale.

The guide test described earlier is also good at uncovering awkward rhythms. If the distances between the guides seem to vary willy-nilly instead of falling into a sensible pattern, you need to make some adjustments.

Margin and Padding

Layouts look more modern, more pleasant, and more approachable when they employ healthy amounts of empty space. **Margin** is the amount of space afforded around an object. For boxlike objects with borders and content, such as a table cell or a button with a text label, **padding** is the amount of space afforded from the border to the content.

On iOS, users expect a certain amount of breathing room for elements, and when it's not there the app feels cramped, cheap, and uncouth. Scrolling is almost free, cognitively and ergonomically speaking, so there is little downside to giving content more space.

Don't Trust Xcode's Guides

Xcode's automatic positioning guides do try to help with layout, but you can't rely solely on them. They're more than happy to blindly suggest positions and spacing that make no sense, given what the layout actually looks like. Remember, optical measurements are what counts, and not the bounds of objects in Interface Builder. Over time, you may develop a reflex of letting Xcode place an object wherever it wants and then adding or subtracting a certain amount of space that you know to be correct for your design.

For margins, you can rely on a scale, as described earlier; put 10 points around everything, and you're in pretty good shape. To make sure you provide adequate padding, though, it's up to you to be vigilant. There isn't a strict algorithm for figuring out how much padding to afford a given bit of content. But a few guidelines can take you a long way. Most of these are based on the cap height of the text involved; that's the height of an ordinary capital letter like "E."

- For a single line of text in a box, give about 100% of the cap height as vertical padding. (See Figure 4.10 for illustrations of text and image padding.)

- For multiple lines of text in a single box, give 50% to 100% of the cap height of the biggest text as vertical padding.

- Generally, the horizontal padding should be between 50% and 100% of the cap height of the biggest text. Once you have your vertical padding as recommended earlier, you can apply a similar amount as horizontal padding.

- Objects that are edge-aligned with each other, especially horizontally, should also edge-align their text by having equal horizontal padding. (Even though the cells in Figure 4.10 have different top and bottom padding, they have the same side padding.)

- Images inside of boxes (such as toolbar buttons) can generally stand having a bit less padding than text. Aim for between 25% and 50% of the height or width of the image.

Figure 4.10   Padding examples for text, in percentages of the cap height) and an image (in percentage of the image height). Orange areas indicate optical bounds; note that the star's optical bounds don't reach all the way to the points, because the points contribute little to the visual weight of the overall shape.

Balance

Even if all the individual details in your layout are appropriately sized, aligned, and spaced, you still need to look at how the whole picture fits together. The main thing to keep in mind when thinking at this scale is **balance:** how the visual weight of the elements is distributed across the entirety of the screen.

A cheap way to get balance is by making your layout symmetrical. This approach is appropriate in a lot of cases, but it isn't the only way. One thing to watch out for is the tendency of the elements that balance each other to seem equivalent or in opposition to one another.

Another way to get balance is by carefully adjusting the visual weight of the elements. Adjust the size or the background contrast (described earlier) of elements to add or remove weight from an area of the screen. You may even subtly shift elements out of strict alignment or consume some of the space reserved for margins in order to achieve better balance. This approach takes a lot of experience and wisdom.

Thankfully, iOS apps can generally bear quite a bit of unbalance before they look bad from it. Vertical imbalance is usually fine, but try to avoid leaving one side of the screen empty while populating the other side.

Understatement

Use the minimum elements necessary to satisfy the needs of the design. In other words, never include anything that you don't need. This is the single most important principle, and it probably seems the most obvious. But it's more subtle than it seems, and it's easy to violate without realizing it.

To separate controls, you usually need only take one step up on your distance scale. There's usually no need for a separator line. When you have two pieces of text separated by whitespace and using different styles, you don't also need to use punctuation or borders to set them apart. If you have buttons organized in a grid, you don't need to draw a border completely around each item; let them share borders like a table, and use the edge of the screen or view as a border, too. Or eliminate the borders if the buttons still end up looking tappable. (See Figure 4.11 for an application of understatement.)

Typography

Normally a design book would need a huge chapter dedicated to typography: how to use type effectively and how to avoid the common pitfalls that make type look amateurish. Luckily, iOS has done a lot of the work for you, making decent typography

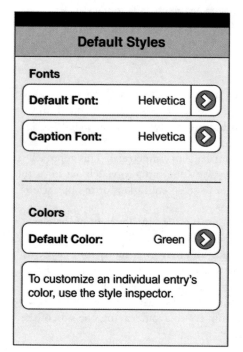
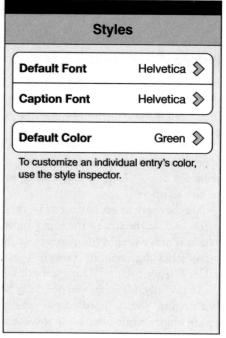

Figure 4.11   A needlessly fussy layout (left) and an understated version of the same screen (right).

easy and poor typography difficult. For most projects, you need only follow a few principles, listed here.

- Many of the principles described in this chapter apply to text as much as to other elements. Text should be balanced, aligned, understated, adequately padded, and so on. A modular scale, described earlier in this chapter, is wonderful for choosing text sizes. See the principles in this chapter that call out how they apply specifically to text.

- Almost all the time, the system font (Helvetica Neue on Retina displays, and Helvetica elsewhere) is all you need. It's a fantastic all-purpose font given the size and resolution of iOS displays, and it's so neutral that anything else tends to feel odd in an iOS interface. One exception arises when you want to put in a bit of branding by, say, using your logotype as a label on your home screen; that's fine, but use the system font everywhere else. The other exception is for long-form reading, spanning many screens' worth of text; in these cases it can be worth switching to a font specially designed for heavy reading; Georgia and Verdana are solid choices. (To learn about hunting down great fonts for inclusion in your app rather than using the iOS defaults, look up Marco Arment's "Introducing Instapaper 4.1 for iPhone, iPad" post on marco.org.)

- Use real characters, not ascii approximations. Habits from the early days of personal computing and the limitations of typical keyboards often keep people restricted to the meager ascii character set. Today's systems have a wealth of expressive characters available, thanks to the Unicode character set, but many people don't even know that there's a difference between, say, a proper apostrophe (') and a clumsy vertical tick ('). Use real quotation marks (" ") instead of neutral ones ("), use en- and em-dashes (– —) instead of double-hyphens (--), and use a real ellipsis (…) rather than three periods. All these characters can be typed with key combinations or copied from a lookup app like UnicodeChecker.

- There's no need to separate sentences with two spaces. It can be a hard habit to kick if you were raised to type this way, but it's just not necessary in the age of modern digital typography. One space is all you need; the carefully tuned fonts included with iOS know how to handle it.

- Generally, columns of the correct width (about wide enough to type the alphabet once or twice) are easier to read than too-wide ones (more than two alphabets wide) or very narrow ones (less than one alphabet wide). If you do have wide columns, you can make them easier to read by putting a bit more space between lines. Then it's easier for the eye to stay on track as it moves from the end of one line to the beginning of the next.

- On an iOS screen, it's rare that you'll have enough words per line to benefit from horizontal justification; instead it's likely to lead to unsightly and random-looking gaps between words. Left-alignment, with a ragged right edge, works well for paragraphs of content. Center-alignment is common for short, stand-alone explanatory blurbs of text that live outside of elements.

For advice beyond this, get hold of Robert Bringhurst's *The Elements of Typographic Style,* or the more adventurous *Thinking with Type* by Ellen Lupton, which are a thrill to read and will put you well on your way to becoming an expert.

Layout: A Place for Everything...

Now that you're familiar with the mechanics of placing elements together on a screen, it's time to think about *where* to put them. This section deals with the semantic (meaning-oriented) implications of how you arrange elements and how iOS helps you convey meaning through layout.

Content and Controls

Recognize the difference, and the relationship, between content and controls. **Content** is the actual stuff that users come to your app to see and manipulate: documents, images, web sites, media, text, and so on. **Controls,** then, are the administrative necessities (such as buttons and switches) that the user uses to tell the app what to do. The content is on the screen because the user wants to see it and work with it. The controls are on the screen because the app needs to get input from the user about how to behave.

This relationship should make it clear that content takes precedent whenever possible. The more you can pull your controls out of the way of your content, the better. That means either putting the controls on a visually distinct layer or presenting them in a temporary form such as a popover or a contextual menu.

Thinking in Layers

Most iOS apps involve some sort of layering, with the visual suggestion that the parts of the screen are actually different contiguous surfaces, each with its own independent position, and often overlapping in the imaginary dimension perpendicular to the screen (usually called the **z dimension**). This book calls these **interface layers** to differentiate them from the layers feature of graphics software. The most basic example of this concept is the way the content of an iPhone app scrolls around while the navigation bar and toolbar stay put. The content appears to be sliding around on its own layer behind the bars. Similarly, the sidebar of an iPad app is clearly its own layer by the way it scrolls independently of the main content area (or slides in from the side, in portrait orientation).

But independent scrolling isn't the only way you can distinguish interface layers. A conspicuous change in visual treatment can also signal a transition from one layer to another. The status bar, for instance, is usually styled differently from the app interface so that it seems more like part of the hardware device than part of the app. The same goes for the keyboard; users understand it as being different from the content area where they're using it to enter text.

The value of interface layers is both practical and conceptual. Practically, of course, it's good to be able to keep some things on the screen (like toolbar buttons) while other things (like content) scroll around. Conceptually, layers can signal the purpose of elements and content. Whatever occupies the center of the screen gets the user's attention, whereas the controls in toolbars, sidebars, and navigation bars around the periphery tend to be more utilitarian, only there to serve a purpose ancillary to the main content. Layers help you avoid polluting the content area with controls and help users' brains understand what's safe to ignore when they're just interested in looking at the content.

Occasionally apps add even more interface layers. An example is the slide-out ruler in the app Pages, which provides further, optional controls related to styling. As you lay out a screen, think about how to make interface elements feel as if they exist in discrete, modular chunks, grouped and arranged meaningfully around the main content.

Controls in Content Areas

Every rule has exceptions. Even though you just learned that controls should be arranged in chunks around the content, sometimes it makes sense to put controls inline with the content. If a control is closely related to the content, and especially if space is tight in the designated control areas, it might make sense to put the control in with the content.

The classic example of this is a "new item" placeholder presented as the last item in a table. If users tap it, a new item appears right in the tapped cell. Note that this approach doesn't guarantee that the new item button will always be visible on the screen; if you have a long list, it might be scrolled off the bottom. (Putting it at the top would be awkward because new items are usually added to the end of a list, not the beginning.)

The main challenge in presenting controls in the content area is making them look sufficiently distinctive to identify them as controls, without overpowering the precedence of the content. One minor styling difference, such as making text grayish-blue instead of black, is usually enough.

Information Density

Scrolling on iOS is cheap. The huge touch target, the simple gesture, the breezy inertial effect, and the viscerally satisfying animation make it one of the easiest things to do on an iOS device. So putting content "below the fold"—that is, beyond the first screenful of information (analogous to the fold in a paper newspaper)—is not nearly as strong a deemphasis as it was on the desktop in days of yore.

So calm any tendency you may have to cram as much data as possible onto a single screen. In some situations, an info-dense, dashboard-style, at-a-glance view is useful, but it's uncharacteristic of iOS apps. Even on a small screen, feel free to spread out your information as described earlier in the principles of layout. See more about information density in Chapter 12.

Dimensionality

Given the controls you have to lay out and the screen or view size you have to work with, it may seem reasonable to use a two-dimensional arrangement: a grid, a multi-column table, and so on. Especially on iPad, where you have a lot more screen space to work with than on iPhone, you might be tempted to get sideways. Be careful! iOS is generally a one-dimensional platform, because it's harder for users to decipher 2-D layouts.

- Most fundamentally, 1-D layouts are far easier for the human eye to scan and interpret. You can simply draw your eye down the list of available items until it arrives at the correct one. A 2-D layout instead encourages the eye to bounce around the screen haphazardly, unsure where to look next.

- Two-dimensional layouts suggest meaning that might not be there. Each column seems to have a purpose, so the eye looks for a way to group its items. The same goes for rows; anything adjacent appears to be adjacent for a reason, which your brain tries to find.

- Although traditional tables of data are common on the desktop, such as in Finder windows or the classic Mail message list, they are rare on iOS. Instead of laying out cells of data side by side, iOS more commonly provides a couple of important pieces of information, using a supplemental text style, arranged in the same cell as the main title. This makes for a sort of 1.5-dimensional layout, where the items are arranged in a linear list but each item contains information spread out horizontally and vertically. (The 1.5-D message list in Mail on iOS has even made its way to the Mail on OS X.)

Keep Widths Sensible

Especially if you stay one-dimensional, you might wonder how to keep your elements from being comically wide as they try to fill the width of an iPad display. In such cases, you should usually not have the entire width of the display to fill; elements usually appear in a popover, a sheet, a sidebar, or the content area next to a sidebar. But if you find yourself with a content area covering the entire screen anyway, use generous amounts of margin (balanced on both sides) to push the controls inward. That's better than having ridiculously sized elements that fill the space just because it's there. (The page sheet style of modal view, described in Chapter 3, does a good job of keeping things from getting too wide.)

Sometimes, though, going two-dimensional is a fine answer. After all, even the iOS home screen is a grid.

- Two-dimensional layouts work pretty well with instantly recognizable entities. A grid of big, simple, colorful icons should work great. But a grid of tiny text-labeled buttons is a hassle for the mind to process.

- The fewer items you have to lay out, the more likely they are to work in 2-D. A 2×3 grid of 120-point square icons can be understandable and comfortable to interact with. A 5×5 grid of 48-point square icons, though, would be a headache to parse.

- If you can establish a meaningful reason for the columns that helps the user identify the options, 2-D can be nice. Suppose you have three text-oriented options and three media-oriented options in a blogging app; separating them into two columns makes good sense.

- Two dimensions is more often appropriate for content than it is for controls. Don't be afraid to use a 2-D layout to present information if it makes the information clearer. Sometimes it makes perfect sense to lay out information spatially. And if a meaningful 2-D presentation already exists for the content at hand, as in a calendar, even better.

Orientation on iPhone

iPhone apps can be locked to a certain orientation (portrait or landscape), or they can adapt to either orientation. There are four basic options for dealing with device rotation.

- Locking your app to portrait orientation is understandable, but not ideal, for a typical app. If you have to pick an orientation to lock to, portrait is the one. That's the orientation of the iPhone home screen, and it's by far the most commonly used orientation in apps. iOS tends to stack UI elements vertically: navigation bars, toolbars, keyboards, and so on. So some apps are simply too hard to cram into the shorter vertical space of a landscape iPhone.

- Being locked to landscape orientation is odd. A few apps can get away with it because their interface is dependent on a unique and immutable composition of elements.

- Adapting one interface to either orientation is ideal. If you can do it without undertaking a drastic redesign of your entire interface, you should. Users appreciate being able to rotate the device to switch between seeing more items at once and seeing more detail about each item. Lots of people prefer the big keys on the landscape keyboard for typing-intensive tasks. You can even get away with a few rarely used screens being portrait-only, if you must.

- Occasionally, it makes sense to offer a different interface depending on the orientation. If you have two drastically different but comparably valuable ways of looking at the same information, an orientation change may be just the way to switch between them. That's especially true if the normal view wouldn't have benefited much from landscape anyway. But be careful with this approach. Plenty of users simply never think to rotate their phone in order to see something different. Some even keep their orientation locked all the time to avoid accidental rotation, because they never intentionally switch to landscape.

Consider the orientation handling of some of Apple's built-in and App Store apps.

- Clock is locked to portrait orientation, because switching to landscape wouldn't gain you much. The information in each item is narrow enough to be completely visible without needing more horizontal space; switching to landscape would merely reduce the number of items visible at once and would make the already sparse items look even more empty.

- GarageBand is locked to landscape orientation, an unorthodox choice. Of course, GarageBand has an unorthodox approach to its interface overall. It feels much more like a virtual hardware device, like an actual piece of recording equipment rather than a magical piece of software that can reconfigure its layout. It is already pushing hard on the boundaries of what a phone is expected to do; redesigning its painstakingly detailed and surprisingly complex interface to be orientation independent would have been prohibitively difficult, with little to be gained. If your app is as grand and complex as GarageBand, and as astoundingly useful, feel free to lock it to landscape.

- Mail adapts to both orientations, which is an easy choice because of its structure. For the most part, it's a flexible content area bounded by a navigation bar at the top and a toolbar at the bottom. When you rotate the device, the content resizes appropriately, and the bars get a bit taller or shorter. It's a small investment for a big payoff, considering how much reading and typing people do in the app.

- Calendar offers a different presentation in landscape mode: a sort of expanded version of its hour-by-hour day planner that spans multiple days and can be panned two-dimensionally. In this app, rotating the device is more like toggling a view setting than it is like simply adjusting the size of the "window."

Orientation on iPad

The question of how to deal with orientation is quite a bit simpler on iPad. The device is still easy to rotate, but it's not as easy and casual as rotating an iPhone. People tend to pick an orientation and stick with it for a long time as they work with various apps. The screen is spacious enough that as long as you design carefully, either orientation offers enough space to get things done. So it is much harder to get away with not offering the same interface in both orientations. For almost all apps, users expect the app to accommodate them and not to have to rotate the iPad to accommodate the app.

Being locked to either orientation requires a compelling reason. GarageBand and Keynote are both locked to landscape, because their interfaces are so specific to those screen dimensions that it would not make much sense to reinterpret them in portrait.

The Worst-Case Height-Compression Scenario

On both devices and in both orientations, it might seem as if you have plenty of vertical space to work with. But there's a horde of interface elements just waiting to stack up and consume it. Whatever elements you're intentionally including in your design, make sure you consider the other elements that might invite themselves.

- Unless you're hiding the status bar because you have an especially immersive app, it'll always be there, eating up 20 points.

- On an iPhone in portrait mode, if a phone call, voice recording, or tethering session is in progress, then the status bar grows to be 40 points tall.

- On any screen that allows text entry, you must of course account for the keyboard (162 points on iPhone landscape, 216 points on iPhone portrait, 352 points on iPad landscape, and 264 points on iPad portrait). Screens that don't normally scroll may need to scroll when the keyboard is visible.

- Some languages, such as Japanese, also need a completion bar to support text input, so the space needed for the keyboard is actually taller than you think (36 points on iPhone, 54 points on iPad).

- Even if you're designing with the taller iPhone 5 in mind, with 568 points of height to work with, lots of people have older iPhones with only 480 points of height. Every screen you make should be great on the shorter display and even better on the new taller display. This may mean that less scrolling is necessary, or it could mean that screens designed to fill the display afford more space to each element. Wireframe for both heights.

For each screen you wireframe, plan how it will respond to having *all* the possible interface elements visible at once. If it can take all those elements and still have a reasonable amount of room for the content, then you know you're in good shape.

Summary

Wireframing is about figuring out which elements to use and where. It requires thinking in screens: how elements fit onto screens, how one screen flows into the next, and what variants and states of each screen exist. It also requires thinking in points: the dimensions of elements and their placement relative to the screen boundaries and the other elements. There are lots of tools for wireframing. Make sure you choose tools that help you draw precisely and measure accurately.

To get good at wireframing, you should be familiar with the fundamentals of layout, especially the goal of unity and the importance of understatement. These principles will serve you well elsewhere, too: on the desktop, on the web, in graphic design, and beyond. When it comes to iOS specifically, keep in mind the standards of layout that users expect from a well-made app.

The next stage of our journey is an exciting one. It's almost time to turn our modest, utilitarian skeleton of a design into a lovely, charming, production-grade mockup.

Exercises

The principles you've learned in this chapter should serve you well for building responsible, sturdy screens. Work through these exercises to get your own app into shape.

1. Based on reviewing the sketches you made of each screen and referring to your architecture outline, build a wireframe of each screen that includes every element just where it needs to be. Consider all the elements built in to iOS and the possibilities of custom controls. Consider what the positioning, grouping, and characteristics of the elements say about their meanings.

2. Critically scrutinize your wireframes, looking for any elements that are misaligned, unbalanced, or cramped. Use the guide test to bring all the elements into harmony as best you can.

3. Wireframe key screens in both orientations and with all the possible transitory elements visible. Make sure these changes don't cause the layout to break down.

5

The Mockups

At last, it's time to develop and polish the skin of your app. A **mockup** (or **comp**) is an image that precisely (or very nearly) represents your intentions for the final visual appearance of a screen. Ideally, it'd be impossible to tell a completed mockup from a screenshot of the real app. That's the quality commonly known as "pixel-perfect." (Indeed, many a designer has been momentarily puzzled when their absentminded clicks or taps on the controls in a mockup don't yield any response.) In reality, though, mockups often have a few stray pixels or approximate colors here and there. Now is the time to make all the specific visual-design decisions you've been encouraged to push to the back of your mind during the earlier design phases.

At this point, the foundations of your design are good. In this chapter you'll learn how to present that good design in a way that *looks* good, inviting a second look from potential customers and eventually cultivating a long and happy relationship. That mission involves everything from conceiving of an appwide (or even brandwide) visual language, all the way down to refining individual pixels.

When to Mock Up

If sketching is the central activity of design, mockups may be the primary output of design. (Yes, there are also other important documents that describe the philosophy and behavior of an app, and not just its appearance. Some would say prototypes are even more important.) Over time, you're likely to develop a sense of when it makes sense to go ahead and mock up a screen; the decision depends on factors like how confident you are in your layout idea and how quick you are about creating and revising full-fledged mockups.

If you're really fast, if you already have most of the graphics resources you need, and if your graphics workflow of choice makes it easy to revise your pixel-perfect mockups, then you can from time to time use mockups to serve the purpose of a sketch or a wireframe.

If you're revising an existing app, rather than dreaming up a new one, you can often use a screenshot as your starting point—that is, if you're sure the new design will be much like the old one, with only a few adjustments. Rather than carefully craft realistic depictions of existing screens and controls, you just grab a picture of the real thing and start drawing on top of it and nudging elements around.

Just be careful about getting into the habit of jumping straight to mockups for every design problem you encounter. If you don't first explore all the alternatives, you're bound to pour several days of effort into a perfectly rendered image of a design that simply doesn't work. In the worst case, you and your team will implement the bad design because you can't afford to go back and start over. You might even be so enamored of how cool the mockup looks that you subconsciously can't bear to find fault with its usability or appropriateness. Or the opposite: people on your team might not care for the specific visual design of a concept and thus will dismiss the merits of its interactions. So don't do that.

Sometimes you can skip the mockup phase entirely. Perhaps you're working on a screen that you're confident will involve only standard system elements, with no significant customization—for instance, a mundane Settings screen containing nothing but simple grouped table views, buttons, and switches. In such cases, you can probably go straight from wireframes (or even detailed outlines) to implementation, as long as whoever is doing the engineering understands the intentions of the design. For screens like that, once the design is implemented, it's easy to go back and make minor changes to the implementation rather than go all the way back to wireframes.

Styling: The Apparent Design Discipline

For a lot of folks, styling is the only part of design that they're even aware of: Photoshopping shiny buttons, picking color schemes, and applying gratuitous wood-grain textures to the background. Even people in the business of building software have a habit of conflating styling with the whole of design. In reality, styling is only one of the many phases you need to go through to design a pleasant software experience. Steve Jobs said, "It's not just what it looks like and feels like. Design is how it works."

A good graphic designer could probably take a list of the features needed for an app and render a beautiful, hyperrealistic interface. But it takes a user experience designer like *you* to know how an interface actually communicates to the user, fulfills the many delicately balanced demands of the task, and remains rewarding over the long term. Whether or not people ever recognize the toil you've put into evolving the skeleton of your app by outlining, sketching, and wireframing, they will certainly notice the skin of it.

Put another way, you've done your research, rehearsed your speeches, and compiled an impressive résumé, all while wearing your pajamas. Now it's time to put on a sharp-looking outfit and head out the door to the job interview.

As it turns out, the clothing metaphor goes a long way in explaining the importance of visual design in software. It's entirely possible to dress up an unreliable, disagreeable, or malicious person in a stunning custom suit or dress, just as it's commonplace to find a flaky or unusable app hiding beneath a thin shell of superb graphic design. Likewise, the most qualified person in the world could very well walk into a job interview wearing a shabby old t-shirt and hoodie; and a tremendously useful bit of software could have an embarrassingly crude visual presentation.

That is all to say that as human beings we tend to use appearances and first impressions as a way to make a time-saving initial judgment. Failing that preliminary test of resourcefulness and attention to detail by posting shoddy-looking screenshots to the App Store is likely to get you filtered out of the running for further consideration, regardless of how qualified you actually are.

The quality of your styling will depend mainly on three criteria: rendering, communication, and tastefulness.

Rendering

Rendering is how well the pixels on the display convince the human eye that they actually are the thing you intend them to look like, commonly referred to as what the objects **read** as. When people see the standard desaturated-blue toolbar on an iPhone, they generally read it as (recognize it as) a sort of glass or plastic surface, slightly convex, about a millimeter thick, resting atop the content area. Why do people perceive a bar that isn't there? It's because the rendering mimics what a real glass bar would look like, and it tricks their perception into seeing it as one. Human perception is everything; even if a rendering makes logical sense when zoomed way in or when the Photoshop styles applied to it are examined, if the eye doesn't correctly understand it in real usage, then it's wrong. Optical illusions count.

Rendering is the most disposable attribute of styling. By no means is great rendering necessary for an app to be understandable or usable. But it's useful for three reasons.

- It supports the suspension of disbelief necessary for truly graceful interactions, as described in Chapter 8, The Graceful Interface. The more an interface looks as if it has a physical presence, the more readily the mind will believe that it can be directly manipulated and interacted with.

- The amount of care that designers put into rendering is a decent first-approximation clue as to how much care has been put into the product as a whole. It's not a 100% accurate indicator, but it helps people find which apps they'd like to give a closer look. Good rendering sends a signal to people with good taste that the designers care.

- It makes people happy. Unsurprisingly, on the whole, humans find attractive products more pleasant to use than starkly utilitarian ones. Putting a half-point inner shadow on a message count badge to make it appear ever so slightly recessed doesn't help anyone get work done. But it'd be a sorry civilization that only ever cared for efficiency and never took a moment to just enjoy a nice recessed message count badge.

Communication

Communication is a more pragmatic thing, and probably the most important thing, to think about when you're creating the final appearance of your screens. As described in Chapter 9, The Gracious Interface, the styling of an element usually carries cues about its purpose, function, and significance.

A button seems to protrude from the rest of the interface, thereby inviting users to tap. An object that can be freely dragged around has a modest drop shadow that makes it look as if it's resting loosely on a surface. A popover has a diffuse drop shadow that makes it appear to hover above the rest of the interface, emphasizing its transitory nature. Many "dangerous" controls that can cause data loss or other unfortunate occurrences are bright red, and the suggested next step in a guided workflow is often a calm blue or green.

Much of the communication that happens in styling is by association with the styling of existing elements. Flat white controls on a partially transparent, shiny black glass bar can suggest similarity to the iOS media-playing experience, or to the utilitarian lock screen experience. Stoic, simple, desaturated-blue surfaces are associated with mundane productivity tasks like email. As with interactions, if a styling precedent exists for the sort of thing you're trying to create, go ahead and take advantage of it.

Almost everything about the styling of an element communicates somehow. The size and contrast of an element contribute to its visual weight, which sends a message about its importance. Similarly styled elements tend to be conceptually grouped in the perception of the user. Any difference in style seems to suggest a logical difference, which the user's mind will try to decipher.

In short, don't make styling decisions willy-nilly. For any decision you make, ask what you're communicating by making the element appear that way.

Tastefulness

No matter how realistic or clearly communicative a screen is, it can still be ugly. iOS has, on the whole, been a powerful force for tasteful interface design. Yes, there is plenty of questionable or even alarmingly bad design in the App Store, but every week Apple features heaps of remarkably well-done work on the front page. It's up to you to align yourself with those front-page apps and step away from the counterexamples.

It may seem important to communicate the magnificence of your brand, but applying the electric colors of your logo to every element will cheapen users' experience of using your app. It's more iOS-like to omit the branding from of the interface and instead construct an experience that serves the task. Then you can place your logo inconspicuously on the top of the main screen or to put it on the icon and leave it out of the app interface entirely.

Another example: no matter how realistically you render a brick-wall background, it's still inappropriate for placing behind content because it's rough, unwelcoming, and high contrast. On iOS, understatement is the norm. Vivid colors are generally reserved for the user's content, and not the interface itself. Severe depth-generating effects like big drop shadows and extreme gradients tend to look tacky on iOS, where well-styled interfaces rarely claim to be more than a few millimeters deep. After all, even the device itself isn't that thick. (Some designers are starting to prefer especially flat-looking interfaces; see Chapter 15, Rich and Plain.)

Mockup Tools

The graphical assets you create for your mockups will eventually become the production graphics resources that you include in the app itself: backgrounds, icons, source images for custom controls, repeating textures and patterns, and so on. Choosing a toolset for creating your mockups and your production graphics is at least as intensely personal a decision as choosing tools for sketching or wireframing. Take the time to try out and evaluate several options, and always be on the lookout for ways to improve your workflow. There's no shortage of graphics tools and add-ons out there, each focused on making your design job easier and each catering to certain ways of approaching your work.

For sketching and wireframing I could simply list important features that you should look for when choosing tools, because wireframing style is a flexible thing anyway. As long as you can create an image that represents the layout you intend, in a way that's easy for you to create and maintain, the tools for wireframing are pretty interchangeable.

But production-grade graphics tools are full of built-in design decisions, technical peculiarities, and other idiosyncrasies that add up to a heavy influence on how you can work with them. That is, the tools you choose have quite a bit of influence on what kinds of graphics you can easily make. Lots of designers end up developing skills in several apps, and the skills to shuttle data between them, in order to realize their visual ideas.

So here is a short list of commonly endorsed production graphics tools, along with a brief commentary on their strengths. Learn one, learn them all, find an alternative, or even join the many who have taken upon themselves the daunting task of building a sensible and modern graphics app from scratch. Nobody can tell you which tools will work best for you.

- **Photoshop**—This is the huge, venerable, seemingly undefeatable industry standard. The majority of graphics you see around the iOS landscape (and indeed around the world) originated in, or at least passed through, Photoshop. Its often-groused-about interface is unique and nonstandard; its stability is questionable; its feature set is likely ten times bigger than what you'll ever need; and its price tag is preposterous. And yet, it almost certainly can handle the most byzantine and esoteric image-creation tasks you care to offer to it. The most important features it offers for iOS design are its layer styles, vector shapes, masking, and a pixel-oriented workflow (since your final production graphics will probably be PNG bitmaps). Nobody ever got fired for choosing Photoshop.

- **Acorn**—This is the classic Photoshop alternative. As of version 3, Acorn offers an impressive system of layer styles that's in some ways more flexible, and in many ways more sensibly designed, than Photoshop's.

- **Pixelmator**—This is another well-known Photoshop alternative. It does support vector shapes, but it doesn't yet have layer styles, which are central to the workflow described in this book.

- **Illustrator**—Illustrator can do a lot of the same things as Photoshop, but it has a vector- and print-oriented heritage. You can make pixel-precise graphics with it, but it's ambivalent about the concept of pixels until it comes time to export.

- **Paintcode**—This vector illustration tool is especially built for software design. As you draw, it generates the Objective-C code to create the equivalent images in your app. You almost certainly want to use normal image resources for many elements, but this is a great way to ensure that the in-app drawing you want to do is possible.

Color: Thinking in HSB

It's surprisingly difficult to think and talk about color, even though we're surrounded by it. Part of the problem is that color perception and understanding depend on a tangle of photons, neurons, synapses, automatic perception, and conscious thought. So physics, evolutionary biology, engineering, psychology, and art each has its own equally valid understanding of how color works. It's easy to get mixed up and struggle for words, not sure of the precise meanings of words like "vivid," "bright," "saturated," "dark," "hue," "tint," "shade," and so on.

Color models are a concept that aims to help people think and communicate about color in precise terms. When you understand a color model, you can specify any color as a set of numbers. Most color models use three numbers, visualized as a three-dimensional area, to describe the space of possible colors.

Good Old RGB

If you've worked with color on computers, especially on the web, you're probably familiar with the RGB colorspace. **RGB** defines colors based on the amount of red, green, and blue light emitted from the screen. And that's how the technology of cathode-ray tubes and liquid crystal displays actually works: by modulating the amount of those three colors at each pixel. So RGB makes sense technologically. And the cones that detect color on your retina are (roughly speaking) attuned to red, green, and blue wavelengths. Another point for RGB: it makes sense physiologically.

The problem is that RGB doesn't make much sense psychologically. You know, like, in your mind. When you have a dark orange you'd like to brighten, it doesn't intuitively come to mind that you should add red light and green light at a 2:1 ratio. If you have a yellowish green that you'd like to remove the yellow from, it doesn't feel natural to decrease the red component. Yet these are the things RGB asks of us. (Yes, because of the cruel history of HTML and CSS, some heroic web designers have mustered the mental discipline necessary to think not only in RGB space but simultaneously also in hexadecimal. If you know someone who can tell you off the top of her head what color #591e6f is, show her some respect.)

Introducing HSB

There is a colorspace that works more closely to the way your mind does. It lets you simply say you want a color to get brighter, be less yellow, or undergo many other simple transformations. It's called HSB (or sometimes HSL, but HSV is a different model), and it works like this (see Figure 5.1 for examples).

- **Hue** is a number expressed in degrees (from 0° to 360°) that represents a position around the color wheel. The hue doesn't care about how light or dark or vivid the color is, only whether it's red (0°), yellow (60°), green (120°), and so on. When you reach 360°, you're back at red, reflecting the circular nature of color perception. If you work with HSB long enough, you'll start memorizing important hues, such as 210°, the blue with a slight aqua hint that Apple likes to use throughout its interfaces.

- **Saturation** is a percentage that represents how much of the hue is present in the color, as opposed to how neutral the color is. Saturated colors look more pure

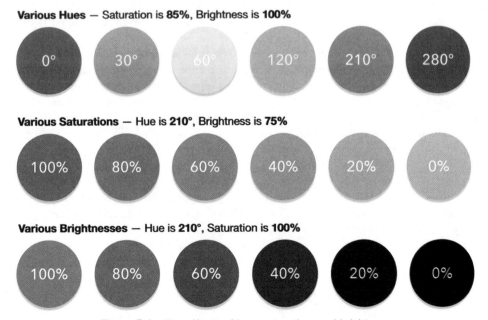

Figure 5.1   The effects of hue, saturation, and brightness

and more vivid; desaturated colors look more muted and gray. At 0% saturation, the hue is eliminated entirely and you're dealing with grayscale.

- **Brightness** (or lightness) is easy. It's a percentage that represents how light or dark the color is, directly depending on how much light is being emitted by the screen. When brightness is 0%, the color is always black, so the hue and saturation don't matter at all. When brightness is 100%, the screen is emitting as much light as possible.

Get used to the difference.

- Blue is a hue.
- Grayish blue is a saturation and a hue.
- Dark, grayish blue is a brightness, a saturation, and a hue.

Once you grow accustomed to thinking in HSB, which should happen fairly quickly, you can speak precisely about colors. You can recognize that what's odd about a certain on-screen element is that it's too saturated relative to the rest of the interface. You can articulate that it's the brightness difference that makes a bit of text stand out from the background. You can even describe colors in the real world in terms of HSB when you're picking out curtains, clothing, or cats.

Get Serious about Value

The brightness that a person actually perceives is called **value**. Note well that the brightness and saturation numbers are not the same as *perceived* brightness and *perceived* saturation.

Different hues have different personalities. You can't just spin the color wheel, holding the other two numbers constant, and expect the resulting colors to be visually equivalent. In fact, each hue has its own unique range of possibilities for human perception. Purple just can't appear as bright as yellow can. Green that's 100% saturated looks outrageously more intense than 100%-saturated blue.

These are facts of nature, related to the historical effects of the evolution of primate vision to find food in the trees tens of millions of years ago. We're well equipped to see a wide range of variations in jungle hues like red and green, but poorly equipped to see the subtleties of hues that don't make much difference in nature, like blue.

This is all to say that just because a 100%-brightness blue has decent contrast against white doesn't mean that 100%-brightness yellow does, too. Yellow is just a light hue. Think of an art project by a first-grader who picks a different crayon to write each letter. The yellow letters disappear into the white paper, becoming almost unreadable. If you intend two elements to have different hues but similar value, you need to nudge the brightness and saturation up or down when you change hues in order to keep the value somewhat stable.

The World Wide Web Consortium (W3C) offers a formula for calculating perceived color brightness, though it's based on RGB:

$$((R \times 299) + (G \times 587) + (B \times 114)) \div 1000$$

If you're uncertain of the relative perceived brightness between two colors, you can put them through that formula for a sanity check. You can even use this kind of algorithm in cases where the text could be of any color, and you need to present it on a sufficiently contrasting background at run time.

Contrast: Thinking in Figure/Ground Relationships

As briefly introduced in Chapter 4, contrast is an all-important concept in visual design. Contrast is the measure of how different two things look from each other. The difference can reflect any visual attribute, such as hue or texture, but **value** (or perceived lightness) is the strongest.

The importance of contrast in visual design can't be underestimated. You have to be thinking about contrast throughout the process of creating your production graphics and mockups. (If you can start thinking about it earlier, in the wireframing phase, even better.) It's the single most important factor in determining a screen's readability, which in turn plays a huge part in how understandable it is and how satisfying it is to use.

It's time for more perceptual psychology and Gestalt theory. One of the most fundamental concepts in perception is that of the **figure/ground relationship.** Whenever your eyes are open and light is present, your eyes and brain work together to decipher the patterns of photons hitting your retina, trying to separate the **figures** (shapes of things) from the background. They do this by finding contrast—differences to serve as clues that a certain area in a user's field of vision actually represents a discrete object. The outline that separates an object from its background, as suggested by the contrast between them, is called the **contour.** Strong contrast creates a crisp, obvious contour. Weak contrast vaguely suggests a feeble, shifting contour, or no contour at all.

Contrast is important because it's the idea that makes electronic displays work at all. Using contrasting colors to illuminate adjacent pixels creates a contour that your mind interprets as a real figure on a real background. The human perception system is great at overcoming difficulties to find hidden or obscured forms, but it's happiest, and under the least strain, when the contrast is strong and clear. Consider the contrast of the objects in your design, and aim to offer unambiguous contours. Camouflage works because it compromises the contour of an animal against the background. If you don't give your elements good contours, you're essentially camouflaging them.

Styling for Good Contrast and Visual Weight

Here's how to get good contrast—that is, to adjust the visual weight of an element to a level appropriate for its role. Try to balance your application of contrast with the layout principles explained in Chapter 4. Sometimes it's worthwhile to give an element a bit of a heavier presence than necessary if it would balance out the layout of the screen. On the other hand, sometimes it's fine to slightly compromise perfect alignment or spacing to give an element an appropriate visual weight.

Look at any iOS screen and recognize the anatomy of each element. Any element should have at least one of the following anatomical components (or two of them, or all three).

- **Border**—This is a narrow line drawn around the edge of the element. On an element with no border, the interior simply stops and the background begins. (A shadow usually doesn't count.)

- **Interior**—This is the surface of the element. An element with a border but with "no interior" is actually one whose interior matches the background.

- **Contents**—This is any text or images inside the element, such as the label of a table cell or the free-floating icon of a borderless button.

Also, every element rests on some sort of **background**. Even if the element reaches to the edge of the display, as with a toolbar, the perimeter of the display serves as a sort of dark background. Figure 5.2 shows how these four components fit together.

It's the contrast between these anatomical components and the background that determines how noticeable and readable an element is. For an element to stand out properly, it must have a sharp, strong contour provided by contrast between the background and either its border or its interior. (For elements that are just contents, such as borderless buttons, the contents must provide the contour.)

There are lots of ways to fine-tune the amount of contrast between an element and its background; here are a few examples (see Figure 5.3).

- The more contrast the anatomical components have with the background, the more weight the element will have.

- Using the interior to get contrast with the background will provide more weight than using the border, because the interior comprises more pixels than the border. It's rare for both the border and the interior to have strong contrast with the background; one or the other usually dominates.

| Border | Interior | Contents | All Three |

Figure 5.2   The anatomical components of an on-screen element

- The more *internal* contrast (between the border, interior, and contents), the more weight the element will have.

- The more saturated the color of an element, the more weight it has. On iOS, saturated colors tend to be reserved for bringing attention to the most prominent items of all, and rarely do more than a few interface elements on the screen have much saturation.

- The more intense, noticeable effects the element has, the more weight it will have. This includes gradients, bevels, shadows, shines, and patterns.

- A more organic and muted texture will slightly decrease its weight. The typical flat or gradient surfaces in interfaces tend to read as somewhat shiny. Adding a gentle texture such as noise, described later in this chapter, actually reduces its weight by making it look matte.

- Some components having stronger contrast can make up for weakness in other parts. A classic example is the text in table views. The message list in Mail, for instance, uses strong typographical patterns to create a sense of regularity from one cell to the next: a large, bold sender name, followed by a smaller, regular-weight subject line, followed by two fainter gray lines of message preview. The strong contrast and rhythm of the text means that the cells can be separated by nothing but a single modest gray border.

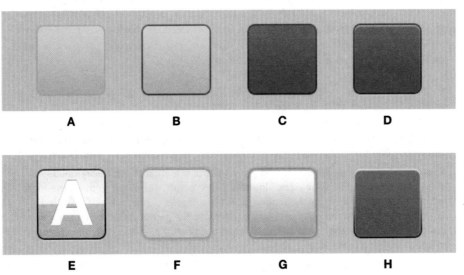

Figure 5.3   Element A has too little contrast. Elements B and C add a border and an interior that contribute to contrast. Element D's highlights improve the contrast. Element E's outrageously overzealous shine compromises the contour of the contents. Element F tries to get contrast from a mere drop shadow, and fails. Element G's weak, muddy gray stroke doesn't contribute to contrast. The stroke in element H is too enthusiastic about its gradient and fails to provide contrast around the entire shape.

A common pitfall when you're applying styling to elements is allowing the styles to compromise the contour of the element. A strong shadow or bevel can easily blend into both the element and the background, harming the contour. A border whose value is midway between that of the interior and that of the background can create a fuzzy transition between the two, muddying the contour. An overzealous gradient or shine effect on the interior can blend into the contents, making them unreadable. In general, the interior of an element should not contain dramatically different levels of contrast with the background, as would occur with a strong gradient or shine.

Good Backgrounds

The most important thing about a background is that it provide a flat, stable environment for content to live on. A good background has low **internal contrast,** meaning it doesn't create any shapes within itself that the eye could conceivably recognize as a figure, nor does it threaten to interfere with the actual figure/ground relationship of the elements. Any texture or pattern should be subtle enough for the eye to ignore as it tries to identify the figure/ground relationships on the screen.

But, especially with the trend for interfaces to imitate real-world surfaces, app designers have a tenacious habit of using photorealistic textures, or even photographs, as backgrounds or even as element interiors. The most commonly found example is wood grain, but you can find anything from corkboards to photos of grassy fields. This kind of background is almost always a mistake. The internal contrast is nearly as strong as, or even stronger than, the contrast between the background and the elements, and that demolishes the eye's ability to make out the correct figure/ground relationship, creating cognitive unease. So don't do that.

How to Get Away With Real-World Textures

But, you might ask, what about Apple's own apps? Apple uses realistic-looking textures all the time. Dark gray linen appears everywhere, notably in Notification Center. The wood-grain trend is apparent in the bookshelf presentation of its own iBooks.

How does Apple get away with this? It gives careful attention to the backgrounds' internal contrast. Apple's "realistic" interfaces are actually *idealized* to avoid the more inconvenient attributes of real-life objects. On the iBooks shelf, look closely at the wood where it meets the edge of a book: thanks to the gentle variations in the value of the grain and to the shadow that helps define the book, there is no way the contour of the book object can get lost.

Next, look at the iBooks toolbar (see Figure 5.4). The contrast between the buttons' dark borders and the whole of the background is several times stronger than the contrast between any two pixels *within* the background. Each button has a partially transparent brown gradient fill that serves to flatten the contrast of the wood texture that appears in its interior. The contrast between the average brown of the interior of those buttons and the average blond of the toolbar is plenty to overcome the variations in

Figure 5.4   The iBooks wood-grain texture has far less internal contrast than most real wood.

the grain. Likewise, the brown of the toolbar title and the white of the buttons' labels are both more than contrasty enough to survive on top of the grain.

Below the toolbar is a strong shadow that crisply separates it from the shelf area. Regardless of whether you like the bookshelf metaphor, Apple's visual-design implementation of it is unimpeachable. If you want to do your own realistic interfaces, study iBooks well.

The choice to use a pattern or texture at all is usually a matter of taste. An app with nothing but perfectly flat fields of color tends to look…digital. A pattern, even a simple one like the standard desaturated-blue pinstripes that appear behind grouped table views, goes a long way. A texture as simple as the noise layer described later in this chapter can also lend sophistication.

The difference between patterns and textures is blurry. Generally, a pattern has a clearly delineated, illustrative style, as if color were applied to a flat surface. A texture uses light and shadow to suggest how the surface would feel if you could touch it and is usually more organic and random. Some backgrounds combine both a pattern and a texture.

Transparency

The trick of the iBooks toolbar buttons' partially transparent fill illustrates a useful, or sometimes troublesome, fact: putting a partially transparent layer on top of anything reduces its contrast. It makes perfect sense if you think about it. Every pixel of the underlying layer gets a bit closer to whatever color the transparent layer is. That is, the colors of all the covered pixels get closer together. By definition, that means they have less contrast with each other.

The good news is that you can put a transparent layer on top of anything to present information or controls without obscuring what's underneath. Or, as with the iBooks toolbar, you can preserve the texture of a surface while putting readable elements on top of it.

Check out the lock screen on your iOS device. It uses partially transparent black glass overlays for the status bar, time bar, and slide-to-unlock control. They're transparent enough to let your lock screen wallpaper show through, but opaque enough to knock down the contrast to a level that guarantees the readability of their content, no matter what crazy wallpaper you use. Transparent layers like these feel more temporary, less obtrusive, and more deferential to the user's content.

The bad news is that you can't have it both ways. You can't expect both the content on top of and the content underneath the transparent layer to be readable. If the layer is transparent enough to make the bottom content readable, then the top content won't be readable, and vice versa.

1+1 = 3

If you use borders to get contrast, be careful when placing your bordered objects next to each other. You can easily end up with the problem of too much contrast in one small space. A single dark border provides a crisp contrast against a light background, but two dark borders close to each other create an area where the value quickly jumps from light to dark to light to dark to light as the eye moves across it.

The thin light area between the dark-on-light borders seems to create a light-on-dark border of its own. Thus, two borders end up looking like three, and that's why the information visualization pioneer Edward Tufte calls this phenomenon 1+1 = 3 (see Figure 5.5).

All this strong contrast in one place creates a sense of jittery, vibrating motion, as the eye tries to figure out which is the foreground and which is the background. That's contrary to the calm, stable impression you're aiming for. So if you're using thin borders, either keep them a safe distance apart, switch to getting contrast from interiors rather than from borders, or merge the neighboring borders into a single border.

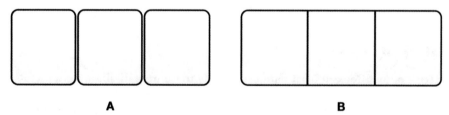

A   **B**

Figure 5.5   Adjacent borders in A cause a 1+1 = 3 effect. B solves it by merging the borders.

Presenting Image Content

Of course, all this careful modulation of contrast is easy for elements you have full control over. What about **image content,** which can be provided by users or procured from just about anywhere? How do you present music albums, book covers, user avatars, photos, illustrations, and the like? These things can have any kind of value and may contain any shapes and patterns. To have confidence that they'll always have a good contour regardless of their inherent visual characteristics, you must take care with their styling.

For all you know, the image that ends up in your screen could be precisely the same value, color, or pattern as the background, thus causing it to blend right in and virtually disappear. A book cover might have a blond wood-grain pattern just like the iBooks shelves. An album cover might be the same light gray as the Music app's album view background (on iPad). And the edges of a photo could easily be the same black as the background of the photo grid in the Photos app (also on iPad). Plus, anything containing an image should be given more visual presence than would be granted by a flat and featureless rectangle anyway.

The answer is that you should never just let image content run directly into the background. You need to provide a buffer at the edge. If you check the apps just mentioned, you'll see that each one solves the problem handily. In iBooks and Music, covers have a nice broad shadow that's dark enough at the edge of the object to provide a nice contour for lighter covers, but transparent enough not to blend into dark covers too much. (Using a shadow alone is a little risky, because some colors might blend right into the combination of the shadow effect and the background. But it's much better than nothing.) In Photos, each picture has a wide white border that provides guaranteed contrast with the dark background, no matter what's inside the photo.

Evaluating Contrast: Posterize It

So the clearest way to create contrast is with differing values. You could meticulously measure the value of every pixel using the W3C formula (discussed in "Get Serious about Value" earlier). You may be a natural-born visual designer with a gift for putting together pleasing, harmonious graphics. But there are shortcuts that can help anyone get to a clear, professional design easily. Here's a way of looking at the visual design of a screen that should help you evaluate its value contrast.

Look at each anatomical component of each element, and judge its apparent brightness as light, medium, or dark. That's right: pretend the entire interface is made up of black, white, and perfect 50% gray. (You might even have planned ahead by using a wireframe style that includes only those three shades and then made your visual design accordingly.) This technique is inspired by the posterize feature in Photoshop, which, like a screen-printed poster, reduces the entire range of colors in an image to a few flat colors. If you aren't certain, go ahead and do the actual posterization process on your design (see "Posterize It for Real").

Ignoring the gentle gradations and subtle color differences forces any weak contrasts to become no contrast at all; a light-gray shape and its light-blue background both become the same flat white. Anything that doesn't have a strong contour simply disappears. When you mentally (or actually) posterize a screen, you're essentially saying that any contours that are not strong enough to survive the process are not strong enough to count as contours.

Posterize It for Real

It takes practice to recognize whether something is closer to black, medium gray, or white, but you'll get the hang of it. In the meantime, or any time you're not sure, you can cheat by actually doing the processing on a screenshot in Photoshop. It's also just plain fun to try it on various screens and put their contrast to the test.

First, choose Image ▸ Mode ▸ Grayscale to remove that pesky color data. Then choose Image ▸ Adjustments ▸ Posterize. For the number of levels, pick three; that forces the entire image to black, 50% gray, and white, just as the mental posterization exercise calls for. Sometimes an excellent visual designer can get away with a design that needs to be divided into four levels (black, 33% gray, 67% gray, and white), but it's safer to force yourself to stick to three.

It's amazing to watch sophisticated, detailed designs get reduced to three flat values and still be perfectly readable (see Figure 5.6). Try it on your own designs, try it on Apple apps, try it on third-party apps.

Figure 5.6   The iTunes app on iPhone, normal (left) and posterized. All the important contours survive the posterization process, which is a sign that the contrast is good.

In a posterized world, there are only three levels of contrast.

- **High contrast**—The values are two steps away: dark on light, or light on dark. Elements with high contrast automatically assert themselves as particularly important relative to other elements of the same size. Any amount of text (beyond a short, seldom-read blurb of explanatory text) should be given high contrast. High-contrast elements tend to grab the attention just a bit more than, and keep it a bit longer than, medium-contrast elements.

- **Medium contrast**—The values are one step away: light on medium, medium on light, dark on medium, or medium on dark. This is the standard contrast level to aim for on a typical element. Although medium-contrast text tends to look svelte and stylish, it is difficult to read for more than a couple of sentences.

- **No contrast**—When you posterize, values that are too close together get smooshed together and the contrast disappears. If the contrast doesn't survive the posterization, it's not contrasty enough. You may be able to see a low-contrast element just fine when you're looking for it, but for people who don't yet know it's there, it will be difficult to spot. Even if a user finds the element, low contrast puts more strain on the eye and on the mind. The element might even seem to be disabled—dimmed out because it's not applicable at the moment. Avoid low contrast. Make your elements clearly and unmistakably proclaim their presence and availability.

Remember that the way you see your app is not necessarily the way other people will see it. Not everyone has perfect vision, and not everyone always has his glasses on or contacts in. Some people prefer to turn the brightness down. Sometimes people hook up their iOS devices to junky old projectors with badly calibrated gamma. Err on the side of making your contours unmistakable.

Make sure to check the internal contrast of your elements just as carefully as you check the contrast between an element and the background. Any element that has contents (such as a button with a text or image label) should have a strong contour between its contents and its interior. It's common to see cells or buttons with text or images that blend into the interior of the element to the point that you can't readily read it.

When your posterization finds elements that don't have enough contrast, you should adjust the design using the guidelines given earlier. Then test it again until it passes without a hitch. Over time you'll be able to tell at a glance whether a screen has enough contrast. You'll even be able to plan and design graphics resources whose values are harmonious with each other before you even have to place them together in a single mockup. Once you've assembled the mockup of the whole screen, you'll likely need to make small adjustments to the contrast of individual elements, but if you follow the light/medium/dark guideline, you'll probably already have values in the neighborhood of what you need.

Contrast Examples

Most of the styling choices you see in the built-in iOS apps, downloadable Apple apps, and popular third-party apps may seem arbitrary at first. It's easy to think that the designers just "make it pretty" and ship it out, then capriciously make adjustments over time to keep it fresh or keep up with fashion and fads. In fact, you can almost always find a good reason for each color, texture, and effect choice if you ponder hard enough. The simplest, most unassuming controls and screens can have the most brilliant design thinking behind them, and most people never notice. That's as it should be. It means the app is communicating clearly and directly rather than drawing undue attention to itself. As you read the following examples, refer to Figure 5.7.

Table Cells

Consider the humble white cell on a light-blue background that characterizes a grouped table view. The white interior is a similar value to the pale background, with the slight difference giving the control a bit of a boost in its weight and presence. The cell gets some of its contrast from the border, but mostly from the high-contrast text contents. This is as it should be. The usually black text on a white interior provides plenty of contrast and is the purpose for the cell's existence.

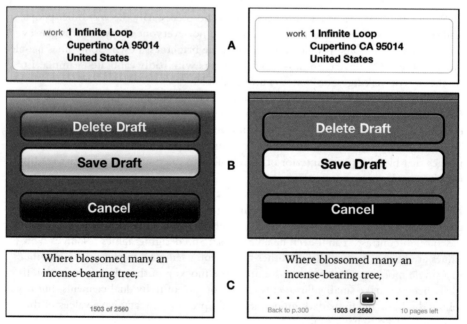

Figure 5.7   A: A table cell, normal (left) and posterized. B: Action sheet buttons, normal (left) and posterized. C: Metadata at the bottom of an iBooks page, in both modes.

Action Sheet Buttons

For another lesson in the clever use of contrast built into iOS, look at the shiny black, white, and sometimes red buttons of an action sheet. (That's the thing that slides up from the bottom of an iPhone screen, or appears in an iPad popover, to provide several commands to choose from—for example, Save Draft, Delete Draft, and Cancel when you try to stop composing an email message in progress.)

The action sheet itself is medium gray, providing a consistent background. That's a wise choice, because it lets the light-interior buttons appear loud and clear regardless of what's underneath.

The three button colors are carefully chosen to communicate cues about their effects. The red Delete Draft button is actually the same value (apparent brightness) as the background, but its intense saturation, especially in the alarming hue of red, pushes it into strong contrast territory. The Save Draft button has strong value contrast with the background, in a safe-looking white, making it look like a normal, recommended option. The black Cancel button has less contrast with the background (and is positioned slightly away from the others), making it blend in and seem to be a sort of meta-option, a "never mind" that nullifies the question being asked.

The white-on-red, black-on-white, and white-on-black text gives the buttons stronger contrast, making them obviously the next thing the user should pay attention to. Meanwhile, a dimming effect covers the screen, reducing the contrast of everything else in order to get the user to focus on the choices at hand. It's modal; there's no interacting with anything else until this question has been answered.

iBooks Page Metadata

A particularly careful case of contrast control can be found in the iBooks reading screen. The app has two main states while a book is open: one in which most of the interface is hidden (to reduce distraction), and one in which the interface is visible. In the distraction-free state, the book title at the top and the page number at the bottom are drawn in a faint beige. Its contrast with the background is low enough, especially compared with the crisp, high-contrast body text, that unless you're intentionally looking for it, you can easily ignore it.

Once you tap the center of the screen to enter the full-on interface state, the beige text quickly fades up to a dark brown, matching the controls that now appear. The moment when you've just explicitly indicated that you want to interact with the controls on the periphery of the screen is a perfect time to bring up that metadata to the same noticeable level of contrast as the controls.

Meanwhile, new metadata appears in the lower corners: a way to hop back to the last section you were reading, and an indication of how many pages are left in the chapter. These bits of information are in the same low-contrast beige as the page number was a moment ago in the reading mode. That styling reinforces their temporary nature, suggesting that they'll fade back to invisibility when the page number fades back to beige. It also correctly matches their importance relative to the other information on the screen.

Birth of a Button

It's time to create your own custom control. Perhaps you've decided that the Capture button in SnackLog (our sample app, introduced in Chapter 1) should have a distinctive, more inviting style than the ordinary number pad buttons around it. This section walks through the creation of a single, classy-looking button in Photoshop, stopping to examine the techniques and reasoning at each step. It's not the only way to create graphical resources for an app, but the easiest, most maintainable method takes advantage of a certain pair of indispensable graphics app features: shape layers (or vector masks) and layer styles.

The workflow presented here is by no means the only way to use those features; it's just a particularly straightforward, introductory way. All designers find their own preferences for using the universe of possibilities that is Photoshop to realize the graphics in their imagination. Likewise, each graphics resource you create will require a unique combination of effects and techniques. This walkthrough is to acquaint you with what's possible. Even though this section discusses the process in Photoshop terms, you can find equivalent features in other graphics tools. And even though this book can't present a full course in graphic design or in the use of Photoshop, these few techniques will take you a long way.

As you work, keep your layers tidily organized and descriptively named. The better your layer management habits, the less irritated you'll be at yourself a year from now when you need to come back and make adjustments to your source images.

Step 0: Set Up the Canvas

Figure 5.8 shows our Photoshop workspace when we're in the middle of creating our Capture button. Whenever you're working on production graphics for apps, you almost always want your vectors aligning to pixel edges. Make sure you have the "Snap vector tools and transforms to pixel grid" setting turned on in Photoshop's General preferences. (In Photoshop CS5 and earlier, you won't see this setting. You have to set up a 1-pixel grid and be vigilant that your points are snapping to it.)

Start a new document, and give it a reasonable size as indicated by your wireframes. In the case of the Capture button for SnackLog, we know the exact dimensions need to be 106 × 60 pixels for the button to fit into the numeric keypad. If you always start by designing graphics at non-Retina resolution, you can be sure that your designs work fine at the lower resolution, and they should scale up and gain fidelity just fine. If you go the other way around, anything you draw has a 50% chance of ending up in-between pixels when you scale down.

Numerous image resources used in iOS apps are bigger than the optical size of the elements they contain. One reason is that having a transparent buffer area around the edges gives space for effects like shadows. For optically small controls, it's easier for engineers if you provide a resource that's already the size that the tap target needs to be; then they don't need to manually assign a larger target to a tiny image. If you need

Figure 5.8   A typical Photoshop workspace, working on the Capture button design

to move an image optically for alignment and balance, you can nudge it in Photoshop and replace the image, rather than ask your engineer to move it in code.

The resources you create need to have a transparent background so that they can be composited properly onto the actual iOS screen. But while composing them, it's helpful to create a solid-color layer to test the contrast against. If you're creating an element that needs to work on various backgrounds, you can even create a suite of background layers to test on.

As you work, you may want to open an extra window on your document. Choose Window ▸ Arrange ▸ New Window for [your document name]. Now you can zoom one window up very close, turn on the grid, and use guides, while the other window stays at 100% and lets you preview how the element will look in practice. There are even apps, such as xScope and Skala Preview, that let you view images from your Mac live on your iOS device as you work. Figure 5.9 shows where you'll go from here.

Step 1: Create a Shape Layer

Select the rounded rectangle tool from the tools palette, and drag across the canvas. When you use one of the shape tools, such as the rounded rectangle, you end up with a shape layer. A **shape layer** is pretty much what it sounds like: a layer that contains a

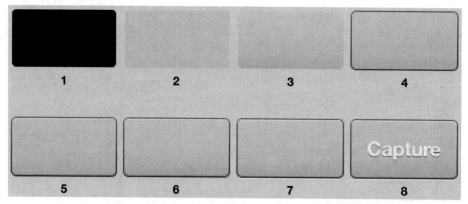

Figure 5.9   All the steps in Birth of a Button

shape, rather than mere *pixels.* The shape is defined by **vectors,** meaning you can scale it, transform it, or adjust its individual points without losing any fidelity. Whatever pixels the shape encloses are filled with the shape's color, and nice antialiasing happens at the edges automatically.

Before the layer-style-based workflow was invented, designers had to create another layer for each effect they wanted to add: a dedicated layer for the highlight, another one for the drop shadow, and so on. Then, if they needed to change the shape of the object, they'd have to update each layer individually. Now, remarkably, the drawing of a single shape is often the only work you need to do on the canvas in order to create an element. All the rest of the work is in the form of applying layer styles to that one shape.

Step 2: Choose a Fill Color

Double-click the thumbnail (not the title or any empty space) of your rounded rectangle in the Layers palette to get a color picker. The color you choose can be thought of as the pure, "true" color of the button before any styles are applied. In reality, objects don't appear as simple blocks of color; they have depth and substance. To simulate those attributes, you'll apply layer styles to the object until it looks real.

From here on, it may seem as if you're adding lots of styles and that the resulting button will be garish. The key is to make each effect as subtle as possible while still achieving its intended illusion. The combined result of all those modest effects should be a pleasing, classy-looking button, without any one effect standing out.

Step 3: Apply a Gradient

Gradients are everywhere in iOS, and everywhere in reality. Very little in the real world appears to your eye as a perfectly flat field of color. Even on a flat object viewed straight on, there's almost always a subtle shift in value as your eye moves across the object. It's hard to tell sometimes, because your eye is good at reading the surface as flat. But if you want to see how different two apparently identical points on an object can really be, use Photoshop's eyedropper tool on a photo. Without at least some faint gradients, interfaces tend to look purely digital, which conflicts with the general iOS aesthetic. (Again, there are exceptions—see Chapter 15.)

Double-click an empty area of the row that represents your shape in the Layers palette, opening the layer style editor. (Yes, you get different results from double-clicking the thumbnail, the title, and the empty space of a layer in this palette; welcome to Photoshop!) Click Gradient Overlay to turn on the gradient and see the gradient controls. There are a lot of gradient controls, but don't stress about them just yet; for now you only need to care about a couple of them. You'll probably see the default gradient—white on top to black at the bottom—totally opaque and obscuring your beautiful fill color. That's not very helpful.

But try slowly dialing back the opacity on the gradient to reveal the fill color beneath. With the gradient at just 20% or so opacity, it lends a lovely sense of depth to the previously flat object. You don't need very much of a gradient to create that illusion of depth. In fact, very conspicuous gradients are out of place on iOS and tend to make a design look cheap and dated. And remember that a strong gradient will make it harder to maintain internal contrast with whatever contents you end up placing in the button. For many surfaces, a mostly transparent white-to-black gradient like the one we've set up here is plenty to give it the depth it needs.

One problem, though, is that putting 20% worth of that *totally desaturated* white-and-black gradient onto your element significantly desaturates your fill color. You carefully chose your original fill color to have just the amount of saturation you wanted, and now it's being polluted by the gradient. That's where Photoshop's many blending modes can help you. The "Light" modes—Soft Light, Hard Light, Linear Light, and Vivid Light—interpret the white, gray, and black pixels of the gradient as lighting effects rather than as literal colors to be blended, as is the case with the Normal mode. Each one has a unique effect on the brightness and saturation of the underlying pixels. Try changing the blending mode for your gradient in the layer style editor, looking at each of the Light modes and adjusting the gradient opacity to get the range of brightness and saturation you want. Soft Light and Vivid Light also tend to shift the hue in addition to the saturation and brightness, and that may or may not be the effect you want.

Step 4: Add a Stroke

We're already planning to put this button on the dark background of your number pad, and we intend to get contrast from the difference between that background and the green fill. But adding a dark stroke exaggerates the darkness of the background, giving you more contrast and defining the button even better. This approach is especially important because the black background will be partially transparent, with the camera view showing through underneath; you want to make extra sure that the button is well defined no matter what the camera is pointed at.

If it's not still open from applying the gradient, open the layer style editor by double-clicking (some empty space in) the rounded rectangle layer in the Layers palette. To apply a stroke, click the checkbox next to Stroke; then switch to the controls for adjusting it. You almost always want the size to be 1 pixel, unless you're going for a unique visual effect. A 1-point stroke tends to read as almost invisible, or as a thin groove that emphasizes the contour of the element. Anything thicker tends to read as some sort of illustrative outline that conflicts with an otherwise realistic rendering.

Even at 1 pixel, though, a pure black stroke will usually read too heavy. Backing off the opacity to somewhere between 60% and 85% lets the stroke blend into the background somewhat, getting darker on dark backgrounds and staying reasonably light on medium backgrounds. For extra sophistication, you can use a gradient stroke: more transparent black on the top, more opaque black on the bottom. That approach tends to give a gentle drop-shadow effect and blends in better with the range of interior colors provided by the gradient. For extra *extra* sophistication, you can use a dark, desaturated variant of the fill color instead of black for the stroke, also with a gradient from more transparent to more opaque.

Step 5: Add a Bevel

If the stroke reads as a groove around the button, then realistically there should be a highlight where the light hits the top of the button heading into the groove. Click the Bevel & Emboss layer style to turn it on. The default settings are overkill. They'll make anything look as if it belongs in a local grocery store flyer from 1998. Changing only a few settings should tidy it up nicely.

First, change the shading angle from 120° to 90°, and make sure that Use Global Light is selected. For whatever reason, Photoshop loves its 120° lighting angle and uses it as the default for every new document, making everything look as if it's lit from above and to the left. Everything on iOS, though—everything—is lit from directly above. Any other lighting angle is a dead giveaway that a designer wasn't paying attention. If Use Global Light is selected, the change you make here will affect all other styles that use the global light setting, such as drop shadows and inner shadows.

Next, knock the size down to 0 pixels, giving you a nice, crisp, single-pixel highlight. If you must create a protruding effect, you can keep it at 1 pixel. Anything beyond that is likely to look as if it's trying too hard to pop out from the screen. You can experiment with the chisel techniques, but for bevels as small as you'll be creating, you usually don't need to worry about them.

The highlight and shadow opacities need to be carefully tuned to the point that they help the button read as being a three-dimensional object but they don't shout it. The default 75% is often good for the highlight. Because it's easy for the shadow to disappear into the bottom stroke, you should pick a faint opacity like 15% or less, or even just drive it all the way down to 0%.

Step 6: Add Texture

If they're well rendered, almost all flat or gradient surfaces with no texture applied read as shiny plastic or glass. (If they're poorly rendered, they read as, well, poorly rendered Photoshop layers.) Those perfectly smooth surfaces are fine, but occasionally you may want to mix up the textures in your app. A bit of texture can make a huge difference in the sophistication and professionalism of a design.

The most standard texture you can add is a matte surface. And the way you make a surface look matte is with a noise layer.

- Create a new layer above the button. Call it "Noise."
- Fill the new layer with 50% gray; you can do this by choosing Edit ▶ Fill.
- Choose Filter ▶ Noise ▶ Add Noise.
- Choose about 15%, Gaussian, and Monochromatic, and then hit OK.
- Set the opacity of the noise layer to something very low, like 3%. Anything that makes the noise noticeable without a very close look is too much, and it tends to make your element look fuzzy or just plain wrong.
- With the noise layer selected, choose Layer ▶ Create Clipping Mask. Now the shape of the noise will conform to the exact shape of the layer below it, which is your button.

The faint noise adds tiny imperfections and fluctuations to the brightness on the surface of the button, making it look more like a real object scattering light in various directions. That's just the best effort-for-impact texture you can make. If you cultivate your Photoshop skills, there's no end to the textures you can dream up and apply to your elements.

Step 7: Add an Underhighlight

Finally, this button needs a bit of style to communicate its relationship to the background. Just as we needed a bevel highlight to make the button read as being surrounded by a groove, the background below the button needs a highlight to complete the illusion. Here you're essentially adding an effect to the background, rather than to the button, to make the bottom edge of the groove look as if it's reflecting light.

Open the layer style editor for the button, and choose Drop Shadow. Normally, a drop shadow is a dark, blurry effect below an object, but for an underhighlight, you need to misuse it slightly.

- Change the blending mode from Multiply (which creates a darkening effect) to Normal, or else your white shadow won't be visible at all.
- Change the shadow color to pure white.
- Change the size to 0 to get a crisp, tight underhighlight.
- Change the distance to 2. (Normally you would only need to set it to 1 to get the single pixel of visibility that you need, but because there is a 1-pixel stroke outside the shape, you need to add 1.)

- Adjust the opacity down to about 25% to match the bevel highlight on the button.

Now the button will appear to be embedded in any background you place it on.

Step 8: Add Contents

For the purposes of making mockups, you have to add your own contents: text labels, icons, and so on. Once the app is a reality, that will probably be added in code. This Capture button needs text that says "Capture."

Choose the Text tool, and click somewhere outside the button. (Otherwise, Photoshop tries to add text to the button itself, and you want a dedicated text layer.) Then move the text into place. Type "Capture," and use the Character palette to choose a color, font, and size.

In the layer styles window, add a small, dark drop shadow above the text to match the style of most light-on-dark text in iOS.

It's good practice to create text layers in Photoshop with the styling that you want, so that you can describe the effects to the engineer who will implement it: "We need a 50%-opaque black drop shadow, with no blur radius, 1 point above the text."

Onward

The skills you learned here can be applied to almost every graphics resource you need to create for an iOS app. Backgrounds, toolbars, buttons, fields, and bezels can all be created with shape layers and layer styles. They all go the same way.

- Create an appropriately sized canvas.
- Add shape layers.
- Apply layer styles.

Mockup Assembly

Creating mockups involves two tasks: building an image of a screen that looks like the real thing, and exporting the custom image resources needed to make it happen. There are a couple of ways to go about reaching those two goals.

Some designers like to work with a full-size mockup of a screen in the same document where they create their image resources. In this way, they can design each element in context and watch the entire screen evolve at once. In practice, it means creating a Photoshop document that's the size of an iPhone or iPad screen, then creating layers for each element, and then slicing up and exporting the individual pieces for use in the real app. You can use Photoshop's built-in slicing tools to get the resources out, or you can use the fabulous third-party utility Slicy to do so in a much more organized fashion.

Other designers prefer keeping a separate Photoshop document for each type of control they're building and assembling them on another canvas. They make one document for 44-point-square icons that go in table cells, another one for stretchable toolbar buttons, and so on. Within those documents, each resource goes into its own layer group. Once you've created your resources, you can export them as the PNGs that will eventually go in the app and drop them onto a screen-sized canvas for final arrangement. (OmniGraffle works great for assembling individual resources into a coherent screen; you can even drop Photoshop documents straight onto the Omni-Graffle canvas.) This is the workflow assumed in this chapter.

Resizable Images

For any image resource that might be called upon to hold content of different sizes—for instance, because it's used in multiple situations or because of localization—you can use resizable images. A **resizable image** (or **stretchable image**) has some portion of itself designated as being stretchable or tileable in order to change its width, its height, or both. The "Tips for Creating Resizable Images" section of the *iOS Human Interface Guidelines* does a good job of explaining how to create them; this is just a reminder that they exist and that you should use them whenever the size of an element is not fixed. Even if you aren't planning on it yet, if there's any chance an element will need to stretch later, someday you'll thank yourself for making it resizable.

Retina Resources

Once you've built your image resources, you need to create Retina versions of them. The most basic way to do this in Photoshop is to use the Image Size command to simply increase them to 200%, making sure to enable the Scale Styles setting. This makes all your layer styles grow along with the rest of the image. You may need to adjust some layer styles to adapt them to the new size, because what works well at standard resolution doesn't automatically look right when scaled up. If you have any bitmap layers, such as the noise texture we created, you'll need to re-create them at the bigger size.

Save your new source image with "@2x" appended to the name, export a PNG for inclusion in the app, and see how your screens work at Retina resolution. You can build a Retina mockup, or you can wait until the app is actually being built and run it with the Retina resources. There's no rush to perfect the high-resolution resources if you're still working on the lower-resolution ones.

You can use Slicy to convert lots of resources to Retina resolution. Every time you save, Slicy can export both resolutions for each resource in your Photoshop file. This workflow assumes that you don't have to make any layer style adjustments for the higher resolution and that there aren't any bitmap layers to reimplement. In those cases, you have to maintain two versions of each source image—one for each resolution.

When you do have Retina screens to test, always make sure to test them on an actual Retina device. If not on a Retina iOS device, at least run your interface in the simulator on a Retina Mac. Often, @2x graphics that look fine blown up on a standard-resolution display look wrong at high resolution, and vice versa. Tools (such as xScope and Skala Preview) that can broadcast a window from your Mac to an iOS device are invaluable for checking on a resource's appropriateness for Retina displays while you're building it. Otherwise, you need to do the dance of trying an edit, exporting, sending to the device, and checking it. Every. Time.

Designing for Layers

In Chapter 4, you learned how to think in interface layers. Much of the job of the visual design in your app is to communicate and reinforce the interface layers that describe each screen. Notice how standard iOS apps such as Mail use contrast to indicate the difference between, on the one hand, the navigation bar and toolbar on the periphery of the screen and, on the other hand, the main content area in the center. See how drop shadows subtly encroach on the content from the navigation bar and toolbar, emphasizing that the bars are on top, and the content can be scrolled around beneath them. When you look at a standard app, you see the medium value of the top and bottom bars, and the light value of the content area, and immediately recognize them as separate interface layers.

Color, texture, and other styling also help communicate how an element fits into the screen. In Mail for iPhone, the Search field has cues that suggest it is somewhere between content and control. (See Chapter 4 for more about the relationship between content and controls.) Its background has a value that's between that of the white content area and of the blue navigation bar. It also has a gradient like the top bar, but it's desaturated like the content area. This in-between styling reflects the in-between role of the search field. Normally, it scrolls along with the content. (In fact, it starts out scrolled off the top of the viewport.) But as soon as you tap it to start typing, it's promoted to become the top bar, gaining a scope bar below it to help you narrow your search. During the search operation, it takes over the top of the screen and no longer scrolls with the content. All the styling of the search field supports its role and its purpose in the message list screen.

If you're trying to define interface layers in your screen, you need to pay attention to the way the eye groups elements by contrast. If the surfaces of a single layer have drastically different values, or if surfaces of different interface layers have very similar values, then the contrast may be working against your layer structure instead of reinforcing it.

Be vigilant about the style of control you use on each layer. Occasionally in third-party apps, you'll see the shiny, desaturated-blue segmented control that's intended for use in a toolbar, sitting casually in a table cell. You can almost hear it whistling as it glances around innocently, hoping nobody notices it doesn't belong there. Likewise, flat white table-cell-style buttons certainly don't belong in toolbars.

Summary

During the mockup phase, you define the outward appearance of your app. You start by creating an attractive graphic design that will get a good reaction from customers browsing the App Store, but your work doesn't stop there. You need to pay attention to the ways the color, contrast, and texture of your elements affect each screen's understandability and usability. Contrast, in particular, is important, because it's what human perception uses to identify figure/ground relationships. Visual weight is the attribute that determines how consequential an element seems.

You also need to create standard- and Retina-resolution iOS image resources and assemble them into a mockup that represents your intentions for the final implementation of your app.

Exercises

Getting good at visual design and mockups in the iOS style is a never-ending journey. Try these exercises to develop your Photoshop chops.

1. Pick a standard iOS element (such as the bordered toolbar button or the blue detail disclosure button) or even a distinctive control in a third-party app (such as the bottom tabs in Tweetbot). Try to re-create its style as closely as possible using Photoshop layer styles. You may need to add more than one vector shape layer, but aim to use the fewest layers possible.

2. Take any custom element you've created (in following this chapter, in the preceding exercise, or otherwise) and create variants of it. Try creating a version that maintains the same visual weight but has a different color. Try keeping the original theme but making a much heavier or much lighter version. Try creating a version that works better on a different background value (if your original control has a light interior and is intended for a dark background, try the equivalent dark control for a light background).

6

The Prototypes

Pictures of software have served you well so far. Especially if you have a good imagination, you can often get a reliable sense of how a screen or an interaction would work if it were implemented. But you can't rely on good imagination for everything. Sometimes you need to see something in motion, or feel the interaction happen. Often, your own opinion of an interaction that exists in your head isn't enough, and you need to let other people try it out. But as long as an idea is only in their heads, people often just talk past each other as they misunderstand what everyone else is getting at. As Bill Buxton points out, a sketch *provokes,* but a prototype *resolves.*

A **prototype** is a rendering of a software idea that functions in some way. It can be as limited as a test of a single animation, or as elaborate as a full-on early working version of the real app. It can be as low fidelity as pencil on paper, or as realistic as a pixel-perfect mockup. Just as sketching lets you communicate the appearance and idea of an app, prototyping lets you communicate the feel and flow of an app.

Some designers consider prototyping to be the ultimate design practice, because a realistic prototype most accurately represents their true vision of the product. In this view, all the other work you've done up to this point has been preparation for the creation of the prototype. This is especially the case in design firms whose final product is an interactive prototype. They hand off a prototype and a stack of design documents, and then it's up to the client to either implement it or hire someone to implement it. (I've heard firsthand of clients who didn't want to bother to develop the real thing, so they shipped the prototype itself as their actual product. Zounds!)

Test on the Device

This should be mentioned up front: when you're designing apps for iOS devices, you have to do everything you can to find out how they feel on iOS devices. You need the experience of holding that object in your hand. You need to see precisely how big the elements are. You need to find out how it feels to reach for each tap target with your fingers, rather than mousing to it and clicking. Looking at mockups on a Mac screen gives you a rough idea, but sooner or later you had better get it on a device (or a reasonable facsimile of one). Prototypes are, after all, about interaction and experience more than appearance.

If you want to get serious, get yourself one device of each currently available display size, or at least become good friends with people who have the devices you don't have. That means the tall iPhone 5 and the shorter prior versions, a normal-sized iPad and an iPad Mini. It's also good to have access to both Retina and non-Retina devices, so that you can see how your final images work in real life.

Kinds of Prototypes

Various kinds of artifacts can be labeled "prototypes." The thing they have in common is that rather than being static, they have some sort of *behavior*. They can be **low fidelity,** like sketches, requiring imagination to see how they would really appear as finished software. Or they can be **high fidelity,** with an uncanny resemblance to a polished product that might even fool someone for a few minutes. These definitions leave the possibilities wide open, and all the following examples are likely to be useful at some point.

- **Paper prototypes** are just what they sound like—bits of paper cut out and stuck together to create a semblance of a software interface. Generally you put them in front of a user willing to humor you, and swap out the bits for them as the user indicates how he would interact with the real thing. You'd be surprised how useful this seemingly childish pursuit can be.

- **Wizard of Oz prototypes** are generally electronic, but like paper prototypes they involve a designer acting as moderator—either "behind a curtain" or in plain sight. Rather than program real interactivity, the moderator manually swaps out mockups based on the user's inputs.

- **Motion sketches** are quick tests of an animation or a transition to find or communicate the right feel.

- **Preemptive demo videos** are a way to create a holistic, polished vision of what an app could be like. It gives you something to work toward.

- **Interactive prototypes** use a design tool such as OmniGraffle, Axure, Balsamiq, or yes, even PowerPoint, to add interactivity to pictures of software.

- **Proof-of-concept software** is in some ways your ultimate (that is to say *last*) prototype, because with enough iteration it will eventually become the real app.

Paper Prototypes

Even at the early stages of figuring out interactions and workflows for an app, you can benefit from prototyping. Paper prototypes are a low-fi way to get a feel for how an app might work. (See Figure 6.1.) More important, paper prototypes are a way to get feedback about interactions with a minimum of visual-design or technical investment.

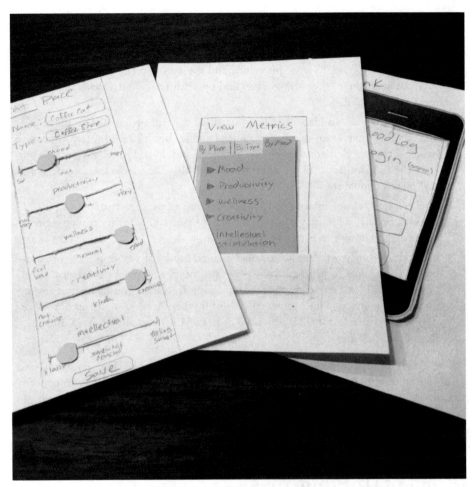

Figure 6.1   An ambitiously full-featured paper prototype with
working controls, created by Dan Shank

The method consists of drawing or printing paper scraps representing all the screens
and interface elements and then shuffling them around in front of people as they
pretend to interact with it. The process is much like the usability testing procedure
described later in this chapter, but instead of putting software in front of people, you're
presenting slips of paper. Invite them to touch the elements with their fingers just as
they normally would. As they make choices, you can swap out screens and elements
as necessary. Meanwhile, narrate any animations, effects, or experiences that you can't
readily reproduce on paper.

Paper prototyping takes creativity. Any combination of the following approaches is
valid; it's up to you to decide which ones work best for the job at hand.

- Sketches of whole screens, each on its own page, which you swap out as the user taps around. This works best for static screens that flow from one to the next.
- Individual interface elements cut out and assembled interchangeably. This is great for alerts, modal views, popovers, and the tabs of a tab view. If you get too granular with these, though, you can end up with UI confetti that's impossible to keep organized.
- Blank cells, fields, and labels that can be filled in with pencil. When the app asks for text input from the user, go ahead and let her write it in. If you need to make or change elements on the fly, go ahead and do it. Do what's necessary to keep the test running and preserve the conceit that the user is interacting with a real piece of software.
- Stickers, tape, clever folding contraptions, spools of paper that scroll within a frame, or any other artsy-craftsy endeavors that make your prototype more believable. Having fun is allowed.
- Hardware prototypes: iPhone- or iPad-shaped hunks of wood, plastic, or cardboard. (You can also just tape your paper prototypes to a real device that's been turned off.) If you're testing what a mobile app feels like, you had better test it on a mobile device. This is especially helpful when Apple announces hardware with a new form factor (like iPhone 5 or iPad Mini) and all you have until it ships is a list of specs.

The idea is to keep things as cheap, fast, and casual as possible. The less formalized and finalized the interface looks, the more willing the participants will be to concentrate on the interactions. The low fidelity should also prevent premature criticism of the visual design. Thus, you need to recruit testing participants who have good imaginations and can picture what a real piece of software based on the paper scraps in front of them would look like.

Wizard of Oz Prototypes

You can think of Wizard of Oz prototypes as being like paper prototypes, except on screen. Start by preparing several sketches or wireframes in the design app of your choice. As with paper prototyping, make sure you have all the needed screens and elements in the form of documents, canvases, and layers.

Sit the participant down in front of your initial screen, and explain that you'd like her to pretend that the picture of the app is a real app. Have her try walking through the tasks you give her, but instead of actually interacting with the software, she'll indicate to you what she intends to do.

As she points to where she'd tap, your job is to swap in the next screen, change layer visibility, move objects around, and otherwise create the (admittedly not very convincing) illusion that she's interacting with a real app. Thus, this sort of test also requires a bit of imagination on the part of the participant. If she's game, though, you can learn a lot about the expectations people have and the ways new users are likely to try interacting with your design.

Oz Prototypes on the Desktop

Against the normal advice to run tests on the platform you're designing for, you may want to run your Oz prototypes on a normal desktop or notebook computer instead of on a touch device. One nice thing about running the test on a computer is that as long as you're OK with having people touch your screen (some people aren't), you can invite the participant to pretend the interface actually is touch. He can poke and swipe and smudge his fingers all over your monitor while you shuffle the cursor around and make the right things happen. (Or you can hook up to a projector and let him touch the projected image.) The other benefit, of course, is that desktop design software makes it a lot easier to navigate, switch canvases and documents quickly, add elements, and so on. If you want to run a desktop-based Oz prototype on an iOS device, you can use the lock feature in xScope to disable taps on the device's screen.

If you haven't guessed yet, the name of this method comes from the climactic scene in *The Wizard of Oz* where (spoiler alert) the great, fearsome floating wizard head is revealed to be an illusion, operated by an ordinary fellow.

Motion Sketches

A **motion sketch** is hardly a prototype at all, because it generally has a bare minimum of interaction. But it fits here because its purpose is to test out the feel of an animation, rather than only the layout, organization, or appearance of a screen.

iOS includes plenty of standard, built-in animations.

- Stepping through a navigation controller hierarchy uses a horizontal push, with the new screen moving the old one out of the way.

- Alerts appear with a quick forward zoom and then a bounce back, as if emerging from behind the screen, to emphasize their unrelatedness to anything else on the screen.

- The default animation for most modal views is a slide that, in contrast to the navigation slide, doesn't move the old screen out of the way. This design emphasizes that once the modal view has served its purpose, the old screen will be back.

Occasionally you might want to use a transition or animation other than the standard ones. If you do, make sure not to trample the metaphors and visualizations already present in the operating system. Don't present screens floating or rearranging themselves in a black void, for instance, because that's used by iOS to visualize app launching and app switching.

Another thing to pay attention to is animation curves and timing. Check out Chapter 8, The Graceful Interface, for advice about fine-tuning animations. For the moment, here's all you need to know.

- Most iOS animations tend to be about 100–250 milliseconds (0.1–0.25 seconds) long, depending on the size of what's being animated (100 for a small portion of the screen, all the way up to 250 if you're animating most or all of the screen).

- Most iOS animations use an ease-in/ease-out animation curve, which starts out slow, reaches maximum speed in the middle, and then slows down at the end. This subtle curve adds a lot of realism and personality to iOS.

Luckily, most of the animations you may want to try simulating can be done in Keynote, Apple's own presentation software, which can double as an affordable prototyping tool. (See Figure 6.2.)

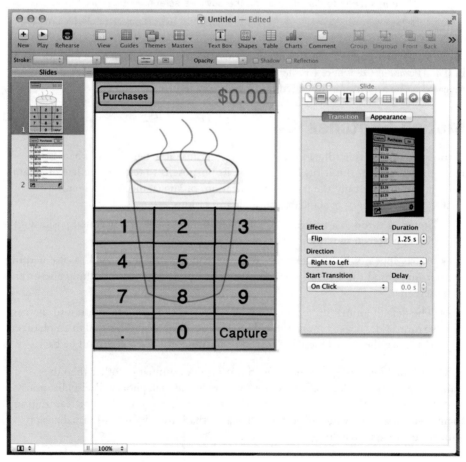

Figure 6.2   Creating transition animations in Keynote

Here's a quick introduction to prototyping animations in Keynote.

- Build an iPhone- or iPad-sized slide deck by picking Custom from the Slide Size pop-up menu in the Document inspector.
- Add some objects to the slide, either by dropping in mockup images or blocking out a wireframe with shapes and text in Keynote itself.
- Select an object, open the Build inspector, and switch to the Action tab.
- Choose Move from the Effect pop-up menu.
- Now you can customize the animation curve, the path, the speed, and even the order (for multistep animations).

For full-screen navigation animations, you can use the built-in slide transitions, such as Push, Move In, Reveal, and Dissolve. Those transitions very closely match the animations for navigation (Push) and modal views (Move In and Reveal) on iOS. For exotic transitions, you can use Cube, Flip (for the iBooks-shelf-like "multiple personalities" architecture described in Chapter 3), Page Flip (for an iBooks-page-like experience), and Swap (if you ever need to simulate app switching).

When you test your animations (on yourself or others), the main thing is getting the speed right. Imagine how many times a user will invoke the animation in a given session with your app. An animation that feels fine the first time might be infuriatingly gratuitous the tenth time. Moving normally from screen to screen should be fast enough to feel snappy, but slow enough for the animation to register as motion to the eye.

More substantial animations can take a bit longer. You're not likely to switch back and forth between the iBooks shelf and store many times in quick succession, so it's all right for that big flip animation to take a second and a half. Those bigger animations can have multiple steps and feel a bit busier, too. The unlock animation for an iOS device first slides the top and bottom bars away and then zooms the home screen up. It all happens pretty fast, but it feels consequential and appropriate, as if the full functionality of a powerful device has been, well, unlocked. The **weight** of an animation is related to how frictiony it feels (see Chapter 13, Friction and Guidance).

The other key feature you want is **coherence.** Does the animation make physical sense in the metaphor of the app? Users can tolerate a bit of magic in their interfaces. Maybe they move right several screens, but then tapping the Home button to get back to the top level only appears to move one screen to the left. That's fine. But stretching the metaphor too far can break the illusion. (See the Custom Navigation section in Chapter 3, Getting Familiar with iOS.)

Preemptive Demo Videos

If you're good with After Effects or another video or animation tool, you can often take a mockup one step further by putting it in motion. You can even go quite a long way with the animation tools built in to Keynote. (And you can do the same with sketches or wireframes.)

Typically, the marketing video is the last thing to be made before an app ships. But here's a trick to help you and your team know what you're working toward: make the video first. Imagine that the product is finished, and all you need to do is show it off; then create a video for software that doesn't yet exist. Choreographing each step in a typical workflow will force you to confront a lot of seemingly small design decisions and is sure to chase some difficult design problems out of the shadows. You can't just wave your hands and say, "Then we switch to this other screen" or "Then all these items disappear." You have to actually show it.

Making a marketing video pushes the boundaries of what counts as a prototype, because it's not actually interactive; it only *looks* interactive. In fact, it's a carefully scripted set of steps that reflects what you as a designer think would be a normal flow through the app. So it's unlike a prototype that you can put in front of a random person in your target audience and find out how he would interact with it. But you can find out what a person thinks of the way the app reacts at each step, even if they're not the exact steps he would have taken. You can also get a sense for the overall personality of the app: how the screens fit together, whether the navigation feels fussy or simplistic, and whether each screen presents a good balance of functionality.

For the most part, the video should look precisely like the app would if someone were really interacting with it. One thing that's helpful to add, though, is an effect that shows where the hypothetical user is tapping, dragging, or entering other gestures. An abstract dot or circle or glow works fine; superimposing an actual disembodied hand is more realistic and reminds you that part of the interface will in fact be obscured, but it can get a bit creepy.

You can, of course, create videos for anything from a seconds-long motion sketch (described earlier) all the way up to an entire several-minute session with the app. The main constraint is how much time and effort you're willing to put into a visualization artifact that in the end probably won't resemble the final design. The iterative, cyclical, and somewhat chaotic design process is bound to leave you with something quite different from what you originally animate in an early video. Remember that the video serves mainly as a conceptual inspiration, and not a moving blueprint.

Interactive Prototypes

For most folks, **interactive prototypes** are the main event, the artifacts that best represent the practice of prototyping. Interactive prototypes can look like anything from lo-fi wireframes to perfect hi-fi mockups, but what makes them special is that they respond to input—even if in a limited way.

You have several options when it comes to creating interactive experiences.

- **Prototyping tools**—At the specific end, you have products, like Balsamiq, that are intended for software prototyping. These are good if you want something that's dedicated to the task of creating prototypes and if the visual-design capabilities of the tool match the sort of prototypes you want to make. The aptly named app Prototypes on the Mac, and the paper-sketch-oriented POP on iPhone, are designed for quick and exploratory prototyping.

- **Keynote**—One step up is presentation software that happens to be useful for prototyping, specifically Keynote. You can do a surprising amount of design work in Keynote, even if it's slightly off target from the product's supposed purpose. Use the hyperlink feature, present in both the Mac and the iOS editions, to jump from one slide to another whenever a specific object is tapped.

- **Design apps**—A half-step in between are general-purpose design apps with interaction features, such as OmniGraffle. The main advantage here is that you can use the same tool for many of the phases of design. In OmniGraffle for Mac, you can use the actions feature to jump to a certain canvas or change layer visibility when an object is clicked. There's a big community of users out there sharing stencils and templates for software design. To run these prototypes on an iOS device, you'll need a desktop-to-iOS previewing tool that sends taps to the host computer as clicks. An example is LiveView.

- **Code**—At the most generalized end, you have quick, visually oriented development platforms like the team of HTML5, CSS3, and JavaScript. If you're a quick developer, and especially if you can make use of time-saving technology like jQuery, you can create pretty realistic and complete prototypes. After a few hours' coding, however, you may start wondering whether Keynote or OmniGraffle would have done the job nearly as well in a fraction of the time, or whether you should have just gotten your engineering team involved to start building the real thing.

When you build an interactive prototype, it's unlikely you'll be able to, or want to, re-create the entire range of possibilities of the app in prototype form. So each time, you have a decision to make: do you want to go wide, or go deep?

- **Wide prototypes**—These cover a broad range of screens and experiences in the app, but with minimal detail and interaction at each step. They can be as simple as linking a series of top-level screens so that when the user taps a tab or sidebar item, the correct screen appears. With a wide prototype, you get a good sense of what an app feels like at arm's length, when you're casually wandering around its architecture. If you created a wide prototype for SnackLog, it might consist of one canvas or slide each for the capture screen, the purchases list, and the purchase details screen—a sort of interactive version of workflow sketches. Going a step deeper, you might present variants for the capture screen during the typing of a price and for the purchases screen in Edit mode. See Figure 6.3 for a simple example from SnackLog.

- **Deep prototypes**—These stick to a small number of screens, or only one screen, but allow for lots of fine interaction. A deep prototype usually requires either (a) a prototyping technique that allows you to show and hide objects or layers on a single screen or (b) the creation of lots of very similar screens with slight differences. In that way, you can simulate the steps of text input, interstitials such as action sheets or alerts, or similar step-by-step experiences. A deep prototype of SnackLog might include the tap-by-tap process of entering a price and pressing Capture—like a live version of an interaction sketch. In a typical prototype-interaction corner-cutting measure, you could make a tap anywhere on the number pad always enter the next in a predetermined sequence of digits. That's fine! Going to the trouble of building an infinitely variable number entry system into your prototype would not really serve its purpose of figuring out how the interaction feels.

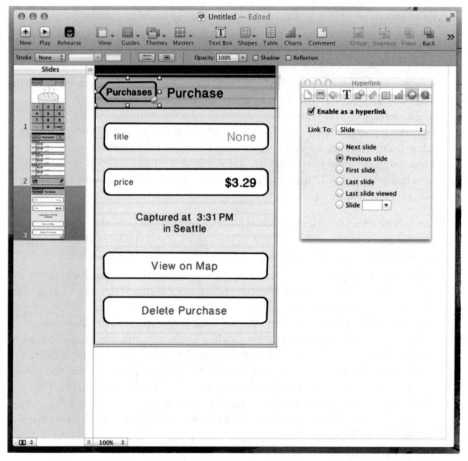

Figure 6.3   Using hyperlinks to build an interactive prototype in Keynote. Because this is a wide prototype, there is only one example of each screen, and it's taken for granted that all data are placeholders.

Proof-of-Concept Software

The best software prototype you could ask for is an early version of the real thing. When you can get your hands on "alpha" software depends heavily on how your team and your organization work. But once you have it, it's fundamentally different from other kinds of prototypes because it's the thing that, after a long process of development and adjustment, will actually *be* the app you're designing. This means that the way you evaluate it needs to be fundamentally different, too.

Although building the real thing is often the best way to test interactions, it can also drain your resources unnecessarily. If you can use a quicker method, you should avoid the temptation to spend a bunch of time and effort only to find out whether an idea feels right. Some of your ideas will fail; make sure they fail early, before they've consumed too much of your time. The same principle that applies to premature visual styling applies to interaction: get it right in a quick, low-fidelity way first, and then polish it.

Evaluation of alpha software is special, because it comes in the form of bug reports. Over there, you've got how the app should work. Over here, you've got how it really does work. The difference is called a bug. The challenge is to define what the bug really is and how to get there from here. Often, the biggest difficulty is figuring out what kind of bug it is. To that end, here are a few of the genera of design-related bugs that you and your team may need to write up.

- **Engineering bugs**—The app doesn't look or behave like the design, but the design still represents what you want. If this is the case, then engineering work needs to be done to make the app work as designed. For example, a button doesn't give feedback when tapped, a label is not positioned as shown in the mockup, or an animation is using the wrong curve.

- **Design bugs**—There's a situation in the app for which no design has yet been made, or there is a design but it is no longer what you want. This means you need more design work to decide how the app should work. For example, you have yet to provide a wireframe for how an app behaves in landscape orientation, or usability testing has determined that a gesture is too hard to discover.

- **Documentation bugs**—Sometimes you spend a bunch of time and effort trying to serve a specific uncommon or advanced use case. (A **use case** is a description of an interaction that should be possible in an app.) To support it, you find yourself compromising the experience in the common case. Eventually it dawns on you that it's not worth it to keep trying to make it easy in the interface. Instead, you should let it be difficult, but offer some documentation for the few people who need it. Most of the time, this happens when you're trying to maintain compatibility with outside technology that you don't control. For example, it would be impractical to try to present an experience in your app that satisfactorily and comprehensively reflects all the idiosyncrasies of how iOS location-based notifications work. But you can present something that makes sense most of the time to most people and offer a "Learn More" button that links to extensive documentation about the fussy details and ways to work around them. If you find yourself trying to communicate ever smaller and rarer corner cases, get that stuff out of the interface and into the documentation.

- **Marketing bugs**—You may find yourself trying to make a feature more prominent than it needs to be just to make sure people know it's there. This is especially the case for features that took a lot of effort to design and build. But sometimes it's best to let those features work quietly in the background, and make sure to promote them outside the app—in your App Store description, on your web site, and in your screencasts. For instance, suppose you built a robust iCloud-based backup system into your app and determined that it doesn't really need any interface to set up. Proclaiming that users' data is safe with your app because of the cloud backup is a marketing bug. (And telling users how to get their data back in the case of an emergency is a documentation bug.)

- **Negotiation bugs**—Often, it's just not clear what the solution is. When that happens, the best you can do is to make it as clear as possible what the problem is, and have a discussion. Different team members may suggest different solutions that reflect the notion that it's one (or a combination) of the types of bug just described. Negotiation bugs tend to emerge from usability testing, and they tend to start out as vaguely phrased sentiments like "account setup is too hard," "rearranging items feels slow," or "people can't find the delete command." From there, it's back to the creative processes like outlining and sketching to try to find better approaches.

Bug reporting is an art form. Getting good at describing what's wrong with software, in a clear, helpful, nonaccusatory way, is one of the most crucial skills you can develop as a designer. If you haven't yet, you'll someday come across a tiny interaction whose description requires multiple pages' worth of writing and visual aids. Many of the bugs you write will be little collages made of the sort of outlines, sketches, and wireframes described earlier in this book, this time directed toward a single element, screen, or interaction.

Priorities

Most bug-tracking databases use a priority field, and bugs in which the engineering doesn't perfectly match the design are often labeled low priority. It can be a challenge to convince your team to work on seemingly minor aesthetic or experience-related bugs, such as improperly drawn elements or slightly glitchy animations, when there are "high-priority" bugs to fix and new features to implement. They might argue that it's not as pretty as it could be, but at least it works. They might argue that nobody has complained about it.

Fight back! Point out that an apparent lack of attention to detail in your app is embarrassing to your organization, especially when compared with the highly polished apps people expect on iOS. Point out that an engineer taking 15 minutes to fix a rendering detail will pay off in more positive perception of your app by every single person who uses it. Remind them that no matter how many stressful, "high-priority" situations you have going on in your life, you still brush your teeth every day—a seemingly minor, but still very important, act of maintenance.

If you're a designer/developer, you're in the fortunate position of being able to create your own prototype interfaces in the app proper. As long as the app is building and running properly and the large-scale infrastructure is there, you can dive in and make it happen and then try it out. You can fine-tune visuals, animations, and interactions in between runs. If the app isn't ready to bear experimental UI code, you can create little bespoke disposable demo apps that exhibit a single, self-contained experience.

If you're not a Cocoa developer yourself, foster a happy and close relationship with your team members who are. It'll never be as immediate and frictionless as building your own demos and working directly with the code. But you can team up to do the same sorts of experiments together and see what works.

One of the best favors your friends in engineering can do is to give you parameters. Sweet, scrumptious parameters. Rather than pepper the code with specific numbers representing specific colors, sizes, distances, timing, and other values, they can break all those numbers out into variables and collect them in a header file. (And even if you're a designer/developer hybrid, you should know not to hard-code values like those; you should be parameterizing anyway.) If they're tidily organized and commented, then you, the designer, can go into the code and adjust them yourself—slow down that zoom animation, make that green a little brighter, or nudge that icon 3 points. Then you don't need to bother an engineer every time you want to make a tiny change, and you don't need to tread into the spooky territory of the source code files, searching for the right number to adjust. If there are any values in the design you think might need to be adjusted along the way, make them parameters. Everyone will be happier in the end.

Why Do Usability Testing?

It's invaluable to get your app in front of someone who wasn't involved in creating it and watch her try to get something useful done with it. The ways your painstakingly designed, perfect interface can fail at this stage are many and can be grimly amusing. You can't measure usability, but you can expose usability problems.

Usability test participants find inscrutable the interactions that seemed simple to you when you designed them. They gloss over the most essential elements on the screen. They ignore the workflows that you thought to be obvious and reach their goals in a different, unexpected way. They spend minute after agonizing minute trying to find a certain feature while you stare on and smile reassuringly, wishing you could scream at them, "Just hit the dang *circley thing!*"

Part II, coming up, takes a look at software design through the lens of the three levels of cognition identified by Donald Norman: the visceral, behavioral, and reflective levels.

Usability testing is fantastic for evaluating how your app does at the behavioral level, which is described in Chapter 9, The Gracious Interface. If there is anything wrong with an app's minute-to-minute interaction and understandability, it will come out in these kinds of tests. What people often miss, though, is that usability testing isn't very good at showing problems at the other two levels.

People are generally hard pressed to articulate whether an app is satisfying at the visceral level, because that stratum of experience is happening below their conscious awareness. (This level is explained in Chapter 8, The Graceful Interface.) Unless they're trained software designers, they probably can't specify that what makes an animation unconvincing is that it's 100 milliseconds too slow or that a tap target needs to grow by 2 points. (If you have sharp eyes and a strong sense of empathy, *you* may be able to spot such problems by paying close attention to the screen and to the user's reactions.)

And judging quality at the reflective level (described in Chapter 10, The Whole Experience) takes much more time than a usability test can feasibly cover. People can barely get acquainted with an app during a testing session, let alone develop long-lasting feelings about it.

So for the most part, you're looking for improvements you can make at the behavioral level: conscious communication between the app and the user. How well does each screen tell the user about its purpose and suggest the options for interacting with it? What kind of mental model is the user creating about how the app is organized, and how accurately does it match the one you tried to portray? That's what Chapter 9 is all about.

How to Do Usability Testing

Usability testing doesn't have to be formal. Once you have a working build of your design (or a reasonable facsimile in the form of a paper or software prototype), you can ask some people to try it out. If your target audience is casual iOS device users, you can recruit pretty much anyone. Ask coworkers who aren't directly involved in building software, along with family members, fellow coffee shop patrons, or anyone else you haven't yet done a test with. The less familiar they are with your project, the better. (Make sure you follow your organization's rules about intellectual property disclosure.)

If your target audience is more specific, you need to find people who fit into it. You may need to rustle up filmmakers, retro video game aficionados, balletomanes, or cockatiel owners.

Run your participant through this rough script.

- Tell the participant (not the "subject"!) that you'd like him to help you improve your app. Make it clear that you're testing the software, not him, and it's impossible for him to make a mistake of any kind. Anything that doesn't go smoothly is a fault of the app, not of his personal aptitude. (Keep this in mind when asking people to participate, too. You want someone closer to the average person who'll be using your app, not someone especially "technical.") It's hard to convince people of this, but keep at it.

- Ask the participant to talk out loud as much as possible while he uses the app. You will probably need to remind him of this several times, because it's not very natural for people to think through a new experience and talk about it at the same time. But you need to know as much as you can about why he's making the decisions he's making, what he's looking for next, and what thoughts he's basing his decisions on. This makes it easy for you to seem annoying and intrusive; after all, the user is trying to think. Part of being a good test moderator is developing the ability to balance data gathering with the comfort of the participant.

- Give the participant a realistic task or situation to work through. Naturally, don't explain it in terms of the app's interface. Tell him in terms of real life. That is, don't say, "Use the photo screen to add an entry to your database." Instead, say, "You just bought this latte," possibly waggling a real-world prop in front of him for believability, "and you want to use this app to record the purchase." Let him take it from there. You'll probably have several tasks or scenarios to test; try to give them in order of increasing complexity.

- Don't coach the participant. It is excruciating to watch someone struggle with something you designed, when you could be explaining it to him. But don't give in. Your real customers won't have the designer sitting there, walking them through each step. You need to know how a real person will experience launching your app and trying to get something done with it. Just remind him to keep talking as he thinks things through, and only help him if it's obvious that he's never going to finish otherwise. (You may need to do a *little* bit of coaching to let the user know when he's trying to interact with something that isn't really hooked up in the prototype.)

- Take notes on everything that happens. Note the painful parts, of course, but also note what seems to work well. If the participant seems to enjoy using a certain metaphor or flow, you'll want to find out why and take advantage of it. You'll need the notes later to jog your memory, because there will probably be numerous revelations to process.

- Be grateful. What seems to him like ten minutes of weird, awkward poking around with an app is pure research gold for you. Without him, you're designing for some imaginary, idealized user and not for real humans.

Not only can your usability tests be casual, but also the conventional wisdom is that you don't usually need to do more than five of them. For any given design, the sixth person you test isn't likely to find anything that the first five didn't. So you can confirm what works, get to fixing what doesn't, and do another round of tests. But you should get fresh participants for each test so that they don't come into it with preconceptions from their last experience.

When you look at your results, don't get worked up about fixing every little snag. If one person had trouble in a certain spot, you aren't obligated to change the entire design to avoid that problem. One reason for doing multiple tests is to find out what trips up *everyone* so that you can focus on fixing those pervasive problems. Any design is bound to take some getting used to for some people. That's fine! Focus on patterns of trouble and on especially problematic moments, not on isolated fumbles. In the end, you're the designer, and it's up to you to consider all the input available. User testing is only one of many valuable sources.

For a treasure trove of advice on how to get serious about usability testing, check out *Handbook of Usability Testing* by Jeffrey Rubin and Dana Chisnell.

Summary

Prototypes are your chance to get a sense of what the software you've been designing feels like. This phase spans the transition from ideas to actual software. The ultimate prototype is an early version of the real app.

Prototypes can span a wide range of fidelity and functionality. Anything that can be made interactive, from Keynote presentations to web pages to stacks of paper, is fair game for prototyping. Use what makes sense for the resources you have and the kind of feedback you're hoping to get.

Usability testing is key to finding out how your designs are communicating and how people will try to interact with them. It's easy to get wrapped up in your own ideas as you work on design, so from time to time, make sure to get them in front of someone with fresh eyes and no preconceived notions. Use that feedback to get a sense of what you might have missed and to inform your next round of designs.

Exercises

You can start prototyping at any stage and get insight from real people about the direction your app is headed.

1. No matter how far along your own app concept is, create some paper prototypes for it and run a usability test with an unsuspecting friend or colleague. You'll probably gain insight about the design, but, more important, you'll get experience in administering a usability test. Can you set the participant's expectations and encourage her to explore the prototype? Can you get her to use her imagination and pretend the app is real?

2. Choose a digital prototyping tool that seems to align with your skills and goals. Use it to create both a wide and a deep prototype for your app. Then run a usability test as described in this chapter.

7

Going Cross-Platform

An app that stands alone on iPhone or iPad can be an eminently useful thing. But an app with multiple incarnations on a combination of iPhone, iPad, other mobile platforms, desktop platforms, and the web can be exponentially more valuable. It's getting rare to find an app that exists only on one platform; almost anything worth building on iPhone or iPad is worth building on the other, too, at the very least. Many apps are worth building somewhere outside iOS, too.

Or you may be thinking of bringing an existing app from another platform to iOS. In that case, similar considerations apply, but in the opposite direction. This chapter covers both situations.

Platform Catalog

Taking on another platform is a big commitment, and every product has its own complex of needs and benefits that affect which platforms make sense for it. You'll need to evaluate the relative virtues of all the platforms.

- **iPhone**—The main win here is ubiquity. It's hard to deny the value of being on the platform that users have access to every waking hour of their lives. iPads get put away, and desktops get left at home, but an iPhone tends to stay in the purse or pocket all day. It's also attractive because the constraints on its display size and processing power mean that you have a neatly defined set of boundaries to work within. Unless the nature of the app idea precludes it, iPhone is a marvelous place to be.

- **iPad**—This gives you many of the advantages of iPhone, except that it's less likely to be available to a person at any given time. In exchange, the generous display means that you have a lot more freedom to create powerful productivity tools or immersive entertainment experiences. The similarity in design and development process means that you can reuse a lot of your work on an iPhone app in the iPad edition, and vice versa. That makes iPhone plus iPad the most accessible cross-platform combination.

- **Other mobile platforms**—There's a surprisingly common belief that mobile platforms are more or less the same and that it makes sense to design a single interface that can be deployed without adjustment on iPhone and Android (and Windows Phone, and BlackBerry, and Symbian, etc.). In reality, any interface that feels at home on another mobile platform will feel a bit alien on iOS, and vice versa. What's more, the development tools that promise this utopian, run-anywhere vision tend to result in watered-down experiences that run anywhere but look good and feel good nowhere. (The major exception is games, which usually define their own user-experience bubble rather than conform to the system standards, anyway.) The lesson is that if you want to develop for other mobile platforms, you should be ready to redesign your app with each platform's unique idioms in mind rather than simply port its design unchanged. The primary advantage of offering your app on multiple mobile platforms is reach; if your team has the resources necessary to maintain several independent interfaces, the desire for a big audience, and the wherewithal to support that audience, you can reach a lot of people (and for social or communication apps, reaching more people increases the value for everyone).

- **Mac**—You will probably be able to maintain common back-end code between iOS and Mac editions of an app. And because lots of design lessons are making their way "back to the Mac," as Steve Jobs put it, some of your UI design work may even transfer. You should reconsider the design of each individual feature from scratch, though, even if sometimes you end up imitating your iOS editions. On the Mac, powerful features like interoperability with other apps, advanced configuration, and multitasking feel at home. You can also take advantage of bigger displays, precise pointing, and guaranteed presence of a hardware keyboard. If you have "power user" features that you want to offer somewhere but seem too fussy for iOS, the desktop is probably the place for them.

- **Windows**—It's less common than having a Mac version, but some iOS apps offer a Windows counterpart. You get a lot of the same power-user advantages of having a Mac edition but without the benefit of sharing much code or interface design philosophy. Windows 8 brings a mobile-like interface model to the desktop, but it's based on Windows Phone's "Metro" design language, a departure from the design of iOS. This is another platform that's attractive because of its reach.

- **Web**—This gives you the biggest return on investment for making your app available to more people in more situations. Everyone with access to the Internet can benefit from a web app. And for most teams, web apps have a gentler ramp up from idea to implementation than native desktop apps. The iPhone plus iPad plus web combination is a popular one, because it maximizes availability to users while requiring only sane amounts of redesign and reengineering. And because the interface expectations on the web are diffuse, you can often get away with creating a web app that follows the same design philosophy as your iOS app, thus saving precious resources. The drawback is that (flame-resistant suit on) web apps still aren't nearly as system integrated and satisfying as native apps. Noble efforts have been made to change that, notably Cappuccino and the increasingly impressive Google Docs, but we're not there yet.

Standalone, Mini, and Companion Apps

A good decision to make early is whether you want your various editions to be dependent on one another.

- A standalone app is useful all on its own. It may sync or otherwise share data with other editions on other platforms, but a person who installs only that one edition can get plenty of utility or enjoyment from it. It may offer features that other editions don't, and vice versa, but the core functionality is mostly overlapping.

- A mini app is a reduced-functionality version of something that exists elsewhere. Often there's an edition that provides the full functionality that an app has to offer, usually on a bigger-display platform, and a mobile edition provides on-the-go access to only the most commonly needed subset of features. This is also sometimes called a "lite" version or, in the famous case of Panic Inc.'s Coda, the "diet" version. Sometimes a mini edition has features that work only if they're synced or otherwise sent over from the full edition.

- A companion app assumes that you have some other edition of the app and acts as a sort of accessory to it. The companion offers a feature that the original couldn't easily offer on its own. The classic example is an iPhone app that acts as a remote control or a data input method for a desktop app, such as Keynote Remote.

This distinction isn't black and white. The functionality of a suite's various editions can overlap any amount (see Figure 7.1). The decision of how much functionality to

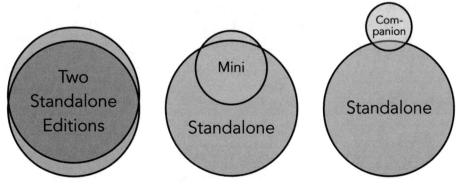

Figure 7.1   Feature overlap for various combinations of standalone, mini, and companion editions of an app

include in a given edition of an app is explored in more detail in Chapter 11, Focused and Versatile. Determining what falls within the scope of each edition is part of the fun of going cross-platform, and the rest of this chapter will help you decide where to draw those lines.

Start from Scratch

The key notion to keep in mind when you contemplate your cross-platform venture is that you're not porting an existing app over to a new display; you're designing a new app—with a lot of helpful background work done in another app, which you can mine for precedent and inspiration.

If you already have one platform covered and it's time to move to another, try treating the two editions as separate products. Take the opportunity to set aside all your sketches, wireframes, and mockups for the first edition, and start fresh with the new edition. It's a rare chance to reconsider all the design decisions you've made, all at one time.

If you're pursuing both editions at once, you should still try to treat them as separate products. Doing so will keep you in the right mind-set for giving each platform the dedicated design attention it deserves, rather than just making the same thing twice at different sizes.

It is possible that your final decision is to match the existing edition quite a lot. Maybe it's nearly the same result you would have gotten if you had decided to imitate the existing edition from the start. That's fine. But you should arrive at it honestly, and not start by taking it for granted. Apps that are blindly ported look and feel like apps that were blindly ported, and that's always a bad experience.

Back to the Outlines

The good news is that you don't really need to start all the way back at the beginning. "Start from scratch" is only a phrase meant to motivate you to set aside your developed designs. When you're thinking about a new platform, you should go back to the outlining stage. That's when you first thought about what your app was for (and whom it was for) without yet getting into the details of how it would serve those goals. That's when you figured out what features you'd need, without worrying about what they'd look like.

You can use that abstract understanding of your app to build a new interface that suits the new platform and serves your intention to build a standalone, companion, or mini app. Here's how to use your outlines.

- Dig up the outlines that you wrote for the first edition of the app, assuming you did so.

- Look at your requirements outline, and think about how each item fits with the new platform. (If you didn't write a requirements outline, hurry up and write one.)

- For any item that no longer makes sense, remove it. (For instance, iPhone-specific requirements such as initiating a phone call don't mean much on iPad.)
- If an item needs adjustment, adjust it. (The one-handed use requirement for an app like SnackLog would be tough to adhere to on iPad.)
- This is the hardest part: think about whether there are any new use cases that need consideration, requirements that emerge, or cool features that become possible because of the new platform.

What does it mean that your app will be in someone's pocket, now that you're bringing it to iPhone? What does it mean that it'll have the luxury of a display with more than 786,000 points on iPad? What about when you bring it to the desktop, where users expect much more customizability? Those are the questions covered in the following case study, which describes three platforms and their unique characteristics.

Case Study: Apple Mail

Mail has always been a reliable source of guidance about Apple's current understanding of how a basic, utilitarian productivity and communication app should work. Because email is a fundamental, universal need, Apple has paid close attention to making a reliable, understandable app that can benefit everyone.

As Mail has been brought to each new platform, we've gotten examples of how Apple intends a basic app to be implemented on different platforms. That makes Mail a sort of prototypical case of how to go cross-platform. The iOS editions of Mail are good examples of standalone apps, because they implement all of the most commonly needed functionality from the desktop edition, omitting only the features that don't fit on iOS anyway.

Your app is likely to be more interesting than Mail. And you're always free to stray from Apple's precedent. But studying Mail's various editions gives you a place to start, something to help you decide to either hew to or diverge from at each step.

The three editions of Mail are presented in chronological order according to when they were released. In addition to describing what the app looks like today on all three platforms, I explain how the app made its way from Mac to iPhone to iPad and back.

Mac OS X Leopard

To set the stage for the journey through these platforms, let's take a look at what Mac Mail looked like when iPhone was originally released: Mac OS X 10.5 Leopard, released in October 2007. Way back then, there hadn't been much time at all for the design philosophy behind iOS (then called iPhone OS) to directly influence the Mac. Remember that here, Mail is serving as a sort of representative for the prevailing design approach of desktop apps from that era.

Mail on the Mac has a long pedigree that goes all the way back to the Nextstep operating system, before it eventually became Mac OS X. Like much desktop software, it has spent decades accumulating features like a wharf accumulates barnacles.

That's part of making software: it's hard to take away features. Every time you add a feature to an app, you're committing to either keeping it indefinitely or upsetting the people who rely on it when you eventually take it away. Whether you call it "bloat" or "feature creep," it means desktop software that's been around a long time tends to have a lot of features. It's messy, but you can't hold it against those desktop apps if along the way they gave in to pressure for more functionality or decided to offer users choices. It should be interesting to see how iOS software compares in a decade or so.

The amassing of features is most evident in a desktop app's preferences window. It doesn't help that email is an inherently complicated and temperamental technology and a mail client needs to communicate with a huge variety of servers with nearly infinite configurations. If you look at the eight panes of preferences that Mail has on the Mac in Figure 7.2, you'll notice that each of them has a unique layout.

- **General**—Right-aligned labels attached to left-aligned controls, except at the bottom, where three checkboxes hover uncomfortably to the left without aligning to anything.

- **Accounts**—A list that intersects with a three-way tab view, each tab with its own layout of labels and controls. (And you can open a sheet of outgoing servers, containing yet another list, intersecting with yet another tab view, *and* there's a multistep sheet for adding a new account.)

- **Signatures** —A three-column layout, with the width of each column customizable, containing your accounts, the signatures for the selected account, and the text of the selected signature.

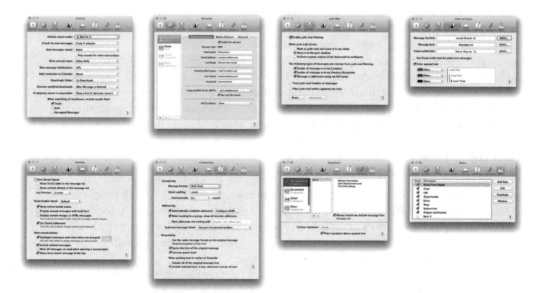

Figure 7.2   Mac Mail offers eight panes of preferences, each with its own layout and logic.

And so on. After looking at iOS apps all day, it might seem overwrought, but this is just the way things are on the desktop. Unique and custom layouts, each one using its own logic that users must decipher, are the order of the day.

The main window of Mail, especially here, before its redesign for OS X Lion, is a good exhibit of what traditional desktop interfaces are like. It has a unique geography. The hierarchy flows from the sidebar on the left, to a message list at the top, to a message view in the lower right, as you can see in Figure 7.3. The sidebar itself can contain an arbitrary hierarchy in the form of an outline showing mailboxes within mailboxes. The message list is presented as a typical table view that requires reading across a long row of data, with the position and width of each column left up to the user.

As with almost any desktop app, users are free to resize and reposition the window and its panes to accommodate their display size and work around other apps they have open. And because of the huge range of display resolutions, desk setups, and work environments, the fonts and presentation of the sidebar, message list, and messages are customizable. (Papyrus and Chalkduster are both fair game.)

The presentation has had a lot of color taken out of it by this point, as compared with the shiny, candylike treatment of early-2000s Mac interfaces like v10.2 Jaguar. But there are still touches of red, brown, and blue in the toolbar buttons and sidebar icons.

Menus are a major part of the Mac experience and have been since 1984. In Mac Mail, only a few common commands are available as toolbar buttons, but a great many more specialized commands are available from the nine menus. There are more than 200 menu commands, give or take a few depending on how many accounts and mailboxes you have set up. In a Mac app, many menu commands are synonyms for actions

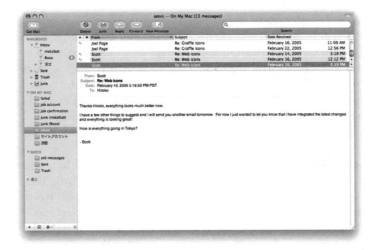

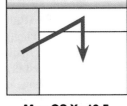

Mac OS X v10.5

Figure 7.3   Mail on Leopard presents the information hierarchy with a unique layout.

that are more easily performed via buttons, drag-and-drop operations, or contextual menu commands; the menu serves as a sort of in-place catchall documentation to help users figure out what's possible. And anything that appears as a menu command can be accessed via keyboard shortcut or AppleScript so that power users can customize their workflow.

Thus the menu is a conglomeration of functionality that's intentionally disconnected from the stuff it operates on. In this way, it can live in a single consistent location (always at the top of the screen), with a single consistent presentation (mostly plain-text lists of verb phrases). Many menu commands are like those preferences that accumulate over time: they're there because somewhere along the line, it became apparent that some small number of users really needed a certain command, and tucking it away deep in a menu was the least disruptive way to offer it.

Here's what it all means for traditional Mac design, in oversimplified bullet-point form.

- Lots of desktop apps are old, and thus they have lots of features.

- Even the newer desktop apps are likely to get away with having quite a few features, because it feels right at home among those older apps.

- Users expect to have a great deal of control over how an app works, from preferences to menu commands to font controls to window arrangement.

- The main window of an app often shows most or all of the information hierarchy at once, in a unique arrangement that may take some getting used to.

- Data is often presented in a tablelike fashion, arranged in rows and columns.

- Commands are not necessarily visually connected to the objects they affect.

iPhone

January 9, 2007! In one of his most iconic keynotes, Steve Jobs introduced iPhone. In fact, the original idea within Apple was to create a multitouch tablet-sized device like iPad, but bringing that experience to an iPod-sized device was found to be a better first step, based on where Apple was at the time. That's telling. If Apple had been designing downward from the Mac, it would have been easier to do the more computerlike iPad first. But it was instead designing upward from nothing. So the smaller, simpler iPhone was the sensible stepping-stone. So it's time to look at how it has designed Mail for iPhone, a flagship of the suite of "desktop-class applications" Jobs introduced that day.

The huge number of features and extensive customizability of Mac Mail have been replaced with a streamlined set of the most commonly needed ones. The Mac's complement of preferences on a variety of topics is replaced by a screen of essential server settings, along with another screen or so of advanced settings, for each account (see Figure 7.4). These settings are stowed safely away from the main functionality of the app in the dedicated Settings app. Other settings that are covered in the preferences on the Mac side (such as Notifications) live in other parts of the Settings app. Rather than

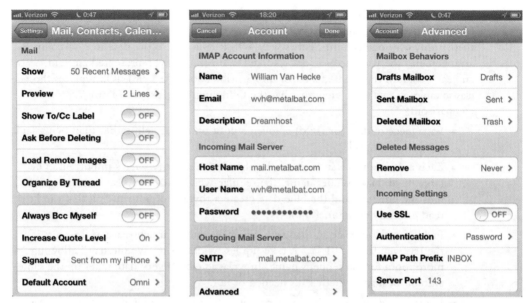

Figure 7.4   Mail on iPhone has a streamlined set of preferences, all arranged in standard grouped table views.

have custom layouts (as do the preferences panes on the Mac), all the settings appear as standard grouped table views, with stacks of cells and labels that resemble the other settings screens on the system.

Settings for customizing the appearance or behavior of the app itself are nowhere to be found. Instead, the app shows confidence that the way it works and the way it looks will be good enough for most people to adapt to. After all, when iPhone first came out, no one had yet established her own preferred workflow or appearance for iPhone apps.

Instead of a customizable interface, Mail on iPhone has a deliberately designed, consistent presentation that aims to make the best use of the iPhone display. That's possible in part because, unlike on the Mac, there's only one display that the designers need worry about. Font customization is less of a concern, because users can usually move the device into whatever position makes the text most legible for them. Designing for one possible layout and presentation is far more likely to yield a consistently good result than trying to design for arbitrarily numerous combinations of layouts and presentations.

The information hierarchy is presented as a navigation controller, the systemwide convention that provides a screen-by-screen walk from broader categories on the left to specific content on the right. Rather than ask the user to decipher the entire architecture at once, iPhone tends to offer one level at a time, a much quieter way to take in information.

On the message list screen, each message is represented by a carefully laid-out table cell. If you thought it was odd that these things were called "table views" when there's only ever one column, here's why. iOS is reluctant to put data in row/column arrangements the way the Mac always liked to do (each row represented an item, and each column represented a bit of information about the item). iOS replaces those classic tables with a table view that has the following benefits (see Figure 7.5 for a comparison).

- Each piece of data (or **field**) is given a position in the cell, rather than being laid out in a strict grid.

- Each field is given a style that helps the viewer identify what's important. The large, bold, black sender name, the regular-weight black subject line, the gray message preview, and the blue date create a rhythm of information that can be read carefully or scanned quickly.

- Fields can share space so that each one takes only as much space as it needs; if the received time is "1:11," it takes up less width than "Wednesday," allowing more room for the sender's name. In a classic table, every date takes up the same amount of space, whether it's needed or not.

- If a field is empty (e.g., the attachment indicator), it simply doesn't appear at all, rather than leave a gap in the grid.

- Resizing is necessary only when the device is rotated between portrait and landscape orientations.

The result, compared with a classic table, is a more compact, more efficient sort of table that feels more one-dimensional while still using some 2-D layout within each cell. The iOS table is much more comfortable being quite narrow and quite tall, scrolling vertically if necessary but never horizontally, a perfect fit for the iPhone display. Horizontal movement can be reserved for moving in the hierarchy. The same philosophy of dedicated layouts that are aware of the display dimensions is carried over to the message screen.

What's more, the presentation of commands is greatly simplified on iPhone: commands tend to be attached to the objects they operate on. The commands that are most central to the purpose of the app (Compose, Reply, Delete, etc.) are toolbar buttons. And the only toolbar buttons to appear are ones that make sense given the current context. (When you're not viewing a message, for instance, Reply is absent rather than disabled.) The toolbar buttons are attached to the messages they affect in the sense that they live in the toolbar of the screen that represents an individual message. Text-related commands appear in a contextual menu attached to the selected text. Contact-related commands appear on a dedicated contact info screen that you can reach by tapping the contact's name. The disconnected, menu-based command scheme is gone.

Figure 7.5   Mail on Mac OS X Leopard and Mail on iPhone, with the fields identified by color. The Leopard table requires reading across rows, whereas the iPhone uses clever layout to present each item as a compact, self-contained rectangle.

Time for the bullet-point takeaways.

- Going from the desktop to iOS is a chance to reboot users' expectations of the features and customization that should be offered in an app.

- Rather than creating endlessly fluid and flexible layouts and offering fine control of fonts, you can focus on designing a single, stable, consistent layout and presentation that works flawlessly in the very few display dimensions that exist on iPhone (portrait, 3.5-inch landscape, and 4-inch landscape). This is very much a conscious choice on Apple's part. It carefully chose a tiny handful of resolutions and stuck to them; everyone who designs for iOS benefits from that decision.

- The same information hierarchy that is spread across a single window on the Mac, with the selection state determining a pathway through it, is instead broken down into an individual screen for each level. The concept of selection doesn't need to exist in the iOS edition at all; the message you navigate to is implicitly selected.

- Data is shown in a compact, adaptable layout rather than with rows and columns.

- Commands are almost always visually connected to the objects they affect.

Attaching Commands to Objects

The contact-related commands in Mail for iPhone offer a good lesson in attaching commands to objects. In a naïve first-pass guess at presenting commands on the message screen in Mail, one might think that it would make sense to put an Add Contact button on the toolbar. After all, adding a contact to your address book is an important feature. But Apple reserved the toolbar for commands that are actually *about the message,* along with an ever-present Compose button for quick access. If you think about it, Add Contact isn't about the message at all; it's about the contact. So the designers came up with a hybrid content-plus-control style for the sender's name, and thus they turned what was a mere bit of metadata into a button. When you tap the contact name, you are taken to a special contact-info screen with everything the system knows about that person. A dedicated screen means that you can not only add them to your address book but also make a phone call, send a text message, mark them as a VIP, and so on. This good experience is brought to you by the designers' recognition of what the command is about and by their giving related commands a common place to live.

iPad

January 27, 2010! When Steve Jobs got up in front of the world to introduce iPad, he presented it as something between a notebook computer and a smartphone and better than either of them at certain key tasks. The design is inspired by iPhone, and plenty of smart alecks spent the first couple of weeks after the announcement joking about how it's only a larger iPod Touch (and should have been called "iPod Big"). Remember, as mentioned earlier, that Apple started working on iPad first; if either device is a size-adjusted version of the other, then an iPhone is a tiny iPad. As usual, it's easy for people to misunderstand what the big deal is in a new Apple product, and even to dismiss it—especially before it sells tens of millions of units.

The fact is that something subtly momentous happens when an iPod Touch gets huge. A 10-inch screen opens a lot of possibilities that don't exist on a 3.5-inch screen. Suddenly, the device is much more prepared to replace a notebook computer for key tasks like web browsing, email, and video. All the simplification and freshness of iPhone—no file management, dead-simple app installation, focus on one app at a time, the multitouch interface, and so on—were suddenly on a device that felt as if it could replace a *computer.*

Desktop OS developers have done a great job of hiding complexity and power from average users while exposing it to advanced users. But after decades of desktops, we take a lot of silly things for granted. The weird way some Mac apps stick around when you close their last window and others don't. The need to check the menu bar to find out what app you're in. The difficulty of focusing on what you're doing, and getting rid of stuff you don't care about. The way your ~/Library gets clogged up with residue over time. The need to know what the heck a ~/Library is in the first place. The unfortunate fact that sometimes, your system gets hosed for some unknown reason and you need to start over. iPad is a big deal because it uses the fresh start of the iPhone and applies it to a computerlike device, overcoming nearly all the technical and design cruft that had been building up as computers were incrementally improved over the years.

Designwise, iPad is a lot like iPhone—close enough that you could write a single book about designing for both of them. But there are important differences, and you can see them in the iPad edition of Mail.

The most significant difference is the way the navigation is relegated to a sidebar, with a main content area for the main content. This design increases the number of hierarchy levels visible at once from one to two (although it is often only one in portrait orientation).

With the navigation bar safely stowed in the sidebar, the main toolbar migrates to the top and leaves the bottom 44 points open for more content. In what might at first seem an arbitrary change, the toolbar and navigation bar have gone from the standard desaturated bluish-gray on iPhone to a totally desaturated light gray. There's a good rationale for that change. With the greater space of the iPad display, those bars are bigger, and more of their area is left empty—and big swaths of saturated color are noisy when you're trying to read. The iPad generally aims to give a more immersive experience than iPhone, betting that you might spend hours using it at a time. So the quieter the interface can get, the better.

The most obvious difference? The big display means iPad can show more content and be more expressive. On one hand, that means you can see more of your email at once; on the other hand, it means that the app needs to be careful about keeping your text areas narrow enough to be readable. (It's tiring to read wide lines of text, because it's hard for your eyes to go from the end of one line to the beginning of the next.) That lesson—keeping the bigger screen from making an overwhelming amount of information visible at once—is an important one. The larger screen also means that the app can do whimsical things like pile up messages loosely in the content area as you mark them for editing in the sidebar.

To sum up.

- iPad endeavors to replace computers for many users' day-to-day tasks, whereas iPhone was meant only to provide a portable companion.

- iPad often presents two levels of hierarchy at once—usually a pane for navigation and a second pane for content.

- The overall presentation on iPad is quieter and more immersive, especially for apps that a user may spend a lot of time with.

- iPad can put more content on the screen at once and be more expressive with it. But it's up to you to make sure that "more content" doesn't mean "too much content."

Back to the Mac

On October 20, 2010, Apple held a media event in which Steve talked about bring-ing design advances from iOS "back to the Mac." If you're thinking about bringing an iOS app to the Mac, or updating a Mac app to feel more in line with the iOS-like apps of recent years, read on.

So far, the update of Mail on the Mac has been at the surface level; the feature set hasn't been reduced. Apple has made quite a bit of headway in simplifying and mod-ernizing the main message window of Mail, and it could very well do the same for the preferences any revision now. But until then, the preferences window remains largely unchanged, except for one illustrative exception. Rather than simplify its preferences, the bit of iOS goodness that came back to Mac Mail gave it one *more* setting: "Use Classic layout." Users can reject the new iOS-inspired three-column layout and go back to the familiar—because changing things out from underneath people on the desktop is still a dangerous proposition.

The new layout of the main window logically presents the same three panes as before, but they're now in an orderly three-column arrangement (see Figure 7.6). It has the same straightforward left-to-right progression as an iOS app, with relatively narrow views that scroll vertically, but with all the levels visible at once. The design encourages hiding the sidebar, though, reducing the layout to only the message list and the message view. The message list itself uses a table view very much like the iOS one, compressing the relevant information about each message into a neat little rectangle rather than spreading it out along a wide row.

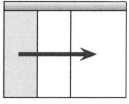

Mac OS X v10.8

Figure 7.6   Mail on Lion presents the information hierarchy with a straightforward three-column layout.

The system-standard full-screen mode introduced in Lion makes it easier for users to focus on one app at a time and stop worrying about window management. The menu bar and Dock disappear in full-screen mode, and some apps hide other UI elements until the cursor hits the edges of the screen. Especially on smaller displays, it can make a Mac feel a lot like an iPad. But as a designer, you can take advantage of the full-screen feature but you can't count on its being the only way your app will ever be seen, as you can on iOS.

The desaturation of the Mail interface is now complete, except for a few very small touches. Blue still appears as the sidebar theme color and is applied to a few key bits of information. Flags still show their color coding. And the occasional green Messages status appears next to a contact's name. But the Mac seems to be fully embracing the iPad's insistence that vivid and multihued color should be reserved for the user's content and not for the interface—at least in serious productivity apps, where people are apt to spend a lot of time working.

Here are the points to keep in mind when you're going back to the Mac.

- If you're updating an existing Mac app, be careful about changing things too drastically and irreversibly unless you are ready to defend yourself against users who liked things the way they were.

- Take inspiration from iOS in simplifying and compacting your data display and making your overall layout more logical and spatial. You may be able to use screen-by-screen navigation instead of showing multiple levels at once, or hide levels when they're not needed.

- Think of your app not only as a window floating among dozens of other windows but also as a possible full-screen app occupying its own space. Think about how you can focus on content, showing peripheral UI furniture only when it's needed.

- Consider whether you should make your interface quieter to put more emphasis on content.

Summary

The best, most responsible way to go cross-platform is to seriously consider the needs and capabilities of each platform from scratch. You may end up deciding that the various editions of your app should have similar or wildly divergent feature sets, and nearly identical or unique presentations.

Mac, iPhone, and iPad are three distinct platforms, and each requires unique thinking and design. They overlap in certain areas, and you need to know which areas so that you don't betray users' expectations. As a rough approximation, iPhone apps like focusing on portability; iPad apps like focusing on carefree replacement of casual computing tasks; and Mac apps like focusing on power and flexibility. By no means should you feel restricted by those tendencies, but you should be aware of them.

The design of Mac is converging somewhat with that of iOS, with most of the convergence happening toward iOS. Some things about the Mac, though, aren't likely to change soon: its window orientedness, its precision mouse cursor, and its hardware keyboard, to name a few. So don't get carried away trying to turn your user's Mac into an iOS device.

Exercises

If you're considering going cross-platform with your own app, try these exercises to get thinking about how the platforms fit together and how you can make the most of each one.

1. Think of your own app or of any app that exists only on one platform. Sketch how you think it might serve its users' needs on another platform. Are the needs the same everywhere, or are they different depending on the platform?

2. Pick an app that's already cross-platform, and decide where you think it fits into the standalone/mini/companion space. Imagine what it would be like if it were one of the other types. Could it do some jobs better? Do you think the designers made the right choices about how much functionality to include?

3. Choose an Apple app that's available on iPhone, iPad, and Mac. As is done in this chapter with Mail, examine how each feature and experience is designed to feel right on the platform where it lives.

Part II

Principles

The Graceful Interface

This chapter describes the nuts and bolts of what makes a software experience feel good under the fingers. Psychologist Donald Norman identified three levels of cognitive processing that are relevant to design, and the concerns of this chapter can be roughly correlated to the first, the **visceral** level: both the unconscious, automatic, mechanical interaction of a person sliding his fingers across a piece of glass, and the immediate feelings produced in his brain by the way the software under the glass responds.

The goal is to craft a **graceful** interface, one that produces a viscerally satisfying experience for the person using it. The gracefulness of an interface can be separated from its other merits or failings—even if it's graceful, perhaps it's also glitchy, garish, useless, or condescending—but those are questions for other chapters.

Suspension of Disbelief

The Holy Grail when you're designing for grace on iOS is the ability of the user to suspend her disbelief that she is actually interacting with some kind of magical mechanism. This magical device reacts appropriately to how she touches it, seeming to create a direct conduit from her mind to her fingers to the screen. Note well that the magic in your design should still make sense and should respond to the user's intentions. It shouldn't be the sort of inscrutable, unpredictable "magic" characteristic of a device that seems to have a mind of its own.

For a long time, technology was obviously just a mess of pixels frantically blinking on a screen, in a crummy representation of abstract data in a bunch of memory registers that kinda vaguely represented what you were trying to do but weren't very helpful in helping you accomplish it. iPhones and iPads behave more like devices dedicated to the task you're working on, with buttons and switches and movable surfaces that respond directly to your hands.

iOS devices are better than desktop computers at maintaining the suspension of disbelief, for two reasons. First, they are more immersive: you get one app at a time, pushed out to the edges of the screen, monopolizing the input and output capabilities of the device. This is a huge deal, because, as Adam Engst pointed out, "The iPad *becomes* the app you're using." You're touching the technology directly with your hands, those primary human conduits of interaction with the world for tens of millions of years, rather than via an abstraction such as a mouse or a keyboard.

That leads into the second reason: touch-based interaction works well on iOS because the system prioritizes the responsiveness of the interface over almost everything else. If surfaces scroll like butter the instant you drag them, buttons depress the instant you poke them, and switches flip the instant you swipe them, the software can really feel like a physical object. You can forget that you're using software at all.

Of course, this experience is still presented as what Bret Victor calls "pictures under glass." (Track down Victor's essay "A Brief Rant on the Future of Interaction Design" some time and have your mind blown in the best way.) If while using a touch device you stop for an instant to think about it, it's obvious you're not interacting with a physical object at all, because you can't *feel* it. Someday we'll have interfaces that provide all the tactile expressiveness of objects in the real world and that respond to the full repertoire of input that our hands can muster. But until then, we have it pretty good with our pokes and our drags of stuff under glass. It's good enough to occasionally convince people for a little while that the stuff going on under the glass is real.

It's extremely easy to break the suspension of disbelief. If the software stutters, hangs, or otherwise fails to give instant feedback, then the dedicated, magical mechanism reverts to software inside a little chunk of mundane technology. The spell may be broken more often for you if you run certain resource-intensive apps or if you have an iOS device that's a bit short of the top of the line. But the good news is that there are concepts you can put to use to make your app as graceful and responsive as possible, to the immersion and satisfaction of your users.

The Moment of Uncertainty

A crucial instant occurs every time a user provides a bit of input to a piece of technology, such as trying to tap a button in an app. If the designers have done their part to create a graceful experience, then the instant will pass without notice by the user. The technology responds, the user's expectation is met, and he continues getting done whatever it is he's using the app to get done. But if any link in the chain of app, operating system, and hardware happens to falter, then that imperceptible instant can stretch out into a moment of uncertainty. (See Figure 8.1.)

During the moment of uncertainty, the user has no idea whether his input was successfully recognized. Perhaps it wasn't—touch input is an imperfect thing. Here are examples of **failed inputs** that happen to users all the time.

- A tap was a couple of pixels off from the tappable area of the button.
- A pair of taps was not rapid enough to count as a double-tap.
- A swipe was not quite in the right direction.

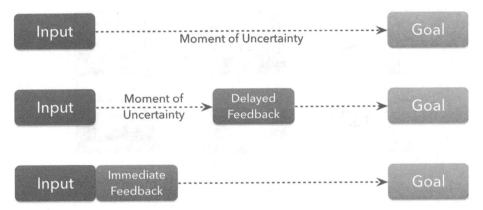

Figure 8.1   A lack of immediate feedback causes a moment of uncertainty.

On the other hand, it's possible that the input was successful, but the app didn't give immediate feedback. These are types of **failed feedback** when the input was successful but the app leaves the user guessing.

- **Silence**—There is no feedback. The tap was in the correct location, but the button doesn't highlight and the app doesn't indicate that anything has changed until it's finished processing the results.
- **Delay**—The feedback comes too late. The double-tap was quick enough, but the feedback highlight doesn't appear until after a noticeable delay.
- **No negative feedback**—The swipe was fine, but the content is already scrolled all the way to the top; and instead of providing the expected bounce-back animation, the app simply doesn't move the content.

Failure to give negative feedback when it's expected is arguably the worst, because it could lead the user to false conclusions. With silence, the length of the moment of uncertainty after a failed tap is however long it takes the user to give up waiting and try tapping again. Delay is common; sometimes it takes a few seconds before a tap yields any kind of feedback, and during those seconds the user isn't sure whether he actually tapped in the right place.

Instantaneous Feedback

The most fundamental way to preserve the illusion of reality that iOS thrives on is to provide instantaneous feedback for all input. When a control is successfully activated, it should glow, depress, darken, or otherwise instantly indicate that it knows it was hit (see Figure 8.2).

Figure 8.2   Several styles of button feedback

The reason for the tap is the **goal:** navigating to another screen, summoning a popover, sending a message, and so on. That final goal may be only a fraction of a second away, making it seem like overkill to highlight the button and then perform the action. But delays can always happen, depending on what's going on with the device, especially on older devices. Even the needed processing—for the system to recognize the touch input, pass the message to the OS, pass the message to your app, and display feedback on the screen—takes around 50 milliseconds. Giving feedback within 500 milliseconds or so feels instantaneous to users and preserves their suspension of disbelief (though even faster is better).

When a single tap and a double-tap have different effects (or even a triple-tap, if you're using one for an advanced shortcut), the system must wait after each tap to find out whether another one is coming. That adds a 300-millisecond delay after each tap. Keep that in mind, too, as you tune your feedback.

Any response that takes more than about three seconds should put up a progress indicator—probably a spinning indeterminate indicator unless there is a lot of work to be done and progress can be easily quantified.

Wait Indicator Threshold

If a process is sometimes quick but sometimes takes a while, you shouldn't immediately put up a progress indicator each time it happens. In the cases when it finishes quickly, you'll be flashing the indicator up and then taking it away faster than the user can recognize it. That sort of frenetic updating of the interface leads to a feeling of chaos and instability. Instead, give the process a bit of time; if it crosses a critical threshold that suggests it will be a while—say, 1 second—then put up the progress indicator. Or just commit to leaving the indicator up for a minimum duration, such as 1 second, even if the process finishes more quickly than that.

It's not unusual for some apps to occasionally take several seconds to perform an action that normally happens within half a second. Those seconds can seem like a frustrating eternity for a user, waiting to find out if the software really did interpret her input as intended. According to the Nielsen Norman Group's "powers of 10" concept, effects that happen within 0.1 second of the input feel as if the user caused them; effects that take a second or more feel as if the computer caused them—a vaguely disempowering feeling that reminds users they're not really in charge. So do everything you can to give feedback to users as soon as possible. If every single control on every iOS device gave instantaneous feedback, then there would never be any question about whether or not input was successful. Successful taps would always be immediately recognizable as successful, and unsuccessful taps wouldn't do anything. The moment of uncertainly would be a thing of the past. In truth, lots of apps, even some Apple apps, are guilty of neglecting to give feedback. Do your part to make iOS a less uncertain place.

Gracefulness through Layout

When you wireframe screens for iOS, you need to consider the principles of layout described in Chapter 4, The Wireframes. But that's not all. You also need to consider the physical and physiological realities of a human being holding and touching a hunk of glass and metal with his hands. Everyone develops his own quirky ways of holding his device, but for the most part they fall into a few basic techniques. These ways of holding the device affect how people see and touch the device.

Consider these basic holding techniques for iPhone.

- **One-handed**—The phone rests across the fingers and palm of your dominant hand, and you touch the screen with your thumb. The easily reachable regions of the screen are described by the **thumb field**, a fuzzy blob centered on the spot where your thumb most easily points (see Figure 8.3). The specific shape

Figure 8.3   The thumb field on iPhone (left) and the steering wheel zone on iPad

and size of the field depend on the size and flexibility of your hand: some people have no trouble reaching the top-left corner (or top-right for lefties) of even a tall iPhone 5, but others must strain a bit to reach it. For some, it's difficult to reach the very bottom corner of the screen near the palm, so a button slightly removed from the corner is easier to hit. (Thus, the bottom middle of an iPhone screen is an excellent spot for controls you want everyone to be able to easily access all the time.) These limitations aren't so great that you should never put anything important in the upper corners of the screen. But given the choice, keep controls that you want to be especially attractive to the touch in the lower three-fifths.

- **Two-handed**—You hold the phone in your nondominant hand while you use the index finger, middle finger, and thumb of your dominant hand to touch the screen. All areas of the screen are equally reachable.

- **No-handed**—The iPhone is resting on a surface, and you can use one or both hands to touch it. All areas of the screen are equally reachable.

Here are basic holding techniques for iPad.

- **Two-handed**—Essentially the same as the two-handed method for iPhone, except that it's harder to keep an iPad steady with one hand.

- **No-handed**—The same as no-handed for iPhone, except that it's much more common. People stand up their iPad on a desk, rest it in their laps, or otherwise alleviate the eventual strain of holding up a pound and a half of magic.

- **Steering wheel**—You hold the iPad with one hand on each side, occasionally extending your thumbs to touch the screen.

The steering wheel method is especially interesting, because it makes certain gestures easy and others impossible. A tap or drag within 200 points or so of either edge of the display—the **steering wheel zone**—is comfortable. But to touch anything in the middle of the screen, you need to let go of the iPad with one hand and reach for it. (See Figure 8.3.)

What's cool is that you can design an app around the steering wheel notion. If you place your controls in the steering wheel zone, it opens up a swath of space in the middle of the screen that can be strictly for the user's content. Pushing the UI furniture against the walls means that users can focus on what's most important to them. Once you're aware of this pattern, you'll see it everywhere.

Remember that on touch devices, the display and the input device are one and the same. Whenever users are interacting with the software, there is guaranteed to be something in the way of the screen: their hands. (Yes, yes, unless they have an external keyboard connected, sure.)

Wherever you expect a gesture to happen, be sure to keep any important feedback out of the **hand shadow:** the area most likely to be covered up by the user's hand as she makes the gesture (see Figure 8.4). Generally, this means giving feedback (such

Figure 8.4   The hand shadow on iPad; the equivalent effect also exists on iPhone.

as displaying a contextual menu) *above* the spot where the touch happens, or making the feedback big enough not to be covered by the hand, even if it appears below the touched spot (as when new controls appear based on the state of a higher-up control). Because of the location of the very tip of the hand shadow, borderless toolbar buttons have a big glow effect when pressed; if only the glyph itself changed, the effect would almost always be obscured.

Six Reliable Gestures

When iPhone came along, and especially when iPad came along, the multitouch experience seemed to offer a world of expressive, intuitive, fun gestures for interacting with software. The truth is that even though multitouch gets us closer to directly interacting with virtual objects than ever before, it's still an experience of pictures under glass.

Yes, it feels more natural to poke your fingers at objects on a screen than it does to shove a plastic rodent around on a desk to convince a flea on the screen to hover in the direction you want it to. But poking *at* objects is not remotely realistic enough to replace millions of years of interacting with objects in the physical world. It's still very much an abstraction to reduce all the things you can do with an object to a variation on poking it or smearing your fingers across it.

If we can't reproduce the real experience accurately, we need to resort to a few abstractions that we know are effective for most people. In reality, there are only a few gestures you can count on to be reliable. These reliable gestures are discoverable, meaning that people already know about them or can guess they exist. And they're usable, meaning that you can expect most people to succeed at performing them most of the time. Here are the six reliable gestures, in descending order of reliability.

- **Tap**—This is the principal gesture: a touch and immediate release. By far the easiest, most natural way for users to express their intentions to your app. Unless you have a great reason to require a more sophisticated gesture, the tap should be your default choice for all input.

- **Drag/Swipe**—This is a touch, a move across the glass, and a release. A drag is deliberate: the finger touches the glass and then slides around while the user watches the resulting movement and decides when to let go. A swipe is quick, with the finger usually already in motion when it touches the glass, and coming off the glass while still in motion. These gestures are almost always reserved for scrolling or for moving things around; the swipe-to-delete convention is an exception. A common temptation is to use swipes in various directions to signify various commands; resist it! It's too arbitrary and undiscoverable to expect users to guess that they should swipe unless their intention is as simple as "go in this direction."

Those two gestures should constitute the immense majority of the gestures required to interact with your app. Sprinkle in the remaining four sparingly.

- **Touch and hold**—A finger touches the glass and stays there. Touch and hold is the "do something else" gesture. If you need to offer more functionality than a simple tap will get you, the touch and hold is a safe place to put it. It is somewhat equivalent to a right-click on the desktop, especially in that it often opens a contextual menu for performing various actions with the item you tapped. Sometimes a touch and hold is necessary to pick up an object at the beginning of a drag to distinguish it from a normal scrolling drag.

- **Double-Tap**—This is two taps in rapid succession. It's not nearly as commonly required on iOS as double-clicks are on the desktop. For uneditable, zoomable content, it means "zoom in." If there are discrete objects or clear boundaries on the screen, that zoom should try to fill the screen with the tapped object, as Safari does. (Otherwise, it should just zoom in, as with Maps.) For editable content, it usually means, "Start editing this thing." Its two accepted meanings are pretty well understood; any other meanings you try to assign to it will likely seem odd.

The last two are the hardest to perform, because they require two fingers moving in concert. And they both have set meanings; trying to use them for some other purpose is just asking for confusion.

- **Pinch/Unpinch**—Two fingers touch the glass and move toward or away from each other. This gesture almost exclusively means "zoom out" and "zoom in."

Users strongly expect a zoom from this gesture, with the content following the movement of their fingers precisely; using it for anything else is sure to be puzzling.

- **Rotate**—Two fingers touch the glass and move radially around a center point. Performing it successfully is rather difficult. This gesture has exactly one meaning: rotate. Users expect it to rotate an object (as in iWork) or the entirety of the content (as in Maps).

These are the same six gestures that were introduced with the iPhone in 2007. Even the arrival of iPad, with its big screen, didn't make any significant change in the complexity of gestures that we can count on to be reliable.

Conveniently, those gestures have been documented in the form of advertising. Apple's marketing style tends toward simply showing the products in action, so the parade of iPhone and iPad commercials has educated people about what's possible on an iOS device even before they meet one in person. This is a huge boost in the discoverability of the six standard gestures, and a case against introducing any new and exotic gestures beyond them. (But if you really want to invent your own, check Chapter 14, Consistency and Specialization.)

The Sandwich Problem

Every function of your app should be accessible using the most basic gestures possible. If you require any complex gestures (two-fingered or even two-handed) for any of the core functionality of your app, you will run into what HCI researchers at Brown University call the **sandwich problem.** (Others have called it the burrito problem; either way, it's a problem.) Users are not guaranteed to have all their fingers on both hands available to perform the gestures you ask of them. In fact, you should assume that users want to use one of their hands for some unrelated task, whether it's eating a sandwich, holding on to the handrail on a train, or gesticulating as they make a point to a colleague.

Then any extra usefulness they get from having both hands available is a bonus and not a requirement. The mobility and all-around casual interaction of iOS devices means that people are using them in all kinds of situations, and we can't expect them to dedicate the sort of concentration and dexterity that we expect on the desktop.

The Maps app is a fascinating illustration of the sandwich problem in conjunction with the difference between reality and the ideal. The canonical way to zoom out on iOS is the pinch, a gesture that requires two hands. So you can't actually do it while eating a sandwich…and it's extraordinarily dangerous while driving a car. But it's one of the most crucial interactions in the whole Maps app. True, you're not supposed to use an iPhone (or an iPad) while driving; it's unsafe, and in lots of places it's illegal. But many people do it anyway. Should Apple make it easier to operate the Maps app while driving, to avoid making those people even more dangerous? Or is its current difficulty of use preventing even more people from trying to use it while driving? It's a moral puzzle with no obvious answer, and Apple seems to have made its choice. Sometimes in design, lives are on the line.

Exotic Gestures as Shortcuts

Now that you've been convinced that you shouldn't use exotic and specialized gestures, here's when it's actually fine to use them: when they're shortcuts. If you're comfortable with desktop software design, it's helpful to think of those more difficult gestures as being like keyboard shortcuts—quick ways of getting at advanced functionality for advanced users.

Every function that you offer a shortcut for should also be accessible using more basic gestures and ideally should be discoverable via a visible control or cue. After all, you can't count on people to read your documentation, watch your intro video, or read your blog post about your cool and intuitive gestures. So you can't expect someone to guess that a two-finger double-tap might do something useful like zooming to 100%, but that's exactly what it does in several Apple apps, including Safari. Did you know that? You never needed to know it, because you can always use a series of pinches to reach the same goal. But if you learn it, you can trade a little cognitive load and manual dexterity in exchange for saving a bit of time.

Similar to the concept of gestures as shortcuts is the idea of **fallback gestures.** If you intend for a more difficult gesture to be the "normal" way of doing a certain task, you can sometimes offer a slightly less sophisticated interaction when you receive a slightly less sophisticated gesture. This is best illustrated with an example: the iWork apps on iPad offer a popover for inserting graphics, such as colored shapes, charts, or photos, into your document. If you touch and hold one of these graphics, it lifts off of the popover and you can drag it to the precise desired spot in the document. But even if you aren't aware of that touch and drag gesture, you can simply tap the object and it will be placed in the center of the document, where you can then reposition it. If you intend for an object to respond to any gesture more advanced than a single tap, make sure a single tap does something, too: either a fallback behavior or an animation cue such as the camera icon's vertical bounce on the iPhone lock screen (described in the Cues section in Chapter 9).

Realistic Gestures

Gestures such as drags and pinches are more demanding about feedback than taps are. Whereas a tap that responds with feedback within 500 milliseconds feels more or less instantaneous, drags don't have as much of a grace period. A tap followed by feedback happens over short span of *time,* but a drag with feedback happens in time *and space.* The eye can plainly see the gap that appears when the object being dragged is not actually keeping pace with the finger dragging it (see Figure 8.5).

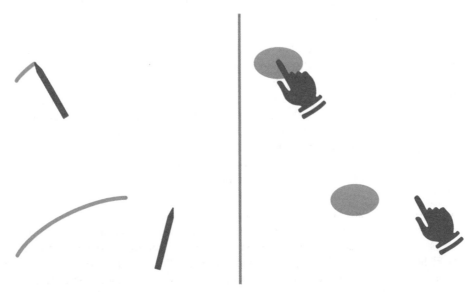

Figure 8.5   Lagging behind a drag gesture, with a stylus and with a finger

So as hard as you try to make taps give immediate feedback, try even harder to make drags happen fast. Unfortunately, there is a minimum lag of between 50 and 100 milliseconds caused by the inherent speed of iOS devices. So brisk strokes with a touch stylus in a sketching app, for instance, can't feel nearly as satisfying as sketching on paper. (The extra length you get from a stylus can make angular movement faster, amplifying the effect.) But you can do your best to make more deliberate drags feel good, and you should.

Not only should drags keep up with the fingertip as much as possible, but also you should take care that the location of the dragged object or point doesn't get out of sync with the fingertip. The exact point (or for a pinch, points) that was under the finger when the gesture started should stay under the finger at every point along the course of the gesture. If there is any drift, the illusion of manipulating an object, as if pushing it around on a table with your fingers, is lost. Drags and pinches that get out of sync with the fingers are a telltale sign of an app that doesn't understand the value of touch-based interaction.

Hysteresis

There are, of course, exceptions to the advice that gestures should be precise and realistic. **Hysteresis** is an intentional use of imprecision in processing input. This is a difficult concept, but stay with it because it's one of the most important tools you have for serious touch interface design. It's an opportunity for invisibly improving any experience, such as drawing apps, that makes use of delicate gestures.

For the most basic gestures, like a simple tap, iOS does a good job of detecting which gesture is happening and sending the information along to your app's code. But for more "analog" gestures where the timing and movement really matter, such as touches and drags on a canvas that's precise down to a single point, you often need to use a bit more finesse than just blindly obeying the touch events sent by the system.

Imagine an app where you use drag gestures to move or resize objects, like Keynote or Pages. If the app simply took the user's gestures at face value, it would be easy to turn that imperfect input into an unhelpful result, something the user didn't intend. But if the app purposefully disregards certain tiny imperfections in the gestures, it can actually produce a more reliable, more pleasant experience. Slightly disobeying the user's input can actually make the user feel more in control.

Here are some examples of hysteresis in action (see Figure 8.6).

- **Tap**—Often, taps don't actually hit the glass and then immediately leave the glass in exactly the same spot. The finger often moves a point or two across the glass during the tap. When the system is recognizing gestures for you, it does the right thing and hands you a tap. When you're handling gestures yourself, you need to *ignore* any movement below a certain distance threshold, or else almost every tap the user tries to make will instead be interpreted as a tiny drag. He'll end up moving objects around a point or so rather than just selecting them.

- **Drag**—As with taps, drags often have a bit of a jump at the end as the finger is lifted. It safe to assume that a sufficiently tiny jump at the very end of a drag, especially if it's preceded by a pause, should be ignored.

- **Drag to move**—You could interpret drags down to the individual point, and put objects precisely wherever that leaves them. But in lots of cases, you can "snap" to a certain angle or position that makes good sense. If the drag is *very* close to being perfectly vertical or horizontal, you might want to interpret as if it really were. If a drag would put an object within a couple of points of abutting the edge of the canvas, you might choose to have it jump the extra distance and "stick." This approach gives precedence to commonly desired or logical results over blindly accurate results. (Of course, in plenty of cases you really do want

Tap   **Drag to Move**   **Drag to Resize**

Figure 8.6   Hysteresis: the area around a tap that the finger can stray into without becoming a drag (left); the vertical and horizontal grooves for a movement drag (middle); and the groove for maintaining an object's aspect ratio while resizing it

to be as accurate as possible; the brushstrokes of a painting app should faithfully reflect the organic nature of the user's movements and not artificially straighten themselves out.)

- **Drag to resize**—As with movement, it often makes sense to lock the resize of an object to preserve its aspect ratio (the ratio of its height to its width). Rarely does someone want to make just a small change to an object's aspect ratio while dragging its corner. It's much more likely that he wants to keep the aspect but change the size; the iWork apps show a dotted line from one corner to the other during the gesture to indicate the "track" you can drag along. And if you really do want to change the aspect ratio, you can break out of the track or use a side handle instead of a corner one.

- **Pinch to zoom**—If your pinches were interpreted as precisely as possible, you would often end up at odd zoom levels like 103% or just-barely-smaller-than-the-screen. Instead, smart apps snap to sensible zoom levels like 100% and fit-to-screen. This means you can't get to 99% zoom via pinching even if you wanted to, and that's fine. Giving up the ability to do something that almost nobody ever wants to do, in exchange for almost always doing what the user did want to do, is a tremendously good deal.

You can also use hysteresis for guessing the user's intentions for a gesture. In plenty of situations, you end up having several commands that seem as if they should be mapped to the same gesture. In a diagram-drawing app, how should the user pan the view? How should she move an existing object? How should she draw a selection rectangle? The answer to all three is obviously "with a drag gesture"; so when the user drags, you need to interpret which of the three she meant. It's possible to devise a scheme for checking how long the touch stays put on top of an object before moving, what direction the drag is going, how fast it's moving, and so on, in order to guess the user's intentions. Sometimes, it can help to make the boundary between differently interpreted gestures slightly less invisible with a subtle visual cue like an animated bounce, a highlight effect, and the like.

If you decide to use hysteresis to improve input, you had better do a lot of testing against various users' gestural habits and idiosyncrasies to get the detection and guessing logic just right. Otherwise, you can end up with software that seems to yield random reactions to the same input, thus feeling unpredictable rather than magical. But if you succeed, you'll have created a delightful, effortless experience that seems to somehow know what the user wants every time.

Thresholds

Similar to the concept of hysteresis is that of the **threshold:** the point at which a continuous, "analog" gesture triggers a discrete action. The classic example of a threshold is the pull-to-refresh gesture described in Chapter 14. It started in Tweetie, but now it can be found in a great many apps, including Apple's own Mail apps. Pull-to-refresh takes a continuous gesture, the drag, and turns it into a discrete command, refresh.

When the gesture starts, an indicator appears to clue the user in to the idea that continuing the gesture might do something: in the case of Mail, a circular blob containing a refresh arrow slides into view. As the gesture continues, the indicator continuously updates to indicate that it's progressing toward a goal: the circular blob is stretched out like a lump of dough. Finally, the threshold is reached, and the indicator undergoes a quick change: the stretching blob snaps back and is replaced by a spinning activity indicator. If the gesture stops before the threshold is reached, then the indicator disappears and the command isn't triggered.

You might be tempted to use a threshold to do something nice and spatial such as navigate between pages: if the user tries to scroll past the top or bottom of a page of content, then the previous or next page immediately snaps into view. On the face of it, this seems not too different from the way the home screen snaps to pages as you drag it horizontally. But there is a difference. If you use a pull-to-refresh-style threshold, there is no canceling the gesture partway through. As soon as the threshold is hit, the next page immediately appears.

Co-opting an innocent, usually inconsequential gesture like dragging past the edge of a view for a harmless function like refreshing is one thing. Allowing it to take the user to a different screen is probably going too far. The home screen approach is better: dragging between two pages can be canceled at any moment by simply dragging back in the other direction. There is no scrolling halfway between two pages of app icons and then stopping. If you didn't drag far enough to navigate to the next page, then the previous page snaps back into place. The threshold is still there, but you have a chance to go back before ending the gesture. The experience might be even better if that threshold were made visible, perhaps by dimming one screen of icons while bringing the other to full brightness, so that you could know when to let go.

Another pitfall is trying to use a continuous gesture like a drag or a pinch to trigger a discrete command, *without a visible threshold*. The common swipe-to-delete gesture is actually a case of this, but because the gesture is quick and casual, and the feedback is almost immediate, it works out. But trying to use an unpinch for something like opening an item, without live feedback during the gesture, would be very contrary to the way users expect pinches to work. Instead, they are used to the continuous feedback given by gestures like unpinching an album in the Photos app on iPad: the photos spread out in perfect sync with the movement of the fingertips.

Generous Taps

Traditional mouse-based input on desktop systems is pretty precise. On a desktop, with a pointy little arrow, you can actually tell exactly which pixel on the cursor is the "live" one, so there is rarely much doubt about whether you really clicked the thing you were trying to click. (These are excellent reasons to test your app on the device as much as possible and not in the simulator.) On top of that, hover effects on elements can give you an extra cue about when you've positioned the cursor in the right spot. And, of course, desktop systems are much faster than mobile devices, so you are less likely to notice the moment between clicking and reaching the goal. When developers try to simply reproduce a desktop mousing experience on iOS, as has been demonstrated by some direct ports of games, the result is painful and frustrating.

The moment of uncertainty happens on iOS because touch input is imprecise. You never know exactly which pixel was processed as the center of your big fingerprint. Your finger is blocking your view of the thing you're trying to hit. The way your taps get processed feels slightly different depending on which hand you use and which finger you use. What's more, touches are processed slightly differently between iPhone and iPad. The angle matters, because the operating system actually compensates for the way your mind perceives taps by moving each event a few points up from the actual center of where you touched. (That trick is sure to mess you up if you ever try to interact with an iOS device upside-down.) All this is to say that tapping is messy and difficult to interpret. But you can make it feel effortless for your users.

Make your tap targets as generous as possible. The baseline requirement is defined in the *Human Interface Guidelines:* that magical number, 44 by 44 points. With a few exceptions (of course), no tap target on iOS should be any smaller. In cases where it must be smaller, iOS goes to great lengths to ease the interaction: keys on the keyboard pop up a little flag that can be seen above your finger, indicating which key you've hit and giving you the opportunity to slide to a different one. And there's some intense probabilistic adjustment of the tap target for each key, depending on which characters you've entered so far. Moreover, the usually marvelous autocorrect feature goes back and analyzes the whole word (and surrounding words), giving you another chance to get it right when you are finished typing. That's more than enough to make up for the tiny tap targets of the keys.

It might at first seem obvious that for a given target, the active tappable area should coincide with the opaque pixels of the image that represents it. After all, that's how we have been doing things on the desktop for decades. But not so. On a touch screen it helps to afford some extra space.

Consider a table cell with a button on its far right side (see Figure 8.7). If a user taps only one pixel outside the button, in the space between it and the edge of the display, what should happen? If only the interior of the button's graphic counts as tappable area, then the cell behind the button gets the tap, which is almost certainly not what the user wanted.

If you make that thin strip of cell surface around the button count as the cell, you're saying that you expect people to tap in that tiny gap to select the cell—even though there is plenty of space on the left to do so. It's a preposterous thing to expect. By contrast, if the tappable area of the button extends all the way to the top and bottom of the cell, and an equal distance to either side, then any tap in that area is received by the button. That's far, far more likely what users want when they tap in the vicinity of the button.

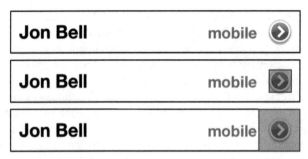

Figure 8.7   A row in the Phone app (top); the same row with a naïve tap target applied (middle); the same row with a reasonable and generous tap target applied

Keep in mind that to balance out this practice, you don't actually want everything to be as easy as possible. In a couple of cases, tap targets are actually smaller than 44 pixels square. One is in Safari, where the system can't help it if you're zoomed out so far that links are only a few points tall. Some people have even gotten shockingly good at precisely tapping those tiny links with the corners of their fingertips, but you had better not expect such precision in your ordinary controls.

Another example is to make certain buttons smaller than standard to avoid accidental taps, because the consequences of a mistaken tap are much worse than on most buttons. The Delete button for apps on the iPad home screen is actually only 24 points square, much smaller than the normal minimum size, and has no extra tappable area around it. You have to really want to delete an app (see Figure 8.8).

Figure 8.8   The delete app button on the iPad home screen, whose tap target is a square with a mere 24 points per side

The purchase button in the App Store and iTunes store is 24 points tall and has a tap target about 32 points tall. You need to hit that unusually small target twice in a row in order to buy an app. The rationale is a good one: Apple doesn't want people to come complaining to it that they accidentally bought something.

As for the thin version of the toolbar and navigation bar on an iPhone in landscape mode, it appears to be only 32 points tall. But that's a trick; the tappable zone actually extends out into the content area, satisfying the 44–point requirement.

---

iPhone and iPad Tap Target Sizes

The HIG insists on 44-point square tap targets at the least, but there's a difference in points per inch between the iPad and iPhone. Yes, a 44-point-square tap target on an iPad is actually physically 52% bigger than a 44-point-square tap target on iPhone, thanks to the magic of two-dimensional math ($\frac{1}{132}^2 \div \frac{1}{163}^2 = 1.52$).

Doesn't it seem as if tap targets on iPad could actually be just 29 points square and still be just as easy to tap? Not really. The discrepancy reflects the famous Fitts's Law: the difficulty of acquiring a target depends on the size of the target *and* the distance traveled to get to it. The bigger screen of the iPad means targets are often farther away, so you're more likely to be making *arm* movements to reach them, and not just hand movements, as on iPhone. What's more, an iPad is more likely to be far away from the eyes than an iPhone is. So the difference in points per inch ends up working itself out: you can use the same point sizes for equivalent elements on both platforms. (As for the iPad Mini, it has the same points per inch as an iPhone but the same point resolution as an iPad; the result is a slightly more difficult time acquiring targets, but not egregiously so.)

Meaningful Animation

One subtle way that iOS cultivates a sense of realism is through pervasive, tasteful animation. Notice that as you tap around a well–designed iOS app, very little abruptly appears or disappears. On the desktop, people are used to the thought that at any moment, the screen they're looking at could suddenly look dramatically different from how it did a moment before, because of some whim of the system.

But that sort of jumpy, choppy experience feels out of place on iOS. Alerts appear rarely, but when they do, they fade into existence and bounce gently toward the viewer, as if emerging from the surface of the screen. Navigation is a smooth horizontal slide from screen to screen. Items tidily reshuffle themselves as you drag them around.

As mentioned in Chapter 6, The Prototypes, polished animation is a crucial part of the iOS experience. This sort of animation isn't just pleasant to look at; it reinforces the sense that you're working with a consistent, realistic system that behaves predictably and according to understandable, if simplified, rules of physics. Some animation catches the eye to convey important information, such as where an object has moved to. Other animation, such as sliding navigation, reinforces a sense of place as you move around an app.

This means that you should animate as many of your app's changes as possible. Seldom is jumping from one state to another preferable to animating the change. (If the "correct" animation for the situation would be prohibitively difficult to implement, a simple cross-fade is probably better than nothing.)

Do everything you can to avoid moving controls out from underneath the user's finger when he might be about to tap. Whenever you plan to animate something that can be interacted with, consider the possibility that you're about to cause some frustration by shifting a tap target. Much of the time you can decide not to move the thing at all, or only move it *immediately* after a tap elsewhere, making it unlikely that the user would have had time to aim for the next target anyway.

Most animations should be quick—even quicker than you think. A one-second animation can feel frustratingly long, especially if users must endure it time and time again as they're trying to get something done. Standard navigation animations take 200 milliseconds to slide the whole screen (or sidebar, on the iPad) over to accommodate the next screen; that's a good upper limit for planning your own animations. For smaller areas of the screen, 100 milliseconds is a safe bet.

Remember that stacking animations one after another can feel especially excruciating for the user; if you need to do two different effects, and it's not absolutely necessary to illustrate that they happen in order, you're probably better off animating both at once.

The progress of each animation is governed by a **curve,** and there are four basic curves available for animations on iOS.

- **Linear**—The simplest animation, it starts abruptly at full speed and continues at full speed until stopping abruptly at the end. It tends to look mechanical and fake, but for small, fast animations it's hard to notice the difference.

- **Ease-in**—The animation gradually ramps up to full speed at the start but stops instantly at the end as if slamming into an obstacle. It adds a touch of realism at the start, while letting you run a slightly faster animation and take the edge off the instant of impatience that users can feel while waiting for an animation to finish. Ease-in also works well when the thing being animated isn't particularly visible at the end of the animation anyway, because the animation has made it become transparent, move off-screen, or shrink to nothing.

- **Ease-out**—The animation starts at full speed but slows toward the end as if friction were causing it to come to rest. It lets you run a slightly faster animation but has a touch of sophistication and realism at the end. Ease-out also works well when the thing being animated isn't particularly visible at the beginning of the animation anyway, because it starts out transparent, off-screen, or imperceptibly small.

- **Ease-in/Ease-out**—The go-to curve for any animation not covered by the other special cases. It looks natural and realistic for almost any animation you care to throw at it, though it tends to look best on slightly slower animations.

Happily, these animation curves are available in Keynote, making that app a great way to do quick tests of iOS animation ideas; see Chapter 6 to learn about motion sketches.

Odd animations are a dead giveaway of an app that wasn't carefully designed to feel at home on iOS. Many good iOS animations use an ease-in/ease-out curve; they start slow, speed up, and then slow down, in a satisfying and realistic way, all in a 250-millisecond span. A linear animation, with no variation in speed along the way, is often (almost imperceptibly) just not quite right, like an exaggeratedly clunky sci-fi robot or an old Terry Gilliam animation. Likewise, even an animation as fast as half a second can feel comically slow and floaty, as if it's drifting under water.

Keep your animation tasteful and understated; the minimum amount of animation needed to get the point across is usually best. When users drop an object into a list, it's informative to see the objects around it zip out of the way. It's not helpful to see them quiver and wobble crazily as they settle back into place.

Making SnackLog Graceful

Let's apply these principles to SnackLog to make sure it's as graceful as it can be. Walking through the interaction for entering a purchase, we can think about each step and evaluate its grace. Every interaction should involve input that's as comfortable as possible and should immediately give meaningful feedback about what happened.

- **The number pad**—We would want to make the number pad as generous as possible anyway, but it's especially so because we expect people to be entering purchases with one hand while they're hurrying off to enjoy their snack and get on with their day. The SnackLog number pad is based on the iPhone lock screen passcode pad, with its big, mashable buttons. And, of course, the big buttons darken when they're tapped, making it easy for a user to see which one she hit (see Figure 8.9).

- **The value bar**—This bar appears at the top of the screen during purchase entry. The clear button is considerably shorter than the standard 44-point navigation bar, but its tappable area fills the entire height. It's easy to poke, and a standard white glow highlight makes it obvious that the tap was registered.

- **Confirming an entry**—When the user hits Capture, a snapshot is created to represent the purchase, and it quickly animates up into the Purchases button as if being filed away. This animation serves to confirm that the capture was successful and to offer a clue that tapping the Purchases button lets you check the results.

- **Switching modes**—SnackLog offers only two modes, so it employs a simple flip-over animation for navigating between them. This encourages a spatial understanding of how the app is organized.

Figure 8.9   The SnackLog number pad buttons are big, easy tap targets, and they give the user feedback by immediately darkening when tapped (right).

Summary

Ultimately, a graceful interface conveys a sense of confidence that everything is working as intended. When your app appears confident that it knows what is going on, that inspires confidence in users that they, too, know what is going on. You can build this confidence by building good mechanics into your app. Targets should be easy to tap and should give instantaneous feedback, so that users always know what the app thinks they're doing. Gestures should feel realistic, as if the user were manipulating an actual object that responds predictably. And animation should tastefully reinforce the metaphors and spatial model that your app uses to organize itself. A graceful experience doesn't feel like software flashing pixels under glass; it feels like interacting with a real thing.

Exercises

Here are some ways to get yourself thinking about gracefulness in interfaces and to work on the gracefulness of your own designs.

1. Pick an app and scrutinize its controls for their competence in giving feedback. (Unfortunately, lots of apps, including ones from Apple, are content to leave

you hanging for several seconds while you wonder whether or not your tap registered.)

2. Go on a tap-target hunt. Explore the interfaces of various screens of a few apps to determine the tappable area of the controls. This is much easier to do on the iOS Simulator, because you can see exactly which pixel you're "tapping" as you poke around, but you can get a good sense on a real device, too. See how big an area around each control actually responds to taps. Try tapping just outside the thin toolbar of an iPhone in landscape mode.

3. Now think about the tap targets for your own app, and determine how you can make them as generous as possible. Draw a map overlay for each screen, indicating which areas should respond to taps. Look for awkward areas, such as thin cracks between targets where taps could fall through to the object below.

4. In Keynote for Mac, or your animation-enabled prototyping tool of choice, fake up some animations. It can be something simple, such as navigating horizontally from one screen to another. Test different timings (and acceleration curves, if you can) to see how they feel. Compare them to the animations in a standard iOS app, and try to find out which intervals work best for different sizes of transition, from full-screen down to tiny areas of the screen.

9

The Gracious Interface

How can you make the mundane steps of interacting with an app seem as sensible and easy as possible? That quest corresponds to the second of Donald Norman's three levels of cognitive processing: the **behavioral** level. (Chapter 8, as you'll remember, deals with the visceral level.) At the behavioral level, people are thinking about the elementary tasks that they want to get done: add, edit, move, or delete an item; move to a different screen; open a document, and so on. A **gracious** interface accommodates those basic interactions so deftly that the user seldom gets hung up on how to do them. In Chapter 8 you saw how a graceful interface makes the instant-to-instant interactions feel good; now we step up a level to look at the minute-to-minute interactions. This back-and-forth communication—between what the app allows and what the user wants to do—is the area of user experience design that's often called **interaction design.**

The behavioral level of cognition involves basic conscious thought on the part of the user—a step up from the immediate, unconscious action and reaction of the visceral level. So you can think about it as communicating with the user's mind, almost like holding a conversation. In fact, there is a school of thought, called **semiotic engineering,** that analyzes software design as an act of computer-mediated communication between the designer and the user. (Check out *The Semiotic Engineering of Human-Computer Interaction* by Clarisse Sieckenius de Souza for an eye-opening academic argument to this effect.) Whether or not you completely buy that viewpoint, there's no denying that you need to think about how your app communicates meaning to users.

Denotation and Connotation

Every message you send possesses both denotation and connotation. The **denotation** of a message is the meaning it explicitly communicates to anyone with the basic faculties necessary to decode it (faculties like vision, color perception, and literacy in the given language). If you label a button "Security," the dictionary meaning of that word is part of its denotation. It's the part of the message that means the same thing no matter who is receiving it. That part of a message is relatively easy to control.

The **connotation** of a message is the associated meanings brought to it by the viewer, and it's trickier to keep a handle on. Some connotations are easy to predict: setting the word "Security" in black Helvetica Neue Bold on a white background makes it seem appropriately neutral—less because of an inherent property of the font, and more because of the associations people have with the font. In this example, the association that's especially strong is the one that summons up familiarity with thousands of other identically styled bits of text on iOS. Other connotations are common but not guaranteed: for many people, a little padlock icon evokes memories of the padlock icon on secure web sites and the reliability of real-life padlocks, and these connotations are probably good for your purposes.

But connotations aren't always predictable. When you design a product for use by any audience bigger than a specific subculture, be ready for surprising connotations to arise that you never intended: there are almost certainly software-using cultures in the world where padlocks are seldom seen (although members of those cultures have probably come to associate padlocks with security all the same, thanks to the prevalence of padlock icons in software).

Speaking of security-related images, think about the way some software uses an icon of a chain to represent a URL or web link. This works linguistically in English, but it doesn't carry the same meaning in most other cultures. An icon of chain links takes the terminology too literally. A more abstract arrow-in-a-circle would be more readily understood to mean "go somewhere." Even a little Safari icon would at least be grounded in the visual language of the platform and suggest "web browser."

Most cultural connotations are harmless, but one of the more famous cases of cultural connotation gone wrong is that of the scheduling software where the names of people removed from a meeting were written in red. In certain countries, notably Korea and Japan, having your name written in red is associated with death and is considered generally inauspicious.

Some connotations are personal and are especially unpredictable. There's probably at least one person out there who simply hates padlock icons because she's an online security expert who is tired of insecure sites bearing meaningless padlock icons. In these cases, there's often little you can do but consider the possibilities and carefully choose the best message you can find.

The avenues of communication available to you can be divided into cues, imagery, and text. The boundaries between these kinds of messages are blurry, but they roughly fit into an ascending scale of how directly, explicitly, and noticeably they communicate to the user—that is, in how much they rely on denotation versus connotation.

Cues

A **cue** is any kind of nonverbal suggestion made by something in your app. (Imagery and text do more than suggest; they *tell*. You can read about those kinds of messages later in this chapter.) Cues rely almost entirely on connotation, because they work by suggesting similarity or connection to other things the user may be familiar with. Because they are mere suggestions, cues are processed at an almost subconscious level and can occasionally go unnoticed. That's fine! Cues are pretty disposable. If the user notices and benefits from them, the app makes more sense and feels more friendly, but if not, the show can still go on.

All the following are **interaction** cues, which you may have heard called **affordances.** Each one invites the user to interact with the interface in some way (see Figure 9.1):

- The horizontal grooves that appear on table cells in Edit mode, suggesting that they can be dragged around (a visual cue)
- The appearance (shading gradient, drop shadow, and highlights) on a button, suggesting that it can be tapped (a styling cue)
- The way a bit of content is cut off at the bottom of the view, suggesting that the screen can be scrolled vertically (a layout cue)
- The way the lock screen of an iPhone bounces vertically to expose a bit of the photo interface when you tap the camera icon, suggesting that you should drag upward to reveal it (an animation cue)

Interaction cues can also be negative, letting the user know what he *can't* do with something (see Figure 9.2):

- The dimming of the interface behind a sheet, suggesting that it can't be interacted with until the sheet is dismissed
- The partial transparency of an Undo toolbar button, suggesting that there isn't anything to undo
- The static, etched styling of explanatory text on a background surface, suggesting that tapping it won't do anything

Figure 9.1   Invitations to interaction: four kinds of cues

Figure 9.2   Discouragements to interaction: three kinds of negative cues

Affordances

Cues about what kinds of interaction are possible are often called *affordances,* a term that started in psychology and was brought to design by Donald Norman in *The Design of Everyday Things.* The way the word "affordance" is used today is usually shorthand for "perceived affordances"—the actions that can be done with a thing or that are apparent from examining the thing (or both). But the word has become so overloaded and misused that it's touchy and difficult to use it without causing confusion. It's also specifically concerned with helping a user understand how he can interact with a technology; cues are a broader category that can help a user understand other things, too.

Cues can suggest things other than how to interact, too:

- The red styling of a Delete button, suggesting that its function is destructive and that it shouldn't be taken lightly
- The presentation of a button as big, friendly, and in an easy-to-tap location, suggesting that it's the recommended next step in a process
- The styling of an interface as dark, dry, and serious, suggesting it's for advanced, power-user features

Software design is full of cues. Nearly every decision you make, every element you lay out, every styling detail you apply, ends up suggesting something to the user, whether you intended it or not. If you're conscious of what your design decisions are saying, you can use those cues to your advantage. If not, your app will be full of accidental cues with unintended connotations. So take the time to scrutinize your designs and consider what each aspect of them is suggesting. The goal should be a design in which all the cues that are apparent to the user are true, and all the facts about the interface that could use help from cues to get their point across have appropriate ones.

Here are some examples of false cues that your design might be sending and that you might find hard to notice.

- A control with insufficient contrast might look disabled or look like a piece of content instead of a control.

- If the layout leaves a clean margin at the bottom of the screen rather than cut off an element, it may not be obvious that there is more to be scrolled to below the fold.

- A sudden animation of an element invites the user to touch it to find out what made it animate. If the element is just a status display and doesn't actually respond to touches, the user will end up confused.

- Colored text among plain text may look like a tappable link, even if it's not.

Of course, it's hard for you to know what sort of suggestions your design is making if you're the one who designed it in the first place and you know how the whole thing works. Finding out whether your intentional cues are successful, and what accidental cues exist, is a perfect job for usability testing (see Chapter 6, The Prototypes).

Imagery

In between subtle cues and direct addresses with text, there is **imagery**. Some imagery ends up fairly vague, giving only a general sense of meaning; other imagery can be quite precise and almost impossible to misinterpret. Here are some examples of imagery.

- The flat, single-color icons assigned to toolbar buttons are a typical example. Given the tiny square space these occupy, they can be of varying concreteness— from the standard Share icon that seems to say, "A rectangle with an arrow coming out, which means something to do with moving a thing somewhere, I guess," to the typical rightward-pointing triangle that says, "Go right."

- A big green arrow pointing at a control carries strong enough meaning ("Touch here!") that it's much stronger than a mere suggestion.

- The various status images in the Weather app on iPhone (sun, clouds, rain, snow, etc.) communicate just as much meaning as text would, but in a more attractive and emotional way.

- A color swatch communicates its contained color infinitely better than text ever could (although you'll probably want a textual description, too, for accessibility reasons; see Chapter 10).

- The battery icon in the status bar directly communicates how much battery life is left via an unmistakable empty/full visualization.

These nonverbal messages are more expressive, more specific, and more noticeable than cues, and yet when they're successful, they don't require as much cognitive effort to parse as text. If you're drawing a picture, think of it as cartooning rather than fine art: the simplest, most universal way possible to convey a concept. Here's a simplified way of thinking of the choice. If you need to communicate something, try imagery as your first choice. But switch to cues when you need to reduce distraction, and switch to text when you need to reduce ambiguity.

If standard imagery exists on the system for what you need to communicate, even better; you're almost sure to get the right connotation. You can use that standard portrayal to get the benefits of imagery while taking advantage of the user's likely familiarity with the meaning. The *iOS Human Interface Guidelines* even have a System-Provided Buttons and Icons section that explains exactly how to use the imagery provided by the operating system. (Some descriptions, however, are curiously weak, such as how the commonly understood Share button is called the "Action" button, for taking "an application-specific action.")

Some bits of imagery, such as the ubiquitous gear, have become de facto parts of the iOS culture because of how often they appear in apps, always denoting "settings." The gear works especially well because it does an OK job on its own of connoting the idea of changing how the mechanics of an app work, and, if you're experienced with the platform, you'll associate it with gear icons in other apps. Always aim for communication that can work well on its own; and when you can, aim to maintain harmony with other apps on the platform, too.

Heavy reliance on imagery in an app can lead to what's known on the web as "mystery meat navigation": an interface that gives users almost no clue about what a given button does until they go ahead and try it. The good news is that on iOS, a well-designed app doesn't do anything untoward when the user taps a button to find out what it does, so there's rarely any risk in just tapping around to see what's what. (The tradeoff is that if you stick to cryptic images, your screenshots on the App Store are less likely to be understandable.) There's more about that iOS "sense of adventure" later in this chapter.

Text

Text is the most direct, explicit way to communicate with your user. It's almost all direct denotation, although individuals or cultures may very well have their own connotations of certain words or phrases. Text appears everywhere in iOS interfaces, in a variety of forms:

- The numbered badge on the Mail app icon that indicates how many unread messages you have
- The title of a element, as on an Edit button
- Explanatory labels that clarify the effects of controls, group elements, or proffer advice

- Alerts that interrupt the flow of the app ("change the subject") to deliver an important verbal message directly to the user

Words can be descriptive, of course, because they enjoy all the infinitely combinatorial expressiveness of language. That's why explanatory text appears on most of the screens of the Settings app, for instance. The sentence, "Swipe down from the top of the screen to view Notification Center" is far better than a doomed attempt to tell users something that complex using only pictures. To create an image to communicate that idea, you would need to devise an elaborate rebus that would end up taking far more of the user's cognitive effort to decipher, when you could have simply asked her to read a sentence.

It's tempting to try to solve your problems without using text; a wordless interface feels cool and elegant (and saves money on localizations). But if you need to use anything more than a simple image, style, or treatment to get an important point across, use words instead. Early on in the history of the Mac, the catchphrase "A word is worth a thousand pictures" became popular at Apple. As it turns out, humans have spent about five thousand years developing a system for expressing arbitrary concepts via visual symbols: *writing*. Sometimes, you can fix the most tenuous, tortured attempts at representing an idea with an attractive icon by simply switching to a single, perfectly evocative word. (If you can't come up with a good word, that's often a sign that the thing you're trying to label is inherently confusing and you should go back to sketching.)

The Grand Tradition of Undo Arrows

Sometimes, third-party developers march ahead where Apple has held back. At the moment, all iPad apps created by Apple use a text button for Undo. That's presumably because Apple's designers decided that hiding such an important, data-rescuing function as Undo behind a possibly unobvious icon would be irresponsible. When you, as a user, find yourself frantically wondering whether you can undo a disastrous change you just made, you probably don't want to be deciphering arrow icons. "Does this curvy arrow signify Share, Back, Sync, Undo, or some other concept?" Seeing the word "Undo" written plainly on the toolbar is reassuring.

But that hasn't stopped other designers from coming up with their own wide array of slightly different swoopy arrows for Undo and Redo. (The popular painting app Brushes even cleverly uses Apple's own Undo arrow icon, used in its original PDA offering from 1993, the Newton MessagePad.) In many of these apps, an icon works fine because it's presented or explained prominently enough, or because the sort of work you do in the app (like sketching) requires you to get acquainted with the Undo feature right away. Whether Undo is better off as a text button or an icon button is ultimately an app-by-app decision, depending on the kind of work being done and the character of the screen it's on.

It's true that a good cue puts very little cognitive burden on the user, because it just looks like part of the landscape, quietly making its suggestion. Text, on the other extreme, demands more attention and requires reading to make its point. As described in Chapter 12, Quiet and Forthcoming, text is visually and cognitively loud. Humans are verbal creatures; when we see words we feel compelled to read them, even if we already know what they say. But that's true only to a point. If we see a lot of words when all we wanted was to get something done, we get irritated and ignore them. So carefully budget your use of text to avoid overwhelming users with the need to read.

Writing: The Secret Design Discipline

Copywriting is probably not the first practice that comes to mind when you think about what software designers do. But being a good designer includes being able to come up with just the right single-word label for a control, compose a perfectly incisive explanatory sentence, or give a feature a compelling and accurate name.

The two main lessons to learn about writing good copy go hand in hand.

- Be concise.

- Don't write like a robot.

They go hand in hand, because usually, writing like a human makes your text shorter, and vice versa. Consider this string:

`Performing the sync operation for account information. Please wait.`

Believe it or not, this is an only mildly fictionalized version of an actual interface string. Imagine that you're a human being speaking to another human being. Would you ever, in any situation, utter those words? Of course not. (But if you try saying it out loud in a ridiculous robot voice, it works.) With some common sense we can trim it down from 18 syllables of robospeak to 5 syllables of plain English:

`Syncing your account.`

Or, if the context of the message makes it clear that account information is what's being synced (for instance, by virtue of this text occurring on an Accounts page), the text could be shortened even further without any loss of useful information:

`Syncing.`

On the face of it, it might seem as if technology should use words like "performing" and "operation" and "information" as much as possible, especially if you grew up in a world where computers were the *future*. Whenever a computer did something, it was a huge deal, requiring a bunch of formalized, self-important fanfare.

But a huge part of the appeal of iOS is that it presents itself as the magical, thrilling *present*. It embraces the idea that technology can be friendly and straightforward and casual. So it's fine with downplaying the awesomeness of what it's doing and just doing it. Syncing your account. No big deal. As for the "please wait" bit, it's superfluous.

If the screen shows a progress indicator while the sync is happening, then the user already knows that he needs to wait. No need to draw attention to the waiting and make the string longer on top of it.

And do the extra work necessary to stay grammatical. The phrase "1 item(s)" has no place on iOS; the device has the power to calculate the number of items and decide whether to use a singular or plural noun.

Some words can be replaced with punctuation. Instead of preceding an extra sentence with "Note:," you can wrap it in parentheses. (And if it's the only sentence in the message, you can omit the parentheses, too.) Lots of nouns can be treated like proper names, so you can write "Notification Center" instead of something fussy like, "The notification center overlay," as long as you're fairly confident the user will have a chance of getting the reference.

Seriously question the contribution of every word and punctuation mark in the message, and get rid of anything that doesn't contribute essential meaning (see Table 9.1). You can also shorten messages and make them feel more direct by wording them as a suggestion ("Tap..."), rather than a condition ("If you tap...") or a possibility ("You can tap..."). For status messages, try to give the user conclusions rather than symptoms. If the user needs to take an action (and you can't provide a control that brings her to the right place to take that action), then the required action should be the focus of the message.

Every now and then, you need to explain an intricate situation, with lots of possible complications and technical limitations. You're not sure which bits of information will

Table 9.1 **Rewriting Messages**

Weak Message	Rewritten Message	Reasoning
(Note: The location services toggle must be enabled.)	Turn on Location Services in Settings.	"Note" and parentheses are superfluous. Reword as a suggestion. Use "Location Services" as a proper name. Remove jargon "toggle." Mention where the user needs to go next.
A response from the server was not detected.	Disconnected.	Give an informed conclusion and not a symptom.
Tap here for more information about settings.	Learn More	Tapping is the default interaction, so there's no need to specify it. If this appears on a Settings screen, there's no need to specify what the topic is. Using the verb "learn" puts the focus on an action.

be useful to each user, so you feel as if you should describe every contingency. But rather than explain everything right there in the interface with a huge blob of text, you might be able to split up the explanation. Give the instructions needed for the common, least complicated case, and then provide a link or button for more information. The button can navigate to a new screen of detailed documentation that clearly explains everything better than a chunk of explanatory text could have done inside the interface.

Redundant Messages

It's helpful to combine cues, imagery, and text to improve their effectiveness. Of course, most styling cues, such as the color and size of a control, are combined with the text or image label on the control. The combination of a big, buttonlike visual treatment and the text label "Connect" makes for an attractive tap target for a user who thinks she is ready to connect. And the combination of the words "slide to unlock" with a horizontally animated glow effect is a classic example of text with a cue built in.

For crucial controls, it can be effective to combine a text label (for precision and memorability) with an icon (for quick recognition). Having both an icon and a name is rare on iOS, though, so anything with both seems important: tabs that control the top-level navigation of an app, the topmost level of items in the Mail app, and so on.

For things that are that important, it helps users to have a *word* to mentally hold on to when thinking about an important concept in your app, especially when they contact you for support: "I'm looking at the Inbox," rather than, "I'm looking at the white boxy thing that's blue inside." But it also helps to have the imagery there so that once people know what the element is and what it's for, they can switch to recognizing its icon.

Communication Breakdown

Any communication you offer in your app is likely to fail at some point for some users. No matter how perfectly logical and clever your design solutions are, they will be misinterpreted or even missed. You can't rely on communication to work flawlessly; the user isn't a robot, and your input into his senses is not code. In reality, different people perceive things differently, and sometimes people are in a hurry or just not interested in taking the time to absorb your brilliant explanations.

So for every communication decision you make, imagine what will happen if it fails. If your app won't work unless the user reads and understands your text, correctly parses your imagery, or recognizes your cues, then you have fundamental design problems to deal with. Put another way, users should theoretically be able to poke around your app without really understanding any of your original imagery or terminology and still be able to make it do its thing.

Here are examples of failed communication and explanations of why they're OK.

- Maybe a user hasn't yet learned the meaning of the horizontal traction grooves on an item in Edit mode. As a result, she can't change the order of the items. But that won't prevent her from using the app effectively; it just means that she must live with the present order until she learns the convention. Thankfully, lots of apps use that convention, so she'll probably figure it out soon enough.

- The partially cut-off item at the bottom of a screen doesn't motivate a user to scroll, for some reason, so he misses out on the functionality below the fold. He might spend a while wondering whether a certain feature exists, although it's probably a less-important feature because you thoughtfully put the most common ones at the top of the screen. Most likely, he'll come back to the screen in his search for the feature and try scrolling sooner or later.

- A user doesn't decipher the icon you devised for your Send button. But when the time comes to send the message she's working on, she's likely to scan the available toolbar buttons for one that seems to match her need. If you've done your job well and made a friendly, reassuring interface, then she'll feel comfortable trying the button that seems most likely to mean Send. If she ends up hitting the wrong one, your forgiving interface should have a way to let her reverse or cancel the effect, back out, and try again.

Guidance at the Point of Need

For a long time, software assumed a lot of knowledge on the part of users. It took a hands-off approach, always assuming that users knew what they were doing and not presuming to offer help. When the time came to enter a recipient address for an email, to take one example, the software sat back and let users type it, unconcerned about whether it was spelled correctly or was even a valid address.

Gradually, software got better at recognizing when it could be helpful and offering its assistance in moments when its particular talents were of most use. Now, rather than impassively watch you misspell an email address, your mail client probably offers a list of known addresses that are similar to what you have typed so far, and it lets you select one to automatically finish typing it. After all, the computer has an address book, and it knows that you almost always write to someone whose address is in it. Why not make that information available at the point of need?

Software often used to rely on documentation and training to let users know crucial information. Now, though, if it's likely that users won't know how to proceed, they can find guidance in the form of a gentle instruction that appears on the screen just as they need it—and that's subtle enough that they can ignore it once they know what they're doing. For example, when you enter Edit mode in an iWork app on iOS, the suggestion "Select a Document" replaces the title at the top of the screen. This brief instruction encourages users to try tapping a document, resulting in a selection highlight and lighting up the Share, Duplicate, and Delete buttons, thus teaching them how Edit mode works and what it's for. Meanwhile, the text changes to "1 Document Selected," hinting that it's possible to select more than one document.

Carefully planned guidance at the point of need (or **contextual controls** and **contextual documentation**) is a hallmark of iOS design. If the system has the information you need and if it knows that right now you're likely to need it, it should offer it to you right now. When you start typing an email address, the Mail app presents an in-place modal view (on iPhone) or a popover (on iPad) to suggest completions. Many text fields across iOS offer placeholder text: hints and suggestions that appear in the field in a subdued font style until you start typing. Each mathematical function offered in Numbers has in-place documentation that you can see by tapping a detail disclosure button.

The challenge is to seamlessly integrate that guidance into the experience. Your goal is to provide guidance in a way that can be ignored if users already know what they intend to do. For documentation, that means presenting it in an out-of-the-way place or with an especially subtle visual style. And, of course, provide in-place documentation only if there really is a need and if users are likely to be unsure what the next step is.

For contextual controls, iOS offers several standard elements. A contextual menu is the shiny black bubble populated with commands that appears in many apps when you make a selection. Contextual menus are excellent for occasionally used commands that apply to content in a content area. When you need more than a list of commands, a popover can be breezily summoned and dismissed, and its stem is a reminder of where it came from.

Some apps provide custom contextual controls, which can be welcome for workflows that deal heavily in interacting with bits of content. The horizontal swipe on a table cell, traditionally meant only for deletion, has become a common way of summoning such controls. Another way is to show floating controls along with, or instead of, a contextual menu.

Visible Status

iOS excels at giving users exactly the right amount of information to keep them informed about what's going on without overburdening them. Although your app probably keeps track of the status of lots of things, you need to decide which of those statuses to make visible, and how. A **visible status** is any situation that the app decides is important enough to make plain to the user visually.

- **Selection** is a common one (although not as common as on the desktop). Many apps allow the user to select some part of the content and then perform an action on it. The item selection is shown with a highlight or other prominent visual effect. It makes sense to offer selection-based interaction when there are more things users could do with an item than would be accommodated by simple tap or touch-and-hold gestures. On iPhone, it's common to highlight the item only momentarily and then navigate to a dedicated detail screen to work with it.

- **Various modes and modelike states** are useful in certain apps. A graphics app may offer a choice of tools, each of which causes touches in the content area to have different effects. "Mode" is sometimes seen as a bad word in interface design because of puzzling modal interfaces in software of yore. Larry Tesler famously campaigned against modality in software interfaces (such as the *vi* text editor) because of the confusion it could bring. But on iOS, modes are not seen as being so terrible as long as they're obvious and temporary. You need to make it apparent that the app is in something other than its normal resting state and offer an easy way out of it.

- **Edit mode** is a commonly used trope in iOS. Users know that if they see a button labeled Edit, usually on a list or grid of items, they can press it to organize or change the content on that screen: reorder, move, delete, make multiple selections, and so on. Edit mode offers occasionally needed functionality as an alternative to what usually happens when the user taps those items. Because it's not the main functionality users expect from the screen, they're fine hopping into a temporary mode to get at it and then hopping out when they're finished. Notice that Edit mode automatically ends when you choose a command; it follows the rule that modes should feel temporary. Edit mode is a valuable concept. Keep it handy when you need to offer auxiliary meta-options on multiple items.

Contextual Status

At the intersection of "guidance at the point of need" and "visible status" is **contextual status**: connecting status information to what the information is about. A strong hallmark of the iOS experience is that status information is closely tied to the element it describes.

On a traditional desktop system, for example, progress bars often appear in floating dialogs that are disconnected from the on-screen objects that the progress is happening to. Throughout iOS, the same experience is instead presented using a progress indicator *on the object itself*, especially if the progress prevents the object from being interacted with: apps that are being updated, iCloud documents that are syncing, and so on.

When there's a problem, contextual status lets users defer their decision of what to do about it. Consider what happens when an iWork app detects a conflict between two versions of a document stored on iCloud. Instead of interrupting the user when the conflict is detected and demanding immediate action, the app quietly **badges** the conflicted document with an alert icon. The badge lets users know that when they have the time for it, they need to do something about that document. Until they tap it, they can interact with other documents as much as they like. Only when users tap the conflicted document does the conflict resolution dialog appear and ask which version to keep.

Contextual Status and Multithreading

The user-interface design idea of contextual status is close to the software-engineering concept of multithreaded apps that don't block user input just because the app is working on some unrelated thing. In an old-fashioned desktop app, it's normal for a user to sit around and wait until some bit of work is finished before they can use other, unrelated parts of the same app. (Ever get frustrated that you can't listen to music, update your developer tools, and sync your iPhone at the same time because of the monolithic, workflow-blocking iTunes?) That's the worst kind of mode: the kind that the software puts you into seemingly because its behind-the-scenes technical needs are more important than your immediate human needs to get things done.

On iOS, and increasingly on the desktop and on the web, it's indefensible to make users wait for more than a few seconds for a process that isn't related to what they want to do next. Just as you should restrict the display of status to the object it describes (showing a download progress bar on the icon of the downloading document itself), you should also restrict interaction-blocking to that object (not letting users open the in-progress document but letting them open other documents).

Invisible Status

One of the many ways iOS quietly serves the user is by using **invisible** statuses. Invisible statuses are hard to notice—because they're invisible. Rather than put on a parade about how helpful and convenient they're making things for you, they work in the background to make your conscious interactions with the app feel as if the device is anticipating your intentions. These concealed considerations are the fairy dust powering the magical experience that characterizes iOS.

Adaptation

Adaptation is the use of moment-to-moment behavior of the user to influence the behavior of the software. Lots of decisions in software design can seem arbitrary, and the choice you make may be determined by a slightly better argument for one answer over another. Adaptation can bridge the gap by giving both those choices a place in the app.

Consider the behavior of the Mail app when users delete or archive the selected message. Normally, the message disappears and users are taken to the next message in the list. It would have been more or less equally defensible for it to take them to the previous message in the list. After all, some people read their email inbox top-to-bottom, and others read bottom-to-top.

Old software might have left it at that and not tried to solve the problem. Or it might have hidden an esoteric preference in a panel, for people who cared enough to find and set it.

But iOS Mail adapts. If users have recently tapped the up or down arrow button to navigate to a different message, this action temporarily sets the browsing direction (see Figure 9.3). Then, when users delete or archive a message, that direction determines whether they're taken to the previous message or the next message. Thus, they're taken in the wrong direction only once. After that, their manual correction of the direction will teach Mail which way they prefer. No preference setting necessary. Brilliant!

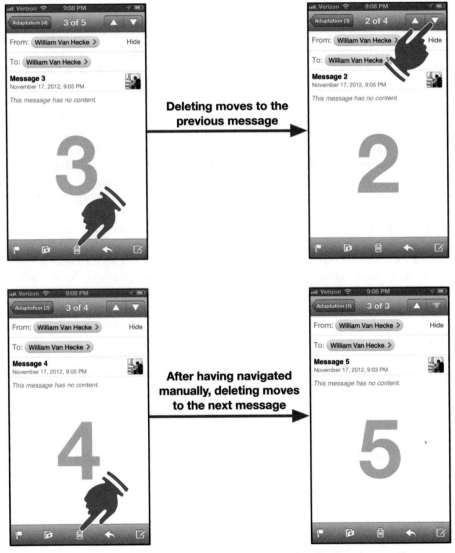

Figure 9.3   Adaptation in Mail. The user's manual navigation changes the direction moved when he subsequently deletes a message.

When presented with seemingly evenly-matched alternative answers to a question, think about whether you can invisibly determine which one would help the user most, and switch to it on the fly. You don't even need to let them know that you're doing it. But there is always the chance that your clever adaptations will come across as mere unpredictability. Lots of user testing can help you decide whether you're being helpful or just inconsistent.

Learning

Learning allows an app to use the behavior of the user over time to influence the app's behavior. The effects of learning take weeks or months and remain in place over the long term, all without any explicit configuration by the user.

A perfect example of learning is the way iOS supplements its built-in dictionary with words based on use of the device. The iOS text input system is aggressive about correcting what it thinks are typing mistakes. But it has a lot of tricks for guessing whether a given word is a mistake. When you type an uncommon name like "Hiroko," a neologism like "retcon," or a whimsical misspelling, the system tries to determine whether that's what you really meant to type. If you have a Hiroko in your address book, you're likely to be referring to her. If you have typed "retcon" or made the same intentional misspelling several times before and you dismissed the autocorrect suggestion, then your habit is remembered and the system lets you carry on typing it without repeating the suggestion. (Apple even uses a fancy text analysis technique called "latent semantic mapping" to use the context to make guesses about words that are likely to go together so that it can offer the suggestion most likely to be correct.)

Of course, you don't need to go as far as maintaining a dictionary and using latent semantic mapping for your app to learn to serve the user better. That's the system's job. A smaller-scale example is the way Mail learns which email addresses you use most. As soon as you start to type an email address, matching addresses from your address book are listed, as described earlier. But the matches aren't just ordered alphabetically; instead, the addresses you use most float to the top. So, say Jon Bell is one of your best friends, and you email back and forth with him all the time. When you start addressing a fresh email message, simply typing "j" or "b" is sufficient to produce a list with his name at the top—even if you have 100 contacts whose first or last names start with *J* or *B*. The system cares about whom you care about, rather than just being a dumb mechanism.

Resourcefulness

Resourcefulness is a characteristic of apps that use the information they can access independently rather than constantly and lazily asking the user to enter it. Here's what the *iOS Human Interface Guidelines* say.

- "Avoid asking people to supply setup information."
- "Get as much information as possible from other sources."

It's mentioned almost in passing, but it's an important lesson: part of the reason iOS seems to work smoothly is that it already knows quite a lot about you and your environment, and it can make good use of that knowledge. Here's a list of things you can find out without having to ask the user to manually enter anything.

- **Contact information**—Instead of making the user spell it out, use the system-provided contacts API (application programming interface) to, for example, show a list of contacts for the user to choose from.

- **Calendar information**—Use the system-provided calendar API.

- **The device's location**—You shouldn't ever have to ask users where they are.

- **The device's orientation, acceleration, or compass direction.**

- **The user's preferred language and locale.**

- **The current date and time**—Some apps, such as Weather and Instapaper, adjust their interface depending on the time of day.

- **Anything else that can be determined via the device's hardware**—These include the proximity sensor (no need to manually switch to another mode before putting an iPhone up to your face), ambient light sensor, or microphone.

- **The hardware specs or operating system version.**

When there is a system-level setting for something, respect it. You might think you're doing users a favor by letting them customize how your app behaves separately from the rest of the system, just in case they have specific app-by-app tastes. Instead, you're doing them a disservice by making them have to worry about those settings in your app in particular, when they already went to the trouble of setting them at a system-wide level. So don't offer language settings or region format settings, for instance, unless you have a tremendously good reason for overriding the system settings.

The Sense of Adventure

B. F. Skinner, the pioneer of radical behaviorist psychology, did many experiments on pigeons. (This has something to do with software design, I promise.) The simple positive and negative reinforcement he studied can't fully explain everything that humans do, but it remains a useful model for thinking about certain patterns of behavior.

In one of his most famous series of experiments, Skinner put a pigeon in a box with a lever that would *sometimes* dispense a pellet of food. The random nature of the reward caused pigeons to associate with success whatever behavior they happened to be performing before the dispensing of a pellet. If they happened to walk in a circle just before poking the lever, and then food came out, they became convinced that it was the circle-walking that did it. Wrote Skinner, "A few accidental connections between a ritual and favorable consequences suffice to set up and maintain the behavior in spite of many unreinforced instances."

For decades, the status quo for software was that unless you were dedicated enough to study the documentation and vigilant enough to avoid making mistakes, you were bound to irrevocably ruin something sooner or later. You'd lose work, get your preferences into a state that causes the software to behave bizarrely, or even wreck your entire system. This situation led ordinary people to a develop a superstitious, animistic relationship with technology. (*Animistic* means that they attributed to technology a capricious and contrary mind of its own.) They'd perform rituals for success, without understanding why, because the systems were so complex and so inscrutable, it was easier to repeat seemingly meaningless patterns of behavior that worked in the past than it was to actually understand them—even if you knew they were erroneous.

You could say that to an ordinary user, the system made about as much sense as a Skinner box does to a pigeon. That's by no means an insult to users. Rather, it's a reflection of the feebleness of technology design to make itself understandable. There is no question that people are smart. But for most of them, it's not worth the hassle to suss out the precise inner workings of the varied and complex technologies they come in contact with every day. It was all they could do to find a series of steps that produced an acceptable result.

These days, we understand a bit better how to present people with an understandable system that they can use to get something done, and we have technology that's better prepared to make it happen. iOS is aggressive about clarifying the user experience while still offering real-world benefits, resulting in an effort-to-results ratio that people find worthwhile. It's not perfect; we still have a long way to go. But it's on the right track.

The opposite of the animistic relationship with technology is a sense of adventure: the feeling that you're in control, that the system exists to serve your will, that if you try you can probably figure out how to make it do what you want. Software that encourages the sense of adventure is not necessarily simpler. In fact, delivering an empowering experience usually requires the software itself to be more sophisticated behind the scenes but deceptively straightforward on the surface. (If you'll forgive this book one car/software analogy: an automatic transmission is a more difficult feat of engineering and design than a manual one, but it results in a much simpler experience for the user.)

Some folks may be out of our reach as software designers; if they've had a life full of bad experiences with computers, there might not be much we can do to ease their trepidation on an iPhone or iPad. But others can be convinced that these devices really are there to serve them and that it would take quite an elaborate series of mistakes to cause any serious harm to them or their data. Happily, there is an entire generation of young people growing up that will always take it for granted that technology is a friendly, useful thing rather than a scary, untrustworthy thing.

Capability

The first step in giving people the willingness to try to get something done with your software is, simply enough, to convey a sense of its capability. Software hasn't traditionally had much problem with this part of the job. For decades, it was the focus of most technology marketing: emphasis on power and versatility without much attention paid to approachability.

It's not difficult to convince people that your app can do something; it's more interesting to think about how to convince people that they can get your app to do what they want it to. There's more about the sense of capability in Chapter 10, because it lives just on the other side of the border, over in the reflective level of cognition. For now, let's look at how to engender a sense of adventure at the behavioral level.

Defensive Design

People have a good reason for fearing that they might mess up their computers—they're probably right! Technology design has long been biased toward nerds like us who actually get a thrill out of figuring out difficult and complex systems. Thus, software has long been more than happy to let users make problematic decisions, leading to harmful situations, all under the claim that they probably know what they're doing and we should give them as much power as possible.

If someone wants to set his default system font to Webdings, delete the system folder, or install hacky utilities that inject code into other apps, who are we to stop him? In reality, of course, sometimes users do know what they're doing, and other times they're adrift, wishing someone would help them instead of offering them more options.

There is plenty of debate to be had about how much power and control should be given to the typical user of a desktop computer because of the grand tradition of creativity, hacking, and personal ownership that the computer world has always had. But even though iOS has plenty of claims to enable creativity, it's skewed toward pragmatic reliability and away from unfettered hacking and personalization.

To that end, iOS offers lots of examples of **defensive design**—erring on the side of keeping people from inadvertently getting themselves into a harmful situation. Here are examples.

- Not only can you not delete important files that are needed by the operating system, but also the file system isn't exposed at all.
- iOS makes the executive decision that presenting a consistent, predictable experience based on a single unified design language is better than enabling the flexibility of applying your own themes to the interface.
- For stability, each app is given its own private sandbox of settings and documents, rather than letting any bit of code touch anything it wants to on the system (and this model is now making its way to the Mac, too).

Thus, users avoid many potentially harmful situations by not having the ability to incur them.

Defensive design is your first bold scalpel swipe toward a focused experience. When you're deciding what functionality, preferences, and options should exist in your app, start by eliminating the ones that are almost certain to lead to problems.

- If integrating with a popular but unreliable third-party service would make your app flaky, save your users and yourself headaches. Find another way to get similar functionality.
- If people could accidentally invoke a rarely used feature and harm their data, maybe you should remove the feature.
- If certain combinations of settings would result in dead-end configurations that can't provide useful results, don't offer those combinations.

Of course, the degree to which you can in good conscience remove "potentially harmful" functionality depends on your target audience and the personality of your app. There is a place for apps that exist precisely to enable the advanced, "power user" audience to do things that other apps don't.

Extreme Defense

I work on a personal task-management app called OmniFocus, which started on the Mac with a strong emphasis on customization. When we first brought OmniFocus to iPhone, we looked at our many view settings and realized that together they offered 67,200 permutations, including numerous ways for users to hide important information from themselves. Plenty of these combinations didn't even make sense; they were guaranteed to result in an empty window—for instance, "Show me all the available items in projects that have no available items." A few users were thrilled by the unrestricted power they had to set up unusual view states, but most were simply overwhelmed. So when it came time to move to iOS, we designed to aggressively avoid the hiding of important information, even if it meant offering "less powerful" view options. With the help of user research and common sense, we settled on *four* carefully curated view settings that covered the great majority of use cases. And people hardly missed the other 67,196.

Once you eliminate the likely harmful options, you can further focus your app by aiming for what the *Human Interface Guidelines* call the 80 percent solution: rather than close your eyes and pretend that all possible options are equally relevant and important, offer those that will be sufficient for 80% of situations. Slice away the rest, especially if the features you leave in can get a user to the same result.

When you're finished, your app offers a focused, understandable set of features, and the options at each step are tailored to what users are likely to want and need. The result is an app that feels trustworthy and empowering, encouraging users to go ahead and put it through its paces. When someone uses a well-designed iOS app, he's eager to poke the buttons and see what it can do. Fear that he's going to ruin something—or get into a bad situation that he can't get out of—is the last thing on his mind. That safe, exploratory feeling is the sense of adventure you're going for.

Much of software design is about balancing the desire to give people lots of features and the desire to prevent the unwanted consequences of having lots of features. What should be possible in your app? How hard should it be to realize each of those possibilities? Part III, particularly Chapter 11, Focused and Versatile, and Chapter 13, Friction and Guidance, offer more guidance in focusing your design on the most broadly useful choices, adjusting that 80% figure for your own app, and deciding when to hand options over to the user anyway.

Forgiveness

Even after you remove the thorniest, pointiest bits from your design, you're bound to have left some possibilities for user regret. After all, even if accidentally deleting an item would be problematic, you can't very well remove the ability to delete items. But people make mistakes: they misunderstand the label on a button, they brush the screen with a stray finger, they get distracted and tap the wrong item without thinking. The more featureful an app is, the more likely it is to have these possibilities.

Users need to be able to take a step forward with the confidence that if they don't like where they end up, they can take a step back. Rather than see "user errors" as not your problem, you need to anticipate them as a normal part of a human being interacting with a piece of technology. You need to recognize user errors for what they usually are: design bugs. People shouldn't feel as if using your app puts them into situations where they are only a tap away from distress. They should feel certain that any mistakes they make will be forgiven. It's up to you to give that reassurance.

The first line of defense is the way controls perform their function when the finger comes off the glass (on touchUp) rather than when it first hits the glass (on touchDown). This gives users a chance to change their mind, correct for a mistap, or start a scroll instead of a tap, by simply dragging away. Make sure any custom controls you provide follow this safety mechanism; controls should give feedback on touchDown but wait until touchUp to do their thing.

Undo

Undo is the classic manifestation of forgiveness in software. If you make a mistake, you can immediately take it back. It's most expected and understood in a productivity context—when users are investing lots of time working on a document or a document-like chunk of data.

In any other, less work-intensive context, such as writing a tweet or configuring a web site account, it'd be odd to see an Undo button staring at you as if the app expects you to make a dire mistake in writing your 140-character message or typing your username and password. It's just not worth taking up the cognitive and visual space for a button that would save so little work.

If you can't justify a dedicated Undo button but you want to offer undo, the next best thing is probably to support the systemwide "shake to undo" gesture—see the sidebar Shake to Undo for more information.

When you offer undo, users have high expectations of it. You need to offer as many levels as possible, and avoid resetting the undo stack except for major, intentional events such as leaving the document. You also need to offer redo. Users often use undo to step back and see where they were, without necessarily wanting to stay there. If they can't get back to where they were before they started undoing, then they have, in a real sense, lost data.

iWork offers redo from a touch-and-hold popover menu on the Undo button—a bit hard to discover, and many people never find it. That design trades away some discoverability in return for visual tidiness. Some third-party apps, especially for undo- and redo-heavy activities like painting, offer a dedicated Redo button next to the Undo button.

If you're a designer working with software engineers, you need to work closely with them to figure out how the undo feature should work. If you're the engineer, you'll have to get your design brain and your engineering brain on good speaking terms for a while. Consider these questions.

- Changes are often grouped for the purposes of undo. When you undo typing in Mail, for instance, the characters don't disappear one by one; a block of text disappears, all the way back to the last time you changed the selection. How will you group edits? What counts as a single change?

- How do you deal with changes that happen in a popover? Does the entire popover editing session count as one undo group, or does each edit in the popover count as its own change?

- What if the change being undone affects an item that's off screen? Can you scroll to it? Will the app switch to the view that was open when the change happened?

Shake to Undo

Shake to Undo is, honestly, kind of terrible. Here's how it's supposed to work. In interfaces without a dedicated Undo button, such as iWork on iPhone or Mail on both devices, you can flail the device back and forth to summon an alert with an Undo button and a Cancel button. In reality, people who know about it can never seem to reliably produce the right flailing motion to trigger the feature, so they end up repeatedly flapping their device about until the alert finally appears. People who *don't* know about it have to live with their mistakes, wondering why the system doesn't offer an undo feature—until one day when they're absentmindedly gesticulating with their phone hand or momentarily holding their iPad at their side while they get on the bus, and then suddenly the thing is inexplicably suggesting that they undo their hard work. If you combine all three situations, you have a feature that's unreliable, undiscoverable, and presumptuous. What would work better? Unfortunately, if that were easy to answer, we probably would have seen it by now.

Manual Undo

Designing and implementing undo support are kind of a pain and yet sometimes necessary. The good news is that they're not always necessary. In lots of cases, the change the user is making is simple enough that she can reverse the change herself without much hassle.

The clearest example of this is a simple switch. When you see a switch that's turned off, you know you can tap it to turn it on, and see what happens. If you don't like what you see, you don't need to undo; you can just immediately turn it off by tapping exactly the same location you just tapped.

This is a bigger deal than it seems. The promise of a switch is the embodiment of the sense of adventure. Emulate that humble switch whenever you can: the easier you can make it to immediately reverse a potentially unwanted change, the better. Often you can't allow a change to be reversed by tapping the *exact* location, but you can keep the reverse setting logically related and visually nearby the original setting. Tapping back to the tab that was just selected a moment ago in a tab view, for instance, is easy.

For every change you let a user make, consider what he would need to do if he immediately changed his mind. To that end, endeavor to make the result of the change immediately apparent. If the user flips an intriguing switch and nothing happens, he may become confused about just what he has enabled. Of course, the label on a button, and the occasional explanatory text, is often the best you can do to communicate its purpose. But if you can, make the switch do something immediately obvious that helps the user decide whether turning it on was what he wanted.

For anything more complicated than a switch, make sure the current state is obvious *before* the change is made. That makes it easier to go back to the previous setting for a user who's changed his mind. If the original setting wasn't visible before he changed it, he may never find it again.

Most important, make sure that there are no side effects for taking action and then immediately reversing it. If the user switches a setting and then immediately switches back to the previous setting, it should be as if she never made the change at all. Don't reset the rest of the interface that was dependent on the original setting. Don't enter a mode that requires the user to understand and undergo several steps to escape. Just accept that experimenting with the interface and poking everything in it is a normal part of a user getting accustomed to an iOS app, and design with that experimentation in mind.

Here are ways you can offer the ability to immediately undo simple interactions.

- For switches or switchlike toggles, users tap the control again to return to the previous setting.

- For multiple-choice controls—tabs, segmented controls, or table views with checkmarks—users tap the previously selected item to reselect it.

- For adding an item, have a convenient way to subsequently delete it.

- For interactions that navigate to another screen or enter a modal view, users hit a Cancel or Back button, usually in the upper-left corner of the screen or view. They should be able to cancel right away without any changes being saved.

Confirmation

Sometimes, you can't offer undo, either with a dedicated button or with a manual reversal. Some actions are final, and they generally fall into two categories: deleting and sending.

After a user deletes something, unless there is a dedicated Undo button, there's nothing for him to interact with that will bring back the now-deleted thing. He can't touch the absence of a thing, so there is no obvious place to tap to undo the deletion. And once he has sent a message bounding across the Internet, he can't politely ask the Internet to take it back; it's gone, man. There are certainly other cases where an action can't easily be made undoable; these guidelines for confirmation apply to them, too.

Confirmation is kind of a last-resort safety net for avoiding disasters. Think about the worst-case scenario. If the action being taken is consequential enough and if an accidental invocation of it is likely to result in true sadness, you probably need to get confirmation. If it's not as consequential, you can let it slide. Messages is happy to let you send a text without confirmation, confident that you've probably scrupulously double-checked it for syntax and content before tapping Send, or at least that you can correct any misunderstandings with a follow-up text.

Ideally, you shouldn't require a lot of confirmation in your app, because even though taps are cheap, it's irritating to have to constantly tap twice to do anything. It's especially irritating if the interaction in question could have been made undoable, but the developers apparently were "too lazy" and tossed in a confirmation instead. So you have a balancing job to do. If you never ask the user for confirmation, she'll eventually make a mistake and then regret it. If you ask for confirmation all the time, then at best your app will be irritating, and at worst it will train users to automatically tap through confirmations without thinking, eventually resulting in regret anyway.

Make your confirmations elegant. The era of popping up an alert every time the user tries to do something—pulling her out of her focus, asking her to read your long, tortured explanation of why that might be a bad idea—is over. iOS provides ways of presenting confirmations *in context,* using the immediately preceding action and the location of the confirmation to get the point across that this action shouldn't be taken lightly. Remember that popping up an alert is most appropriate for out-of-context notifications of things that are happening behind the scenes, and not for referring to stuff going on right there on the screen. Table views, of course, already offer an elegant, in-context confirmation of item deletion: when you swipe to delete an item or tap the circular minus button in Edit mode, only then does a Delete button appear on the item. It always takes two gestures to delete something.

Another excellent way to elegantly confirm an action is with an action sheet. On iPad, an action sheet always appears in a popover, making it easy to keep it closely associated with the element that triggered it. On iPhone, an action sheet slides up from the bottom as if attached to the screen, distinguishing it from an alert and making it clear that it appeared because of the user's last action. Action sheets feel splendidly lightweight. In the iWork apps on iPad, when you try to delete a document you get an action sheet, presented as a popover with a lone action button: Delete Document.

Figure 9.4   The noble one-button action sheet

In a desktop app, it would have been unheard of to show a confirmation consisting of nothing but a single button. A traditional desktop app would throw up a big dialog with an app icon, a multisentence message to the effect, "Are you sure you want to delete this document? This operation cannot be undone," and then, at least two buttons: Delete and Cancel.

The iOS way is to simplify that entire experience to only the Delete button in an action sheet (see Figure 9.4). The button itself expresses the question, "Are you sure you want to delete this document?" After all, every control already comes with an implied "Do you want to…?" question. The button even updates to indicate the number of selected documents, thus elegantly communicating the severity of the deletion you're about to undertake: "Delete 4 Documents." If you really mean it, you can move your finger the one inch down to the Delete button and tap it. If not, the entire remainder of the screen behaves as a Cancel button: tap anywhere else, and the action sheet goes away. And because of the rarity of confirmation on iOS, users learn that anything requiring confirmation is probably not undoable.

On iPhone, the same action sheet slides up from the bottom of the screen. It's not as charmingly elegant; an iPhone action sheet also offers a Cancel button, because there's no popover to tap away from. But the action sheet experience is still far more straightforward and less intimidating than the equivalent dialog in a desktop app.

Making SnackLog Gracious

The capture screen of SnackLog is simple: a top bar with a Purchases button, a camera area, and a numeric keypad (see Figure 9.5). Yet even this seemingly obvious design reflects some thought about how to make it gracious. Let's step through it piece by piece, consider why it's presented the way it is, and compare it to other ways it could have been presented. You might be surprised how much careful attention can be paid to deciding on the way a screen communicates.

The Purchases button is presented as text rather than as an icon. In fact, perhaps an icon of three horizontal bars in a listlike arrangement would have done the job well enough. After all, it takes only one tap to find out where it leads, and every time you capture a photo, it animates into the Purchases button. But this design isn't especially

Figure 9.5   SnackLog at rest

concerned about the noise introduced by the single word "Purchases" in this button. And precedents are many for an upper-corner button, labeled with a noun, that leads to another screen: Documents, Calendars, and Store (in iWork, Calendar, and iBooks) are a few examples. Using text in this case follows the advice, "A word is worth a thousand pictures," and errs on the side of immediate recognizability. The communication is a combination of those precedents and the obviousness that tapping a button labeled with the plural noun "Purchases" would take you to a list of things you have purchased. It even subtly hints that the whole purpose of the app is to capture purchases, and that is a boon for understandability the first time someone sees an app in the App Store or on someone else's device.

The choice of a numeric keypad that's similar to the one used in the Phone app and the unlock screen is intentional. Whenever a user sees a numeric keypad like that, he knows that the next thing he's expected to do is type some numbers. There's no field to tap into and then summon up a keyboard. There's no New Item button to hit before you start typing. The keypad dominates the screen and says loud and clear, "Let's have some numbers." This communication is a combination of the precedents set by those other keypads, along with the visual prominence and appealing simplicity of ten big glossy buttons labeled with digits.

In the corner of the keypad is a Capture button. The presence of this text-labeled button from the initial launch of the app serves a similar purpose to that of the

Purchases button: it helps communicate that the app is all about capturing purchases. Seldom can you actually communicate the entirety of the purpose of an app using the button labels on the initial screen. It sure is nice that we could do so here.

That explains why the Capture button is on the screen immediately, albeit disabled until you type a number, rather than appearing only after you start typing. As soon as you enter a number, the Capture button lights up—a cue that communicates its availability.

At every step, the app suggests the next step. The label could probably have been an icon of a camera, but that image already conjures up meaningful associations of simply grabbing an image; it doesn't go as far to convey the unique nature of the way Snack-Log captures a picture, a price, a location, and a time all at once.

Summary

A gracious interface is one with good communication skills. And communication is important to the behavioral level of cognition, which is all about a person's moment-to-moment conscious thoughts. In other words, communication is how people get information from the app about what's going on and what they can do next. Your tools for communicating to the user include cues, imagery, and text, which contain varying levels of denotation and connotation. Choosing the right one (or combination) for the message you need to convey is your quest.

As much as you can, provide relevant messages at the point of need. iOS puts a lot of importance on context: keeping related elements together and minimizing the need for the user to guess at relationships between the various contents of the screen.

A major part of communicating to the user, and allowing him to communicate effectively to you, is via statuses that affect various interactions. Some statuses need to be visible to the user so that he can react accordingly. Other statuses can be invisible, allowing him to pursue his immediate goals without realizing the underlying logic that's helping him do it.

The result of a gracious interface is a mutually beneficial relationship between the app and the user. The app successfully communicates what it makes possible, and the user can successfully move from task to task without unnecessary friction or frustration.

Exercises

Here are some ways to analyze the graciousness of other apps and then start to think about the graciousness of your own app.

1. Pick an app that seems smooth and effortless to use—you know, a gracious one. Step through a typical workflow. On each screen, note what the screen seems to communicate to you about what's possible and what your next step should likely be. Keep an eye out for communication decisions that seem obvious in retrospect

but that probably had several possible solutions and required careful thought on the part of the designers.

2. Do the same exercise for your own designs, looking especially for places where you made an assumption about how to communicate but where there is actually a decision to be made. Are there ways you could helpfully communicate to the user other than the ways you chose? Even if you conclude that your existing communication is the best possible, at least now you're coming from a position of having done your due diligence rather than from a position of assumption.

3. Go through those same apps and ignore the messages as much as you can. Pretend you're in a huge hurry, you aren't a native English speaker, or you're just too tired to take the app seriously right now. What would you poke to try to make the app do its thing? How far can you get by just blithely tapping around? How likely are you to make something go horribly wrong? What does this experience tell you about how much your app relies on its communication getting through in order to work?

4. Pick a screen in an app that seems to communicate graciously. Design a bizarro-world version of the screen in which every single message that the screen conveys—every cue, image, and bit of text you see—is swapped for a different one. If the screen is well designed, many of the alternatives you swap in will probably be less effective than the originals (although you may occasionally stumble upon a better solution than the official one). An app with all the same features, but with poor or ill-suited communication skills, feels dramatically different and, well, kinda uncanny. Amuse and horrify your friends with your alternate-reality versions of their favorite apps!

10

The Whole Experience

So far, this book has concentrated on improving the practical, routine interactions that people have with your software. Most of what you've read to this point can be classified as product design or interaction design: deciding what the app should do and how. But user experience design isn't only about features, navigation, layout, buttons, and animations.

There's one more layer in Donald Norman's model of cognition, above the two you've seen: the reflective level. The **reflective** level is how you feel over long spans of time as you look back on experiences you've had. It's the feeling that persists long after the app has been quit and the iPhone has been put away. It's the immediate response you have when someone who trusts your opinions asks whether you'd recommend the app. It's how your life has improved, in whatever small way, because you installed and used that app.

The idea behind the discipline of user experience design is that the reflective level counts. UX design looks at the entirety of a person's interactions with a product, and the organization that makes it, as a unified, holistic thing that can be studied and can be improved. In online retail, that means everything from signing up for an account to ordering a product to unboxing the product in your living room. In iOS apps, UX includes everything on this list and more:

- Finding out about the app, whether from the people who made it or elsewhere
- Reading the description at the App Store
- Seeing the app icon on the home screen
- Everything that happens while the app is open
- Reading documentation to learn how to use the app
- Getting help when you need it
- Understanding in-app purchases
- All communication with the people who made the app, usually via email and social media
- Everything you hear about the app and the people who made it in the press and on social media

As you can probably imagine, the reflective level is the biggest, fuzziest, most nebulous part of software design, and it's the hardest to think, talk, or write about. It also happens to be the most important. Most of your ability to make a difference in this area can only come from years of developing your own pantheon of inspiration and influences. But this chapter aims to tackle some of the more concrete topics that can contribute to succeeding on the reflective level. Figure 10.1 illustrates the many disciplines that are touched by UX design.

Because it's about people and their feelings, this chapter is full of advice on topics normally beyond the scope of a design or programming book. But on a platform with a culture as strong as the one iOS has, this stuff is important. It's not meant to be preachy; it's meant only to give you an idea of the zeitgeist of the iOS world and the expectations people have for a great iOS developer.

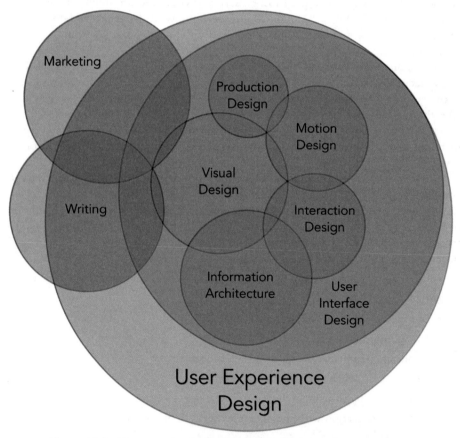

Figure 10.1   User experience design intersects with, and encompasses, a diverse range of fields. This diagram was adapted from one by the marvelous Robby Ingebretsen (http://nerdplusart.com).

Serve the Soul

At the heart of your entire endeavor to build an app is, hopefully, a desire to make someone's life better—maybe even thousands, tens of thousands, or millions of people's lives. Seen this way, each app is an elaborate mechanism for incrementally improving lives. (Yes, there are usually side effects to that happiness, such as the willingness of customers to part with a bit of money proportional to the benefit they get, so that you can keep your enterprise going. But business motivations are another book. This book is about making people happy.) It's healthy to occasionally remind yourself of that ultimate goal at the heart of your project.

iOS is somewhat alone among platforms because of the role it has played in cultivating a market for purely life-improving software. The platform has a huge audience—in the hundreds of millions—and gladly welcomes people who aren't especially tech-savvy. The App Store popularized the idea of very small, affordable apps that are dedicated to solving a single problem and are simple to discover and install. (As the commercial goes, "There's an app for that.")

Of course, business-oriented apps and apps that otherwise aim to help organizations more than they help individuals still exist. There are still apps that people use not because they want to, but because they have to. But because of the expectations that iOS sets, there's pressure on even those apps to do what they can to make the experience of using them more pleasant than it would be on another platform.

There's a little game you can play to get to the bottom of a person's motivation for using a product, and it's called Five Whys. The technique is one of many famous practices that originated at Toyota for the purpose of making good cars but was then widely adopted around the world for a variety of other purposes. Five Whys was originally intended to get to the root cause of a problem, usually a technical one. But you can use it to get to both a person's motivation and the real purpose of your app. Here's how to play.

- Pick a feature or aspect of your app that you think is important to the app's purpose.
- Ask a hypothetical user (or a real one who's willing to humor you) why the feature or aspect is important to her.
- Whatever the answer is, ask why.
- Keep asking why for each answer you get.
- At about five whys, you should find yourself at a root motivation for that user.

Here's a game of Five Whys about SnackLog.

- Why do you need purchase capture to take so few taps? (Because otherwise, sometimes I wouldn't bother opening the app and using it.)
- Why do you want to make sure you always open the app and use it? (Because I want to record every purchase I make, no matter what.)

- Why do you want to record every purchase? (Because I'm trying to maintain a very strict budget.)
- Why are you trying to maintain such a strict budget? (Because otherwise, my spending will get out of control and I won't be able to save any money.)
- Why does it matter whether you can save money? (Because it's my dream to buy a house someday.)

There you have it! In only five steps (sometimes it takes more or fewer), you've gotten from an ordinary interaction design decision all the way down to a core user motivation. You could probably go even farther, although it gets more abstract and harder for people to articulate things such as why they want to own a house someday. Every decision you make in design can be boiled down to a serious, earnest, personal motivation like this one. Although the skin of your app is made of interface and interaction design, those motivations are its soul.

So each app is playing a tiny but crucial part in fulfilling its users' goals. You should keep that in the back of your mind at all times. And occasionally, you should bring it to the front of your mind. Knowing what's riding on your work can help you decide which features to prioritize or can tip the scale toward a certain choice in a difficult design decision. Serve the soul of the app, and you serve the souls of your users.

Conveying Capability

If people are going to use it to solve problems or work toward goals in their own life, they need to be able to recognize your app as able to help. They need to connect your app to a real-life need they have, whether that need is a conscious effort toward a serious goal or a desire for distraction and entertainment. (Yep, even games fulfill needs: we play to destress, exercise our minds, connect with friends, or be immersed in a compelling story.)

There are plenty of ways people can discover your app's value.

- Some people browsing the App Store are happy to use their imaginations to find cool use cases for how a given app they've stumbled across might be useful to them.
- Some people download far more apps than they could realistically use, just to try them out and see what sticks.
- Some people write blog posts, tweets, and reviews of software and thereby inform others about the apps out there and the ways each one might benefit users.

Thanks to all those efforts to uncover apps of merit, as a developer of a good product you may have help in getting the word out. But they all put the burden on someone other than you. To really get prospective users to find out what you have to offer, do the job of selling it yourself.

The Name

Choose a name that balances brevity and catchiness with hinting at what the app can do. "Snacky" would probably be too far in the catchy direction, without suggesting enough about the purpose of the app. "Small Purchases Logger" would probably be too far in the other direction, sounding dull and stodgy. "SnackLog" feels just right.

The App Store allows each app to define one name in the store and a separate name for the home screen, so a popular technique is to be more descriptive in the store name—"SnackLog: Record Small Purchases Quickly" in the store listing, but just "SnackLog" on the home screen. Whatever you do, make sure your home screen title is short enough that it doesn't get truncated. Nothing says the developer doesn't care like an app title with an ellipsis in the middle.

The Icon

In designing an icon, aim for one that's charming and professional and sits happily amid other app icons—maybe even one that could be enshrined on someone's home screen. App icons live in a curious area between user interface design and marketing, and they're the sole bit of identity that your app presents to the user while it's closed. Even if your app is built with strictly standard controls and has a subdued, minimalist presentation, it pays to have a fantastic app icon.

If you look at the icons of Apple's and of the best third-party apps (such as ones featured on the App Store), you'll notice these characteristics:

- Good internal contrast, usually in the form of a single simple contour on a uniform field
- Making the most of the rounded-square format by appearing self-contained and using a layout that embraces the shape, thus looking as if it was created especially to be an iOS app icon
- Relatively flat, with only an occasional small hint of protrusion or recess
- Limited use of color, usually with only one or two simple and vivid colors standing out as the theme of the icon
- Impeccable rendering, with a balanced layout, crisp effects, and not a pixel out of place

In comparison, app icons are easily spoiled by these problems:

- Muddy contours with bad contrast, figures that blend into one another or into the background, and complicated compositions that are hard to read at a glance
- A figure that leaves the frame and thus doesn't appear self-contained by the icon, or otherwise competes with the app icon format, looking like an existing design that was lazily shoved into a rounded square
- Excessive depth, compromising the presentation of a home screen full of icons that appear to be 2 or 3 millimeters thick

- Too many colors, overly intense colors, or even photographs, which look out of place among the sophisticated, simplified, hyperreal color schemes of other app icons

- Unbalanced or misaligned elements, and messy or amateurish visual effects

Figure 10.2 shows some SnackLog icon concepts. The concept is a coffee cup (yes, this author is from Seattle), or an unspecified-hot-beverage cup, to be maximally inclusive to all audiences. Because on-the-go snack choices vary widely around the world, the fairly universal drinking vessel seems like a safer bet than a muffin or candy bar. The first idea was to use the to-go cup made famous worldwide by Starbucks and to hint at the dark-green-on-white branding of that company. But the resulting icon conjures thoughts of disposability and waste and even looks a bit like a trash can at small sizes—not at all a premium, positive association. Instead, the second concept uses a proper mug, with a hint at latte art in the form of a little heart to give it some charm. To match the cozy, warm character of the emblem, the surface was changed to a happy red. Note that the cup isn't rendered as a three-dimensional object resting on a surface that angles away from the viewer, as a Mac app icon would be; instead, it's an *illustration* of a cup, drawn on a flat surface parallel to the display.

Apple's icon guidelines are detailed and specific. Make sure you keep up with the "App Icons" section of the *Human Interface Guidelines,* because new hardware may make it necessary to create versions of your app icon at new sizes. As of the release of the third-generation iPad with Retina display, Tables 10.1 and 10.2 list all the app icon variants you need to worry about.

Figure 10.2   A couple of app icon concepts for SnackLog. They follow the standard formula of a white emblem on a stripy, vivid background, typical of small, utilitarian iOS apps. You can download the Photoshop sources for these icons at the book web site (http://learningiosdesign.com).

Table 10.1   **iPhone App Icon Variants**

Size (in Pixels)	Purpose	Notes
114 × 114	iPhone home screen	20-pixel corner radius
57 × 57	iPhone home screen (Non-Retina)	10-pixel corner radius
58 × 58	iPhone Spotlight results and Settings	~10.2-pixel corner radius
29 × 29	iPhone Spotlight results and Settings (Non-Retina)	~5.1-pixel corner radius
1,024 × 1,024	App Store listings	~179.6-pixel corner radius; scaled to 144 pixels in the App Store
512 × 512	App Store listings (Non-Retina)	~89.8-pixel corner radius; scaled to 72 pixels in the App Store

Table 10.2   **iPad App Icon Variants**

Size (in Pixels)	Purpose	Notes
144 × 144	iPad home screen	~25.3-pixel corner radius
72 × 72	iPad home screen (Non-Retina)	~12.6-pixel corner radius
100 × 100	iPad Spotlight results	2 pixels trimmed from each side; ~17.5-pixel corner radius
50 × 50	iPad Spotlight results (Non-Retina)	1 pixel trimmed from each side; ~8.8-pixel corner radius
58 × 58	iPad Settings	~10.2-pixel corner radius
29 × 29	iPad Settings (Non-Retina)	~5.1-pixel corner radius
1,024 × 1,024	App Store listings	~179.6-pixel corner radius; scaled to 340 or 150 pixels in the App Store
512 × 512	App Store listings (Non-Retina)	~89.8-pixel corner radius; scaled to 170 or 75 pixels in the App Store

If you've read the *Human Interface Guidelines* you should know this, but remember that the system rounds the corners of your app icon for you. The images you submit should appear perfectly square, without any transparency. If you intend to put a top highlight effect on your icon or anything else that follows the contour of the rounded corners, you need to anticipate the amount of rounding the icon will get from the system. This amount starts at 10 pixels for the original 57-pixel iPhone home screen icon and is adjusted proportionally for each of the other variants. Check the app icon tables for the degree of roundedness your effects should have.

You may want to implement your own variation on the typical curved, glassy shine effect that appears on app icons by default. But you almost certainly don't want the default shine effect (the system will automatically apply it unless you opt out of it with UIPrerenderedIcon). That effect puts an intense white layer over the top half of the icon, making it difficult to maintain good internal contrast between the components. Instead, try including your own subtler shine effect (as in iBooks) or a shine that lives behind the main figure of the icon (as in Mail).

On the home screen, icons get a broad drop shadow applied. In App Store listings, they get a very tight drop shadow. Make sure your design works well against various home screen backgrounds and the light gray background of the App Store. You'll need to apply your own drop shadow (and corner radius) for the purposes of marketing materials displayed in places such as your web site.

The web site for this book (http://learningiosdesign.com) has a template you can use, along with the app Slicy, to create perfectly sized app icons. It exports both pointy-cornered versions for inclusion in the app, and round-cornered versions for marketing, and it should save you a lot of tedious work (see Figure 10.3).

Launch Images

While we're on the topic of specifically sized images you need to create, don't forget the launch images that are required for all apps (see Table 10.3). The **launch image**— the image that zooms into view when you open an app—should generally look like a content-free version of the app's interface, causing as little jump as possible from the image to the actual interface.

The idea is that for users watching the animation of the launch image moving into place, rather than just staring at a black screen, the launch feels faster. There used to be some debate about whether it's OK to use the launch image as a sort of "splash screen" by putting branding on it; the consensus, supported by the HIG, is that it's not. So don't do that.

The App Store Listing

After you've spent countless hours designing and building an app, creating its listing in the App Store can seem like a tedious task that you want to coast through. Don't! The listing is your occasion to condense the value of all the hard work you've done into a 4,000-character description and five screenshots.

Figure 10.3   The iOS app icon template for Photoshop, and the output as exported by Slicy. Note how each icon has a square-cornered version (for inclusion in the app) and a round-cornered version (for marketing).

Table 10.3   **Launch Images**

Size (in Pixels)	Purpose
640 × 1,136	4-inch iPhone and iPod Touch
640 × 960	Retina 3.5-inch iPhone and iPod Touch
320 × 480	Non-Retina 3.5-inch iPhone and iPod Touch
1,536 × 2,008	Retina iPad, portrait
2,048 × 1,496	Retina iPad, landscape
768 × 1,004	Non-Retina iPad, portrait
1,024 × 748	Non-Retina iPad, landscape

People browsing the store have already seen your app's icon and title and been intrigued enough to tap through to your listing. They expect to get a sense of what your app is about from casually scrolling down the page and seeing your first screen-shot and your (unexpanded) description. If they're interested, they might expand beyond the three to five lines of description and read the rest of what you have to say, or page through the rest of the screenshots. (If only the App Store allowed developers to upload a video of the app in action, as Google Play does for Android apps, people could get an even better sense of what an app is about without having to visit its marketing site.)

So you need to make those initial tidbits of information count. Your first screenshot is arguably the most important, because images communicate so much more directly than text does. Do everything you can to make sure your screenshots, especially that first one, *communicate* the capability of your app. Capture the app in action, with plenty of realistic, expressive data and not bogus placeholders or (horror) no data. Folks need to see what the app really looks like when it's in use if they're to imagine themselves using it. The meaning of "screenshot" is fluid on the App Store. It's become popular to add concise, friendly annotations (just a quick sentence) to each shot. Some apps even include a zoomed-out image of hands interacting with the app on a device, with annotations or other imagery in the periphery.

If you devised a platform for your app, as suggested in Chapter 1, The Outlines, you already have a head start on what your description needs to emphasize. Cram that mission statement into the very first sentence, as in the following examples.

- "SnackLog is a super-fast, super-simple way to record all those small purchases you make throughout the day—from coffee to candy to parking."

- "With HindSite, you can build gorgeous, clean web sites in no time, and with no code."

- "SnapHeap serves one purpose: saving photos from anywhere to Dropbox with minimum fuss."

You get the idea. Once you've won some awards or gotten some five-star reviews from well-regarded publications (which you're sure to do, right?), you may want to front-load those boasts where people can see them. Just make sure your key sentence is still visible. From there you can go on to list features, expound on the philosophy of the app, and describe use cases. If you've put a ton of work into making some feature work better than the competition, say so. If you designed with a certain workflow in mind, mention it. The more specific, expressive, enthusiastic, and confident you can be in this blob of text, the better. This is the time for modest souls to set aside their humility. Quit being the quiet, modest Woz, and become the confident, boastful Jobs for a while.

Apple has made some refreshingly honest and frank *App Store Review Guidelines* available at the Apple Developer Center. Read them for enlightenment, and read them for entertainment. This "living document" does a good job of telling the story of the heroic App Store reviewers who have, by now, seen just about everything. "22.8: Apps which contain DUI checkpoints that are not published by law enforcement agencies, or encourage and enable drunk driving, will be rejected"—yikes! The App Store review process can be a patience-testing, nerve-racking experience, but remember that in the end, the reviewers are on your side.

The Price

Here it comes: this is as close as this book comes to giving business advice in the guise of design advice. There's a whole conversation to be had among the decision makers in your organization about the pricing of your app. Many of the inputs into that decision are economic ones well beyond the scope of this book. But the price of a product is undeniably part of the user experience, so if you believe in UX as a holistic thing, as a designer you can't ignore it. (This section assumes that you're following something like the old-fashioned "charge money in return for goods" model, not some kind of in-app upsell, advertising, or get-bought-by-Facebook plan. In those cases, you're on your own.)

There's one big, obvious argument in favor of a lower price: more people can and will buy the product. For many people selling on the app store, that's the main consideration, along with the expectation of a greater volume making up for the lower price. That approach has plenty of adherents and doesn't need much cheerleading; much of the App Store has been built on the low-price/high-volume gambit (or the "race to the bottom," as it's disparagingly called). And Apple certainly does its part to set pricing expectations low: the impeccably designed, stunningly functional iLife and iWork apps are a mere $5 or $10 each, and OS updates are free. Apple can get away with it because good apps and a good operating system serve to sell more iPads and iPhones, and that is where it makes its real money. You don't have that angle, of course, but it still affects your pricing strategy.

The arguments for a higher price are easily overlooked. "Higher" means choosing something like $3–5 instead of $1 for a casual app, or $10–50 instead of $5 for a professional app. It also includes decisions like charging separately for your iPad and iPhone editions rather than selling a single, universal app at a single price. Here are some of the arguments in favor of opting out of the race to the bottom, expressed as various ways of spinning a higher price point.

- **Sustainable pricing**—Every product, of course, has its own curve of hypothetical prices versus hypothetical sales numbers. Maybe you really could make more revenue by charging less. But the more copies you sell, the more users you have. To be a responsible app seller, you need to maintain a relationship with those users. That means providing prompt and friendly support, listening to feedback and requests, and allowing the soul of your product to be pulled in a thousand directions at once by the individual opinions of your vast and myriad audience. Raising the bar a bit keeps your audience at a size you can more readily give the attention it deserves.

- **Premium pricing**—There's no denying that the price of a product affects perceptions of it. Whereas some customers are looking for the cheapest tool to do a job, others are looking for the best. A "premium" price is one way to communicate that your app just might be the best. (If your app actually isn't the best, then, yeah, just price competitively and cross your fingers.) A higher price encourages people to take your app seriously. And having people take you seriously means a lot when it comes to the App Store reviews you'll endure. Paradoxically, cheaper apps get worse reviews. It's most likely because expensive apps attract customers who are serious about the product, who've done their research, and who are likely to treat the purchase as an investment that they want to like. When you've paid more for something, you tend to give it time to show its value rather than immediately dismissing it as a waste. (And it probably doesn't hurt that app makers who are more confident in their pricing tend to make better apps.)

- **Fair pricing**—The main reason to charge more than a measly dollar is that a measly dollar usually won't keep the lights on or keep your team fed. When an App Store shopper sees a product that costs a few bucks more, it's a lot easier for him to trust that the company will still be around next year, continuing to maintain and improve the product. It's only fair that you should be paid adequately in return for creating a good and worthwhile thing.

Again, all this is an intentionally biased heap of advice meant to help you calibrate your sense of your app's value—and not a complete lesson in App Store economics. It should help you advocate against undervaluing your work and help you arrive at the right price. There are about a squillion variables to consider, and $1 may very well end up being the right price; just make sure you don't arrive at it by default (or worse, out of fear).

Documentation

The whole idea of documentation may seem old fashioned to an iOS designer. On a platform that prizes focused feature sets and encourages exploration and experimentation by users, documentation may seem extraneous. But there's almost always some form of documentation in place, even if it's not the traditional manual or help file. This section takes a look at the various forms it can take.

Comprehensive Documentation

You may want to provide a definitive document that explains your app and what it can do. It could be a separately downloadable PDF manual, a collection of HTML pages that live inside your app, a repository of knowledge base articles on your web site, or some other comprehensive, browsable text.

Documenting your product in this way is beneficial for a number of reasons.

- Although you can do a lot of design work in the interface to make it understandable, it'll never be 100% successful at making perfect sense to every person who encounters it. That you've done the work to make sure the product is fully understandable is a sign of respect to both the product and the users.

- Some users will be interested enough in your app to explore what you have to say about it even before they've bought it. If your documentation is available separately, then reading it can serve as a sort of preview of the app. Because the platform doesn't support time-limited trials, written docs can make all the difference for a prospective customer who's reluctant to buy until he's sure the app is right for him.

- Documenting each feature is an affirmation that it's worthwhile and deserves to be explained to anyone who cares to learn about it. If you find it difficult to explain in writing why a certain feature exists, that could be a sign it shouldn't.

- If your documentation is good at answering people's questions, you're likely to save a lot on support. Don't get the wrong idea; you shouldn't be reluctant to talk to your users. But if they can help themselves immediately rather than going through a communication loop with you, everyone wins.

- Documenting each feature is a formal process that solidifies your understanding of what it's for and how it works. It requires you to set aside the technical particulars and explain the app with user-facing language and concepts. It gives everything in the app a name and a purpose. This is important: if you find yourself struggling to concisely name or justify a feature, or you resort to explanations of the underlying technology, there is probably a problem in the design. You've probably not done enough to insulate the user experience from the implementation (unless of course the app is intended to help technical people do technical things). For this reason, it's best if you can have the documentation written by someone who wasn't directly involved with the design process. People who made the original decisions are likely to gloss over bits that don't make sense or try to justify decisions that need more work.

- Once you've nailed down a complete and definitive explanation of your app, it serves as a sort of reverse design document. The outlines and specifications you started with describe what you intended to do, but your documentation describes what you ended up with. You can then use it as a starting point for moving forward. Any new features, or reworking of existing features, should probably make sense in light of the way you've already described them.

Problem-Solving Documentation

Even apps without comprehensive documentation typically offer at least some sort of problem-solving help, often in the form of a FAQ on the developer's web site. It's good for covering topics particular to uncommon situations: sales and pricing information, workarounds for technical limitations, or reasons a certain feature isn't in the app.

This sort of documentation is great for addressing specific questions, reducing your support burden, and getting users back on track, but it's not very good as primary documentation. Although you can guess some of the questions likely to be frequently asked—that is, you can pinpoint which parts of your app might need elaboration—for the rest you have to hope users write in and ask—rather than give up and abandon your app. You can't be sure how many people will get confused by an issue and give up before enough users have written in to convince you to make a FAQ about it.

The Silent Majority

Don't fall into the trap of relying solely on user feedback to inform your decisions. For every person who writes in about how he'd prefer to see the app work, or about something that's confusing him, there are dozens, hundreds, thousands of people who keep quiet. They may carry on using the app in a confused state; they may stop using your app; they may complain about what a pain it is to their friends. Or they may love your app and use it happily every day but never write to tell you so. The point is that the communication you get from users who think to write in distorts the reality of the feelings of your entire population of users about your product. Never forget about the silent majority. You need to be proactive about looking for problems by doing your own usability testing and keeping a critical eye on your work.

Tutorials

Resist the temptation to put a big, special, one-time, first-run tutorial overlay on your interface. It's a popular thing to do, and the rationale seems right: if you're going to drop people into an interface populated with unfamiliar buttons and gestures, you'd better give them some guidance. But the typical introductory tutorial, with a mess of labels and arrows and explanations, is more overwhelming than the unfamiliar interface itself—and not more welcoming. People need to try out one interaction before they can move on to learning the next one, but they can't try anything if your tutorial screen is blocking them. At best, they're likely to retain only one piece of information from the tutorial and then be lost when they can't get the tutorial overlay back.

Here are several better ways to introduce people to your interface.

- Create an interface that encourages a sense of adventure, as described in Chapter 9. Most iOS interfaces are welcoming and reassuring enough that they don't need tutorials at all.

- Provide a single hint at the beginning to help people get started. For SnackLog, perhaps a quick prompt like "Enter a price and hit Capture" would do the trick. This hint should coexist with the interface, not obstruct it, and should disappear after the user has followed it successfully once or a few times.

- For a complex app with a predictable layout, you can create a help overlay that's integrated into the interface. GarageBand, one of the most ambitiously powerful and complicated apps on iOS, presents friendly, succinct notes that users can show and hide at any time by hitting the Help button. (See Figure 10.4.) Summoning help doesn't navigate anywhere, doesn't harm the user's context, and doesn't block interaction with the interface. Instead, it offers a bit of guidance and the opportunity to navigate to the comprehensive documentation for greater detail.

- Possibly the best kind of tutorial is an interactive one that users can follow at their own pace. This works best with document-based apps that can present the tutorial as a normal document that's automatically opened on the first run. The

Figure 10.4   iWork (left) includes an interactive tutorial as a document that can be edited normally. GarageBand provides in-context help as an overlay, with links to comprehensive documentation.

iWork apps, for example, include documents that the user can navigate through, following the instructions to edit the document itself (see Figure 10.4). This works well because users can follow along as far as they like, but they can also go outside the lines by trying their own experiments in addition to the recommended steps. And the whole experience exists in the standard interface instead of a dedicated tutorial mode that behaves slightly differently from the real thing.

Release Notes

The App Store offers "What's New," a place to write about updates to an app, which maps roughly to the "release notes" commonly included with desktop software. Depending on how geeky your users are, they may want lots of detail about each release, or they may be overwhelmed by too much detail. Here are two extremes for composing release notes; you will likely want a combination of the two.

- **Concise**—Mention major new features and changes in common workflows. Condense minor changes into summaries like "bug fixes" and "performance improvements." Apple tends to use this style. It keeps the notes short enough that typical users are likely to actually read them. But this approach can be frustrating for people who rely on the app for important work and need to know whether a particular bug was fixed.

- **Exhaustive**—Every single change, down to the tiniest bug fix, is mentioned in bullet points. It helps if you segregate the list into sections for new features, changes, and bug fixes. Some developers even offer access to an archive of these notes for each version, either in the app itself or on the web site, because the App Store notes are ephemeral. Your passionate users who care deeply about the progress of your app will thank you for following this style, but it takes a lot more work. If you're fastidious about using a bug-tracking database, you may be able to edit the titles of your fixed bugs directly into release notes.

Characteristics of Good Documentation

Each type of documentation does a unique job, but there are some ideals to keep in mind while you work on all of them. Good documentation is

- **Complete**—Digging through documentation to find that it doesn't answer your question might be even worse than not finding any documentation at all. Do what you can to make your documentation answer every reasonable question you can think of, and direct people to a reliable way to get support when they can't find what they need.

- **Navigable**—Digging through the documentation should be as quick and easy as possible. Nothing you write is worth anything if the folks who need it can't find it. Create a good index and a good navigation scheme, with reasonably sized pages divided logically by topic. Title each page well. If you can make your help searchable (easier with a web repository than an in-app one), that's excellent. Make sure to consider possible synonyms that people may be looking for, such as "erase" for "delete," and include them in your index.

- **Conversational**—The writing rules for interfaces in Chapter 9 apply just as much (if not more) to documentation. Be concise, and don't write like a robot. It takes practice to write in a way that lays out all the details, no matter how rudimentary they may seem to the writer, without insulting the reader's intelligence. But don't worry too much, and err on the side of being too inclusive. "Be concise" means that you should describe each detail as directly as you can, and not that you should omit details.

- **Illustrative**—It's crucial to explain not only *how* your features work but also *why*. Often, software documentation lays out all the causes and effects ("Tap this button to duplicate the selected document") but none of the reasons ("You can set up a document as a template and then duplicate it for each new document you want to create from it"). For an open-ended feature, make sure your suggestions come across as suggestions, and not as the only sanctioned uses of the feature.

Support

Plenty of big consumer-facing industries are infamous, at least in the United States, for being incorrigibly incompetent, unresponsive, or uncaring after the sale. There's probably a spreadsheet somewhere that mathematically "proves" it's unprofitable to take care of your customers.

But, thankfully, in each industry there's always a number of peculiar companies that pride themselves on their humanity and excellent customer service—the Zappos, USAAs, and Southwest Airlines of the world. As they grow, they maintain their small-company values as best they can. The iOS app development world has a healthy proportion of that sort of companies, probably because many of the developers are still small.

That humanity and that communication are very much a part of the user experience. Users may recommend an app to their friends or leave a good review if it's well designed, but the service they get from the developer has an even stronger effect on their opinion of it. Good service can absolve an app with a few issues that need ironing out, and bad service can besmirch an app that's otherwise unimpeachable.

People are thrilled to hear back from email support within 24 hours, to have access to phone support, or to get support in their own language. Some companies even proactively search Twitter for people having trouble with their product and reach out to them, in a sort of reverse support request.

Not everyone has the resources to promise that level of support. But you can set standards and expectations for yourself and then endeavor to meet them; maybe your email turnaround is two or three days instead of one. Maybe you set up an autoresponder for holidays when you'll be away. But the user who's just sent an email should be given an idea of when she should expect to hear back. If you occasionally exceed those expectations, your users will be even more impressed. If you fail to meet them, though, they'll be extra disappointed.

When you get the inevitable aggrieved messages, *kill 'em with kindness*. Many a frustrated customer, when his irate email gets a calm, apologetic response from a human being, suddenly becomes cooperative and understanding. "I never thought anyone would actually read it!" is a common reaction. If you go out of your way to pay attention to what the customer has to say, show some empathy, and genuinely do what you can to resolve the problem, his attitude will likely turn around. For a person who makes something in the hope it will be useful to someone, "You've earned me as a customer for life" should be a marvelous thing to hear.

Localization

If you can afford to hire professional localizers to make your app available for more locales, you should do it. It'll mean a more comfortable, welcoming experience for many people. For others, it will mean the difference between being able to use your app and being shut out.

iOS 6 itself includes 34 language settings, and the App Store is open in more than 150 countries. There are a lot of potential users out there who could benefit from your work. But be wary of adding anything less than an excellent localization to your app. For someone who knows English as a second language (the case for, oh, about a billion people), a bad localization is worse than no localization. When there's no localization, at least she can muddle through in English. But if a poor localization is provided in her native tongue, she must endure the awkward, vaguely insulting text that the app keeps throwing at her.

Localization isn't only about translating a list of strings into accurate matches in another language. Each platform has conventions for how certain common words (such as "done" and "cancel") should be represented in each language; simply translating them in a way that's technically correct isn't good enough. The translations need to be internally consistent throughout an app. And certain sentences may need to be rewritten if they use metaphors, jokes, or forms of address that don't work for all languages and cultures. In the English-speaking world, for instance, it may seem friendly to call someone by his first name, but in much of the rest of the world, this would be presumptuous, especially for a machine.

The good news is that iOS is admirably well prepared for localization. Unicode has always been its standard text encoding. Most localization should be possible without touching the source code; instead, you can swap in string files and images for each language.

Localization is a huge topic deserving of study well beyond this book. But for now, you owe it to your future international and intercultural users to keep the following basics in mind.

- The most prosaic rule of localization: watch your string length. Any given string in English can easily get 50% longer in famously character-rich languages like German or Dutch. In contrast, long English words can easily become only one or two characters in Japanese or Chinese. So design layouts so that their balance can survive a switch to much longer or shorter strings.

- Keep layouts simple, and keep them ignorant of string contents. Never create a layout that depends on the specifics of line breaking, string length, or the incidental alignment of words between strings; those details will evaporate as soon as you go to another language. If you try to put more than two elements in a row, you're bound to get unsightly gaps or run out of space in the localizations (see Figure 10.5).

- Don't rely on linguistic gimmicks. Double meanings, puns, and language-dependent metaphors (as in the "link" example earlier) will break down in other languages.

- Avoid interfaces that are about building up sentences. Especially for difficult concepts with multiple variables, it may seem clever to present a sentence in which certain words or phrases can be changed by the user; that's how iTunes on

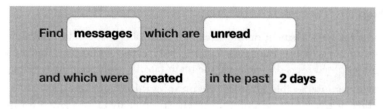

Figure 10.5   What not to do. It may seem friendly and cute to use UI elements to build up a sentence, but the result is unattractive and unlocalizable. In another language, this layout would at best have unsightly gaps, and would at worst make no sense at all.

the desktop, for example, creates smart playlists. But it's likely that the different sentence structures in other languages will make your clever interface seem tortured and alien. Although English sentences are basically ordered subject-verb-object, other languages can have any sentence structure at all. (See Figure 10.5.)

Don't conflate the language that the system is set to and the language of the content being viewed or created. More than half the people on Earth use more than one language in their day-to-day lives; you can't assume that the system language setting matches the content. If you need to show or hide language-related features, it's better to check which keyboards are enabled. Pages, for instance, is more than happy to offer Japanese-specific features like ruby characters (or *furigana*) no matter the system language setting, as long as a Japanese keyboard is enabled.

Accessibility

Accessibility means making sure your software is usable by as many people as possible, including people who have a disability. Because using iOS software generally involves looking and touching, this generally means accounting for vision impairment and physical or motor skill impairment.

You should make your software accessible. It's the ethical thing to do, and it's not prohibitively difficult. (Depending on how customized your interface is, though, it can be somewhat difficult.) Moreover, if you provide good accessibility and your competition doesn't, you gain an advantage among a community of people who love to evangelize for apps that work great.

Like localizability, accessibility support is an area where Apple has done most of the hard work for you. iOS comes with technologies such as full-screen zoom, inverted color mode, and support for assistive devices, but these technologies usually don't affect your job as an app designer very much. The main things you need to pay attention to are VoiceOver (the screen-reading system) and AssistiveTouch (the touch assistance system).

VoiceOver

VoiceOver gives every element on the screen a verbal label that can be read aloud. Users can use gestures to navigate among these labels and interact with them, usually just as richly as fully sighted users do. Here are the main ramifications for you as a designer.

- Everything interactable or otherwise meaningful in your interface gets a name, whether or not it's written on the screen. (Each element also gets a list of traits and a hint that helps users understand its function.)

- You need to decide which elements count as meaningful and thus should be read aloud; mere visual separators, for instance, are not worth reading out.

- Everything meaningful needs to be organized into a sensible, ordered hierarchy that's understandable when stepped through one element at a time. (Note that linearly is not the only way people can access them; that's only a way to get introduced to what an app has to offer.)

If you ignore VoiceOver and let the system guess about the elements in your interface, the resulting experience is bound to be frustrating. Crucial elements end up labeled simply "Button" or are skipped. Some elements report a peripheral bit of information rather than their main title. Meaningless elements are read aloud and must be skipped every time. Often, an app is entirely unusable to visually impaired users because important features are not feasibly reachable via VoiceOver.

Remember that "visually impaired" doesn't necessarily mean blind. Lots of partially sighted users make their way around iOS using a combination of full-screen zoom, VoiceOver, and Siri, to name a few helpful technologies. Some users can see sharply but are color-blind; make sure you don't rely on color to communicate meaningful information (although you can still use it as a cue).

The best way to get a sense of what your app is like for your visually impaired users is to turn on VoiceOver on your own device. Spend some time navigating the system strictly by audio. Try your own app. Frustrating? Imagine if that were the only way you could use it.

AssistiveTouch

AssistiveTouch helps people perform the more complicated gestures that iOS sometimes requires by using only one "finger" (often an assistive device such as an easy-to-grip stylus or a head pointer). Users can summon a menu that offers to simulate the most commonly used gestures on the system.

If you heed the advice in Chapter 8, The Graceful Interface, you're already dealing with the sandwich problem and keeping gestures as simple as possible. But it pays to turn on AssistiveTouch and try navigating around your app with one finger to see what it's like. Perhaps you will find some unnecessarily demanding gestures that you can simplify for everyone's benefit.

Hopefully you're convinced by now that you should go read Apple's *Accessibility Programming Guide for iOS* and get to work making your own app accessible. While you're at it, check out Matt Gemmell's legendary, definitive blog post on the topic (http://mattgemmell.com/2010/12/19/accessibility-for-iphone-and-ipad-apps/).

Ethos

The impressions that people get of your product and your organization are built up over time and through many channels. Often, the individuals who make the apps are available on Twitter, on their blogs, and at conferences. You may be interviewed for a web site or asked to appear on a podcast. People who pay attention to the industry may eventually get to know you and your organization as a personality in addition to your identity as the creator of an app they've used.

If you're in app development for the long haul, cultivate an ethos that you'll be proud to have inextricably attached to your products. When a well-regarded developer announces a new app, his fans often decide to pick it up solely on the merits of previous apps and on the understanding that the developer is decent and trustworthy. That sort of loyalty can't be bought.

More than one app's reputation has been tarnished in the eyes of attentive audiences when one of its developers, in the heat of the moment, published a controversial or unprofessional tweet or blog post. That's not to say that you shouldn't speak your mind; charismatic and iconoclastic developers who tell it like it is can earn a faithful following. But that doesn't mean you can discard respect. Think twice, because everything you say is connected to a product that you're asking people to invest their time and money in. Misunderstandings come easily, especially when you get only 140 characters at a time. The high road is always there for you to take.

Respect

When people install your app, they're welcoming you onto their iPhones and iPads. Those devices are among the most personal and personalized things that people own. People keep their iPhone with them in a purse or pocket all day. They use their iPad right up until bedtime and then go ahead and bring it to bed for some reading. The device is privy to connections with friends and family, to important times and locations, to upcoming appointments, to huge portions of its owner's life. Having your app installed among the other apps that make up a person's digital life is a privilege. The last thing you want to do is abuse that privilege. Happily, iOS has done a remarkable job of establishing and preserving the sacredness of the user's time, attention, and data.

Respect for Time and Attention

As suggested throughout this book, iOS is a triumph of respect for the user's time and attention. The most important consideration is the model of exactly one active app getting the whole screen, along with a unified, customizable notification system for controlling exactly how inactive apps can intrude.

Other contributors are the discouragement of alert dialogs, the reluctance to block the interface while tasks are proceeding, and the overall quiet, subdued, and content-focused design sense. Apps put priority on what the user wants to see and do and not on what the designers thought she should see and do.

As much as you can, follow in that spirit by not interrupting the user's normal workflow. Whatever she is doing with your app right now, chances are it is more important than whatever message or interruption you want to give her. Unless your interruption is directly and immediately related to the work she's trying to do, try to place it out of the way for her to deal with at her own pace. (For example, use contextual status as described in Chapter 9.)

Respect for Data

iOS is also uncommonly respectful of users' data in two ways: presentation and protection. Wherever users' own data appears, it should be treated like the most important thing in the world. While a document is open, it's common for the interface to retreat to the edges of the screen or even disappear. Photos, music albums, word processing documents—if it belongs to the user, it's sacred.

What seems like a cute little touch to the designer, such as rendering an older document as weathered and cobwebbed, could be seen as a small affront to the person who made that document. Scattering album art in a disorderly pile might seem mortifying to a serious record collector who painstakingly imported those albums from his meticulously organized shelves of vinyl.

After the hubbub about iOS 4 caching some location-related information it had collected, even though that data was never transmitted anywhere, Apple went far out of its way to address users' concerns about location tracking. It built much better location privacy into the system and made enabling Location Services one of the very few steps important enough to be included in the setup process for a new device.

A similar thing happened with address book entries, which it turned out some social network apps were secretly and indiscriminately uploading to their own servers; iOS 6 now requires permission from the user to access the contacts database. The system is similarly protective of Twitter and Facebook access, and most data is sandboxed and thus completely off limits to apps.

When you're entrusted with data by a user, do everything you can to make it clear what information is being sent beyond the device, and make sure users can prevent it from being sent if it's not crucial to the functioning of the app. Features that "phone home" to collect information for your own purposes, automatically post to a web service, or otherwise send data on behalf of your user should be well labeled and turned off by default. Anything less would be a betrayal of trust.

Speaking of Betrayals of Trust...

Here's an egregious example that illustrates the difference between an app that respects its users and one that doesn't, even though its creators had the best of intentions. It's the story of an iOS developer that has the license to create app versions of several eminent dictionaries costing up to $55 in the U.S. App Store.

One day, any customer trying to use one of these dictionary apps finds it behaving erratically. Immediately upon opening, it asks for permission to use the customer's Twitter account that's registered with the device. Trying to deny the permission causes the app to immediately quit. Frustrated, and likely needing the dictionary to do her job, her homework, or some other important task, the user finally hits Allow, assuming it's just for some newfangled social feature that she'll never use. With the barrier passed, she proceeds with her expensive, premium dictionary experience.

Sooner or later, the user starts getting confused, concerned, or amused tweets from people who follow her online. As it turns out, the dictionary's antipiracy module has been falsely triggered, releasing its payload in the form of an automatically and silently posted self-shaming tweet from the user's own account. Everyone following that person's account has now seen a message confessing to and apologizing for stealing software. If she has set up her tweets to be forwarded to Facebook or other services, nearly *everyone she knows* may have seen it.

Countless honest customers, who'd decided to give the developer its due and fork over the premium price for a higher-quality app, saw their own online presence turned against them. (People without a registered Twitter account were instead harassed by repeatedly appearing local notifications calling them thieves.) The company behind the apps apologized for the bug and released updates to remove the errant module, but the damage was done. Innocent people had to try to explain themselves to colleagues, family, and strangers.

This incident shows more than a lack of respect for a user's time, attention, or data. It's an injury to his reputation and his dignity. This is an unusually clear-cut case of terrible design decisions in a consumer app causing real and tangible harm to users. You might argue that it would have been fine if only the bug didn't cause the auto-tweet to misfire, and thus it was merely bad programming, not bad design. But *all* code has bugs, and no piracy detection technique is perfect. No matter how watertight you think the system might be, it's bound to hit at least one paying customer, and that's too many. Even if it only ever hit people who really did procure the app illegitimately, who is the developer to say that those people deserve to be publicly shamed by their own online presence? Shutting down the functionality of the app may have been defensible. Leaving the app functional but inserting a sincere plea might have turned some illegitimate users into customers. But presuming to have the authority to hijack the user's identity is going too far, no matter what he did. The feature should never have existed.

Always, always imagine the worst-case scenario for an individual user.

- Your shame-tweeting antipiracy module is accidentally activated for a paying customer the day she sends in her résumé for her dream job; the hiring manager sees the tweet, and the resulting misunderstanding costs her the interview opportunity.

- A new iPhone owner, who doesn't know that alarms are exempt from the hardware silent switch, goes to see the New York Philharmonic Orchestra. During the denouement of Mahler's 9th symphony, the iPhone's "Marimba" tone blares from his front-row seat, causing the conductor to halt the performance. (True story.)

- Upon hearing of a family emergency, a user frantically opens your public transit app to search for the quickest way home. Rather than getting the screen for finding a route, he gets a dialog cheerfully urging him to rate the app in the App Store (and helpfully suggesting that five stars would be a fine choice of rating). In a rush to get past the dialog, he taps OK and is taken out of the app entirely to load the store, losing him several more seconds. (It could happen.)

These are extreme examples, but technology design is filled with tiny decisions about respect. That's especially true now that people are carrying technology around with them and trusting it to help them make their way through each day of their lives. Even if these worst-case scenarios never happen, designing under the assumption that they will results in a better, more respectful product. Family emergency or not, "Rate This App" alerts are just plain annoying.

A Note on the Word "User"

You may have noticed by now that this book has no qualms about the word "user." But the term has taken a beating over the years, usually from well-meaning designers and developers who have a sense that it was vaguely derogatory or dehumanizing. It's valuable to think about how we use language and how we can communicate more clearly and respectfully. I'd like to make the case that even though "user" may be an imperfect word, it's the best one we have. Many words are imperfect, and it's within our power to make them work better for us.

The topic seems to come up every couple of years, and as of this writing the latest conversation about it originated with a post by Jack Dorsey of Square (and formerly of Twitter), who prefers the word "customer." That term is accurate when everyone using your product has paid you money or is about to. It pretty clearly frames the situation of a person using a piece of technology as a *business* relationship. The thing that defines the person is no longer her *interaction* with the product; it's her *transaction* with your company.

That may work great for designers at companies who want to focus on the business side. But it doesn't help designers at public sector, nonprofit, and educational organizations, or hobbyists creating free apps, to name a few examples. It may very well make sense for each organization to think about whether there are more specific words they could use, but it's rare to find one that accurately describes "the people who *use* the product we make."

In the end, we still need a general-use term for talking about the people we're making stuff for. So that we can, say, write books about software design. Imagine if every instance of the word "user" in this book were replaced with "customer." Instead, it uses the general "people" when appropriate, and "user" when making a specific mention of the people *using* the technology as opposed to the people *creating* it. And yes, it uses "customer" when the monetary transaction is the important part of the relationship.

If we use the word "user" disrespectfully, then yes, it *will* become derogatory and dehumanizing. But if we treat it nobly (think *Tron:* "I fight for the users!"), then it will become more noble.

Summary

Software design is about a lot more than just the pixels on the screen. The concept of user experience recognizes that technology is meant to be used by humans, and thus human concepts like emotion and integrity matter a lot.

You should get a handle on what your features are really for, and what your software as a whole is really for, in a holistic, life-goals sense. Then you should put effort into the stuff that surrounds your normal design work and connects it to people's whole experience: marketing, documentation, support, localization, and accessibility. A good designer can't stay siloed in Photoshop and OmniGraffle. You need to stay human and pay attention to every part of your product and company that users come in contact with.

Exercises

Here are a few little things you can do to work on rounding out the personality of your app.

1. Build yourself an app icon using the template provided on the book site (http://learningiosdesign.com). Or at least write up an outline or make a sketch of what you'd like to see a professional artist put together for your app icon.

2. Create a documentation skeleton for your app. Build a document that could serve as a table of contents for a comprehensive documentation resource. It may be trickier than you think. To find out what works best, try dividing it both by task and by screen. If you have a dedicated documentation person, bring it to him to start talking about building the real thing. If not, write it yourself.

3. Once you have a development version of your app running, turn on VoiceOver and run through it on the device. Run through typical usage scenarios to find out how they feel and how you can improve the workflow. Do the same with AssistiveTouch. If your app isn't ready, try it with another third-party app.

Part III
Finding Equilibrium

11

Focused and Versatile

There's an unhelpful dichotomy out there that pits "simple" apps against "complex" apps, with the simple ones being praised and the complex ones being derided. Supposedly iOS is inaugurating a "post-PC" era, because it removes the complexity that was present in desktop systems. Designers and developers are encouraged to "do one thing well" rather than allow feature after feature to creep into their apps. All these things are true in a way, but they oversimplify the concept of simplicity. The word "simple" when applied to software doesn't mean only one thing. There are different kinds of simplicity, and which kind you should aim for depends on the app you want to make.

What are people talking about when they say software should be simple? And when is it fine to create something complex? Although iOS apps are statistically simpler than their equivalents on the desktop, there is plenty of rich versatility to be had in individual iOS apps.

Debunking "Simple" and "Complex"

The two main axes of simplicity versus complexity in software are those of **functionality** and **presentation**.

- Functionally simple apps can be described as **focused**: they follow the exhortation to do one thing well. Think of a dedicated utility app, such as Weather.

- Functionally complex apps can be called **versatile**: they offer lots of possibilities, if you can master them. A productivity app like Pages is the classic example.

- An app of any functional complexity can be presented in a **quiet** way (and thus tend to appear simpler). These apps tuck their functionality away behind a sleek, simple exterior. An example is the famously subdued and undistracting design of the article-reading app Instapaper.

- An app can be presented in a **forthcoming** way (which tends to appear more complex). These apps provide an empowering, dashboard-style interface—for example, the mind-bogglingly featureful web browser iCab.

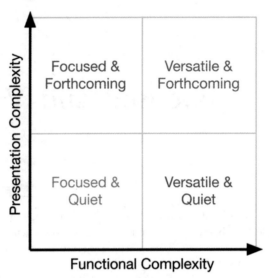

Figure 11.1   The complexity of an app can fall anywhere in this
two-dimensional space, even right in the middle.

Phew! Time for a graph (see Figure 11.1). Notice that having a simple, clean presentation doesn't mean you can't offer a lot of functionality, and offering a focused
feature set doesn't mean you can't offer a powerful, forthcoming presentation. It all
depends on how you intend people to use your app. None of these combinations is
inherently right or wrong.

What's exciting about this huge range of variability is that for a given subgenre of
app, there can be at least four legitimate approaches to solving it (and probably even
more, when you include all the in-between spaces and the other dimensions of possibility described in this book). Four or more apps can coexist, each catering to different
individual user preferences about which features are needed and how they should be
exposed. For a staggering illustration of this phenomenon, check out Brett Terpstra's
massive roundup of more than 70 iOS text editors and their comparative feature lists
(http://brettterpstra.com/ios-text-editors/). Each of those apps has a unique take on
the text editing job, and each one is the best tool for the job in somebody's book.

This chapter looks at the difference between focused apps and versatile apps, and
Chapter 12 looks at the difference between quiet and forthcoming presentations.

The Focused Design

The decision to keep your design focused happens at the outline level. When you're
deciding what your app is about, you have a choice as to its **scope.** You need to draw
a circle around a set of functionality that you've decided is within the purview of your
app, and exclude what you think isn't in its repertoire.

This is probably the most important decision you'll make in your app's lifetime. If your resources are especially limited—say, you're an individual designer/developer hybrid—stay focused. It may save your livelihood and your sanity. If you're part of a bigger company with more resources, you still might want to stay focused. Just because you can summon a herd of engineers to implement a huge list of features doesn't mean you should. Resources aren't infinite, n people are not n times as productive as one person, and every new problem you decide to focus on is an implicit decision that you won't focus on some other problem.

Focused Apps Are About Real-World Goals

To get a sense of how focused your app is, take a look at your outlines (or go ahead and put together a new one). Can you state the purpose of your app in one sentence or so? If so, what kind of sentence is it? As shown in the following examples, the one-line description for focused apps tends to be oriented toward a goal in the real world.

- Dark Sky predicts whether it will rain in the next hour.
- Just Landed notifies you when you should leave to pick someone up at the airport.
- Bistromath calculates how much each person should pay at a restaurant.
- Voice Memos records and plays back audio. (Sometimes the app title alone is a good description of the functionality.)

Each of these apps is aimed toward achieving a specific result in the real world. (Alton Brown would call them "unitaskers.") The story of reaching that goal is written by the designer: "Someone wants to know if it is about to rain, so he looks at Dark Sky and finds out." There simply is no other way to use the app (without getting creative, anyway). The more focused the story of the app, the more readily the developer can serve that specific use case well.

iOS Loves Focus

iOS is, generally speaking, home to focused apps. The reason you hear that you should do one thing well is that it almost always results in a better product. iOS is known for highly polished experiences, the elimination of legacy clutter, and an overall high standard of quality. Compared with desktop equivalents, iOS apps as a whole are focused. (But this doesn't mean that all iOS apps need to be equally focused.)

Massacre Features

Generally, the way to achieve focus is to aggressively prune your list of feature ideas. Especially when you're coming from the desktop perspective, or even creating an iOS edition of a desktop app, you should get ready to eliminate features that initially seem important.

As the classic writing advice from Arthur Quiller-Couch goes, murder your darlings. The more charming and exciting a feature is in your imagination, the more skeptical you should be of its necessity, and the more likely it is you're going to end up having to cut it in order to ship. Think of the concept of the "minimum viable product," and stay focused on it until you have something you can ship.

That doesn't mean you need to resign yourself to making boring, utilitarian apps. It just means you should cut the extraneous stuff so that you can focus on making the core functionality—the stuff your app is *about*—as charming and exciting as possible. When you're enamored of an idea, you can let yourself get wrapped up in finding excuses to keep it in.

When considering features (either features that you're bringing from an existing edition on another platform, or those that you're designing from scratch), ask yourself the following few simple questions.

- **Is the app still useful without this feature?** Would the app still do the job outlined in the one-line description? Would an ordinary user be happy to get her hands on the app sooner, even without it?

- **Without this feature, does the app still offer something unique that other apps don't?** It could be anything—other key features, a cleaner presentation, better interoperability with other apps, and so on.

- **Could you add this feature later without harming the design of the app now?** Is it safe to slice off this functionality for the time being and reinsert it later?

- **Does the feature provide just another way to do something?** You may feel pressure to offer several ways to get a certain task done. But if there's already one way to do it and you're confident that it makes sense, it's unlikely that your time is best spent adding more ways to reach the same goal.

- **Does the feature encourage problematic behavior?** In other words, is it advisable that the feature be used only by a few people? Sometimes developers include a feature not because they think it's a good idea for everyone to use it, but because a vocal few would complain about its omission. As a rule, if the idea of *all* your users using a certain feature is scary, consider not including it. (Philosophy fans, this is the categorical imperative of software design.)

- **Should the feature actually become an antirequirement?** Is it something you should decide you don't ever plan on doing?

If the answers tend toward yes, perhaps you should cut the feature for now, keeping the app focused, and revisit it when you have more time. It's better to plan small and have more time to polish than to plan big and always be racing against the clock.

Consolidate Functionality

Often, two features you think you need can be combined into one feature that's easier to design and implement. Or you can roll in a feature you think you need by making a minor adjustment to an existing feature.

Keynote on the Mac offers similar but separate interfaces for inserting shapes, tables, charts, and media into a presentation slide. On iOS, those four types of objects are given a consolidated experience, all taken care of by a single Insert popover. The lesson? A design becomes more unified when you conceptually group similar features into a single feature with several subcases.

Save It for Later

The good news is that even if you can't fit a feature in now, you can save it for later. All the great feature ideas you don't get to right away can become a to-do list for future versions of your app. If you intend to cultivate the app for a long time to come, you may get your chance to add those features. And getting the app out there in the world sooner, and seeing people use it, may inspire a much better feature than the one you had in mind.

Scaling Back

Another option is to scale it back. Instead of implementing the feature in all its glory, you could find a more modest approach that would offer, say, 80% of the benefit for 20% of the effort. In lots of cases, many users will actually still get 100% of the benefit, because they didn't need the advanced bits you left out anyway. It's true you'll lose a subset of your audience who really needed something in that 80% that you decided not to do, but this is still an effort-for-reward deal you shouldn't pass up lightly. Recognizing such scale-back opportunities is a huge part of developing your designer senses.

Here are some ways to scale back.

- **One not many**—Instead of designing and implementing a feature that allows an arbitrary number of x to exist, allow only one x. In the iWork apps, for example, you can set up only one WebDAV account. Because the number of WebDAV servers used by the overwhelming majority of people is either zero or one, Apple evaded all the complexity of offering maintenance of multiple accounts.

- **The inconvenience hand-off**—Sometimes, you can save yourself an enormous amount of work by asking the user to do a tiny bit of work. Be careful with this one. In most cases, you should go ahead and put in the effort. Imagine how many people in the world will encounter the situation you're designing for, and multiply that by how much effort and inconvenience you would be handing off to them. If it's still smaller than the amount of effort and inconvenience for you to design and implement the feature, then go ahead and hand it off. (If handing off will make it more likely that users will need support, add that to the equation.) For iCloud, Apple could have built an elaborate conflict resolution interface, with side-by-side copies of document versions, and dedicated controls customized for each app to move data between them. This would have required a colossal amount of design and engineering work. Instead, because sync conflicts don't happen very often, Apple presents a simple list of conflicting versions and asks you to choose which ones to keep. Once you have all the versions you want, it's up to you to use the existing document-browsing interface and the copy-and-paste functionality to resolve the conflict and then delete the extraneous copies. You might never end up needing to do this, so Apple didn't waste a huge amount of effort on it.

- **Division of labor**—For lots of features, there is already another app that handles it better than your app could anyway. In those cases, you can concentrate on making sure you can export data to that app and let it do the heavy lifting. Imagine you're considering adding data graphing to an app that isn't really *about* data visualization. Instead of doing all that intensive work, you could make sure your app puts data on the clipboard in a format that Numbers or OmniGraphSketcher can read. Now your users have world-class charting without your having to build it.

- **Read-Only**—If your iOS app shares data with editions on other platforms, or with other apps, consider allowing it to *understand,* but not *edit,* certain types of data. This works great when users might be more likely to create data elsewhere but read it on their iOS devices. Calendar on iPad is more than happy to show you files attached to an event, but if you want to add one, you'll need to do it on the Mac. See Chapter 7, Going Cross-Platform, for more about this kind of decision.

- **Presets**—You can make your own life and users' lives heaps easier by offering some carefully chosen defaults instead of limitless customization. Traditionally, on the desktop, it made sense to offer as much customization as the platform could support and to provide a correspondingly powerful and complex interface. iOS is much more likely to ask a user to pick from a list of reasonable presets. Consider the color palettes in the iWork apps. An almighty color picker, supporting literally every possible color that the screen can reproduce, would be challenging to build and intimidating to use. Instead, there is a simple series of sensible color palettes, offering a total of 24 colors and 5 grays. This is far easier to implement and has the benefit of making it much easier for users to create attractive, tasteful documents. (See Chapter 13, Friction and Guidance, for more on sensible defaults.)

Focusing SnackLog: Labeling

Time for some examples. During the outlining phase for SnackLog, we decided it might be reasonable to include either tags or categories, two different kinds of labeling. To keep track of different kinds of purchases separately, people could label purchases and add up the various totals for each label (see Figure 11.2). This feature is a prime candidate to be cut, as shown by asking the following questions.

- **Is the app still useful?** Certainly. Being able to quickly save purchases is the point; categorizing them would be a luxury.

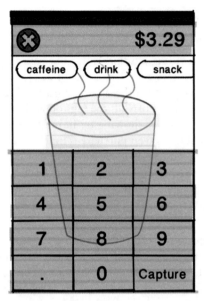

Figure 11.2   A sketch of SnackLog with tags on the capture screen.
Users would have to scroll horizontally through the available tags and tap
each one they wanted to apply. Another possibility would be to insert an
interstitial tag selection screen after each capture.

- **Does the app still offer something unique?** Yep. The concentration on quick-and-easy capture is a good differentiator.

- **Could you add this feature later?** Easily. No other features rely heavily on the interface for tagging, and there is plenty of space (spatially and cognitively) for adding it later if the need arises.

- **Does the feature encourage problematic behavior?** The idea of SnackLog is to be quick and straightforward. But if users see a tagging system, many of them will feel obligated to use it. People tend to abhor an empty field, so they waste time and energy filling out every single one even if they don't need to. Omitting the feature would encourage people to hurry up, capture their purchase, and get out, reinforcing the claim that the app is simple and quick.

- **Should the feature actually become an antirequirement?** Nah. Tagging is getting slightly toward the professional expense-logging side of the spectrum that the app is trying to avoid, but it's not definitively outside the scope of what the app is about.

These answers point toward either saving the feature for later or scaling it back. Of course, saving it for later is the easiest option: just make a note of it, keep an eye on your user feedback, and move on.

Scaling Back on Labeling

Here are applications of the various scaling-back methods to the case at hand.

- **One not many**—Providing *categories* instead of tags would simplify the situation. Allowing an arbitrary number of tags to be applied to each item would require providing a way to turn them on and off (both during capture and later), affording enough space to display all the tags on each item, and dealing with the confusion of a single purchase showing up in multiple lists. But allowing a single category to be applied to a given purchase is much simpler. Instead of turning tags on and off, you need to provide a way to choose an available category (or "None"). Each purchase in the log need only display one label. In reality, even if you offered a full-fledged tagging system, most users might never use more than one tag on a given purchase. So if you're dead set on including some sort of label, categories would be a fine compromise.

- **The inconvenience hand-off**—People could actually do some labeling of their own even if there were no dedicated labeling feature. They could append a label to each purchase title using a scheme of their own choosing (e.g., "Drinks—triple tall latte"). Combined with the division of labor tactic, this option might be useful.

- **Division of labor**—If the user has appended his own labels and then exported his data to a more manipulable format, he can do processing in a spreadsheet or outlining app to generate the totals for each label. The people who really care get the functionality in the end, but you don't need to build a dedicated special-interest feature into your app.

- **Read-Only**—This is not really an option for SnackLog, because we aren't planning on syncing data directly with other apps.

- **Presets**—It might seem appealing to provide a few preset, uneditable labels to choose from. But it would be nearly impossible to offer a set of labels to cover everyone's personal shopping idiosyncrasies. Presets work well only when the choices you provide are close enough to what users have in mind, like choosing a few tasteful colors; it's difficult to do with something as meaningful and personal as language.

The Versatile Design

The iPhone arrived in 2007, and the App Store introduced third-party software to the platform in 2008. In those early days of iOS (or iPhone OS, as it was called), apps were unquestionably far over on the focused side of the continuum.

In 2010, Apple introduced iPad and showed that its little mobile-phone operating system could power a compelling PC replacement. Its iWork suite of productivity apps—Pages, Numbers, and Keynote—made the transition from Mac to iPad and suggested that this touch-based platform could support full-on content creation. Medical apps, educational apps, creative apps, and more productivity apps followed. Gradually, almost full-featured editions of apps like the iWork suite have made their way to iPhone. Building big, powerful iPad and iPhone apps is a real possibility.

The reason for the "do one thing well" exhortation isn't that it's the only way to make a decent iOS app. It's just that doing one thing well is much easier than doing many things well. But it's possible if you have the skill, the resources, and the gumption to follow through. If you end up deciding to make a versatile app, make sure you arrive at that decision honestly, by confirming that a more focused app wouldn't do the job.

Versatile Apps: Bring Your Own Goals

If a focused app is about specific goals, a versatile app is about providing a kit of tools. Again, ask yourself the purpose of the app you're creating. Try to describe it in a one-line statement of purpose. If the user's real-world goal isn't in sight, then you may have a versatile app on your hands. Versatile apps leave the goal up to the user and provide helpful ways of getting there. Their statements of purpose look more like the following.

- Elements is a tool for editing text files in the cloud.
- Penultimate is a tool for drawing sketches by hand.
- Remarks is a tool for creating and annotating PDFs.
- iMovie is a tool for recording and editing video.

What the user does once she has her text file, sketch, PDF, or movie is up to her—the story is only getting started. This, of course, means that the versatile app needs to cover a far broader set of possible use cases and is much more likely to need a complement of features to support them.

It's not necessary that an app with many use cases become functionally complex; you could certainly make a dead-simple, hyperfocused text editor. But those many use cases tend to push at the boundaries of what the app can do and make the app seem to legitimately want a bit more complexity.

iOS Loves Versatility

iOS's love of versatility isn't a contradiction with the previous claim that iOS loves focus. You can build marvelously versatile apps for iOS. In fact, versatile apps feel great on iOS because they're still much more focused than their desktop counterparts.

Consider the quantity of visible features offered by Pages on the Mac versus on the iPad (see Table 11.1). Of course, counting controls and menus isn't an exact measure of the complexity of functionality, but it gives you a pretty good idea.

The complexity of Pages for Mac is reasonable for an average desktop user. It conforms to historical expectations for desktop productivity software.

But iOS has taken the opportunity to reboot those expectations of complexity. It covers most of the functionality needed by most users, with far less need for

Table 11.1 **Counting Elements on Mac and iPad**

Pages for Mac	Pages for iPad
3 panels of preferences	No preferences
10 inspector panes	3 inspector panes
Toolbar, customizable up to 50 items	Fixed 3-item toolbar
12-control format bar	5-control format bar
10 menus	No menus

complexity. This design works because of a funny fact about software featurefulness: once you've included the big, obvious, widely needed features, the remaining ones are minor. Each new feature you add is likely to add decreasing value in return for increasing complexity. Figure 11.3 shows an irresponsibly oversimplified graph.

While versatile desktop apps have been steadily climbing this curve, with less and less return, iOS is so far holding fairly steady at a point of *slightly* less usefulness but *far* less complexity. All this is to say that you can offer a splendidly useful and featureful app on iOS that ends up safely more focused, and less complex, than the equivalent desktop app.

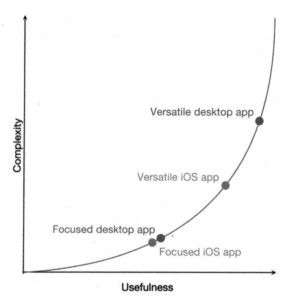

Figure 11.3   Complexity versus usefulness. As features are added, complexity grows exponentially but yields diminishing returns of usefulness.

When to Go Versatile

Getting versatile apps right takes a lot of resources. It takes time and energy to design and build features and usefulness into your app, and that investment gets really demanding really fast. You could probably throw together a perfectly functional app with loads of features fairly easily. But it will be terrifyingly ugly and cognitively impenetrable unless you take the extra time and effort to get the *design* right. That part takes patience.

So before you decide to go for a huge, ambitious project, maybe try a more focused one and see how it taxes your resources. Build up to it. It's entirely possible for a lone designer/developer to build and maintain a big, featureful app, but it's rare. If you think a focused app won't be challenging or interesting enough, you may be surprised. Editing is hard. Keeping a short story short can be as taxing as filling up a novel.

How to Go Versatile

When you're designing an app whose statement of purpose includes a big, wide-open set of possibilities, the primary question should be how to cover the greatest number of possibilities with the smallest number of features. This approach helps you get to a place where you're offering lots of functionality to help people reach their varied goals, but without reaching a desktop-like level of complexity.

Because SnackLog is a focused sort of app, we'll switch to a different sample app for this section. Suppose you're working on an app that can build and publish simple web sites. We'll call it HindSite. The space of possible features and functionality is infinite, because the variety of sites that people might want to create, and the variety of ways they might prefer to create them, is infinite.

Within that theoretical space of possible software, the actual parameters of your design will carve out a certain area that defines what your particular app is about and how it gets things done. Of course, stumbling around in an infinite space and trying to stake out some subset of it as your own is an intimidating task. The good news is that there are ways of trimming the problem to an approachable size.

Triangulation

So you just can't know and plan for all the possible uses of your versatile app, and that uncertainty is the whole point. But you can set out to explore the possibility space to find its boundaries and its center. **Triangulation** is a technique to make sure you cover a healthy range of use cases. It involves sketching several key situations and considering the features needed to support them.

First, pick a center case. You've probably heard of **edge cases,** those tricky situations way out on the boundaries of what the software is supposed to do. A **center case** is the opposite. What is the most mundane, ordinary thing that someone might want to do with your app? For HindSite, it's probably something like

Make a single informational web page about a small business.

For an app that creates documents or some other kind of end product, try sketching those products to get a sense of what you need to support. Don't worry about the interface yet; that comes later. Here we're sketching the sites themselves, without any concern about the design of the app.

Then pick several representative **interesting cases,** and sketch them (see Figure 11.4). These aren't edge cases; instead, they should be well within the boundaries

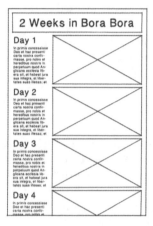

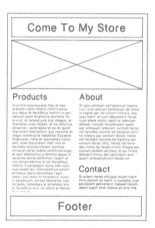

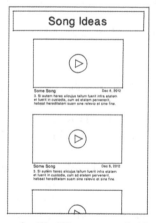

Figure 11.4   A center case for HindSite, surrounded by three interesting cases.
Sketching the kinds of documents you want your app to create helps you triangulate
the feature space you need to implement.

of what should be your app's repertoire. But each one should have something special about it that makes it distinct from the center case. For HindSite, the following are some examples.

- Make a site about a vacation, with a photo page and a journal page that users can update as the trip progresses. This is interesting, because users will revisit the existing site and append content to it over time.

- Make a site for a restaurant, with a menu and contact info. This is interesting, because the menu should have a fairly detailed layout, with prices and nutritional info in their own columns.

- Post a series of videos of yourself playing song ideas on a guitar for your band-mates to watch. This is interesting, because it includes embedded content from a video site.

Each of these cases suggests needs that you'd better support: chunks of text, images, video, links, multiple pages, navigation, updating of existing sites, some amount of layout customization, and so on. Next, you need to figure out the minimum set of features to fill those needs.

Pattern Recognition

Looking over the list of needs for each use case, you may start to see patterns.

- Images and video could be considered "media," and you may want to offer a single type of object to deal with both.

- A navigation menu is probably something you should offer to build into each site, but single-page sites won't need it.

- Separate days in the vacation journal and separate food categories on the restaurant menu could probably both be served by some sort of subsection container objects.

And so on. Now you have a list of features that serve the needs you found, and you can use them to inform your sketches of the site-building experience.

Finding the Boundaries

After you identify the cases you want to cover, you may also want to specify cases that you don't intend to support. If a user wants to go out of her way to force the app to do something it wasn't meant to do, she might be able to. More likely, you can leave that space for competing apps to cover. Often, these **outside cases** are more extreme versions of your interesting cases. The following are some outside cases for HindSite.

- Build an interactive site that allows visitors to comment or otherwise add their own content.

- Build a dynamic site that involves sophisticated JavaScript.

- Build a standard blog with syndication, individual post pages, and archives.

- Build a site with specific and unique layout needs.

This is similar to the concept of antirequirements, described in Chapter 1. Keeping in mind what you've decided not to tackle makes it easier for you to concentrate on doing a good job with your core goals.

Summary

Simplicity is a fine goal to aim for in software, but make sure you know what kind of simplicity you're dealing with. Simplicity when it comes to the functionality of software is a balance between focus and versatility. Another concern is how simply the software's functionality is presented—the topic of Chapter 12, Quiet and Forthcoming.

A focused app is about solving a specific goal that can be summed up in a straightforward purpose statement. The most reliable way to keep an app focused is to aggressively prune any features that don't contribute directly to that goal. You have a variety of ways to check whether a feature should be cut, and a variety of ways of scaling those features back.

A versatile app is about providing a set of tools for working within a possibility space. The goal is provided by the user, so you need to account for a wide range of use cases. You can be confident in your coverage of the needs by triangulating from a center case, some interesting cases, and some outside cases. Then you can recognize patterns and settle on a feature set.

Exercises

Here are ways to play with the space between focus and versatility. They should help you find the right balance for your own projects.

1. Pick a single feature of an existing versatile app, and imagine that you're designing a focused app around that single feature. What is the goal? How can you sketch a focused app to solve it? Can you make it compelling enough to be worth building and selling in the App Store?

2. Find an existing focused app that could be expanded into a versatile app. Can you turn its simple goal into an open-ended purpose statement? Build a possibility space with a center case, special cases, and outside cases. Can you sketch a feature set that satisfies them all with a manageable level of complexity?

3. If you haven't yet, apply these practices to your own app. For it to be the app you envisioned, does it need to be more focused, or more versatile, than you've been planning so far? How can you improve your sketches based on these techniques?

Quiet and Forthcoming

Chapter 11 is all about the functional simplicity or complexity of an app, and this chapter is about the simplicity or complexity of its **presentation.** A versatile app can hide a lot of its functionality, cleverly organizing its navigation to appear deceptively simple; this is a **quiet** design. Or a focused app can put all its cards on the table right away, seeming powerful and full featured on its main screen, because there are no more screens to see; this is a **forthcoming** design. And, of course, any other combination of the two axes is possible, too. Depending on the experience you want to offer and the impression you want to give, all these approaches are available to you.

On the whole, iOS encourages much quieter design than the software most of us are used to. The tools it provides skew toward providing only the elements that are relevant in a given context and requiring users to move around in the app to get at different functionality. That means less stuff is visible on a given screen.

As you saw in Chapter 11, iOS also leans toward consolidating functionality and focusing on an 80% solution (or 90%, or some other big proportion). An app like Keynote, with 20 toolbar items on the Mac, can easily end up with only 7 toolbar items on iPad and 5 on iPhone, as the designers follow the practice of fusing similar features. That tendency alone is a major first step toward quieter interfaces.

The main difference between a quiet interface and a forthcoming one is whether its useful pieces are stacked in time or adjacent in space. The distinction was first articulated in this way by Edward Tufte during his marvelous one-day course on presenting data and information. As the metaphor goes, two elements on a single two-page spread of a book are **adjacent in space,** meaning you can see them both at once. Elements on different spreads are **stacked in time,** meaning you need to travel from one to the other, and you can see only one at a time.

Attention Counts

The reason the topic of this chapter is important, by the way, is that over the decades, technology designers have learned the importance of the human **attention budget.** It turns out that "paying attention" is an especially apt turn of phrase, because we really do have a limited amount of it to spend. The more attention you dedicate to one thing, the less you have for another. When you must choose among a lot of options, you're likely to become overwhelmed and experience **decision fatigue** and **ego depletion**, losing some of your willpower to continue making decisions carefully.

It might seem like a stretch to apply this principle to mere app design, but think about how many hours, tens of hours, or hundreds of hours people may spend in your app. How you present your app's functionality *does* have an effect on how motivated people will be to continue learning it and using it over time. The science is real, and the effects are worth considering.

With this fact in mind, you can and should carefully control the path a user takes through your app as he pursues various tasks. This chapter looks at questions of how much information is presented at once, how that information is grouped, and how many decisions the user is asked to make in a row. (If you're interested in this sort of thing, pick up *Thinking, Fast and Slow* by Daniel Kahneman.)

Adjacent in Space

On iOS, placing usefulness adjacent in space usually means keeping features on the same screen. All the content and controls visible on a single screen are sharing a chunk of the user's attention. That's opposed to elements that appear only when you navigate to another screen, summon a popover, or otherwise interact with the app to make them appear.

The result is an experience characterized by choosing from many options, but with a small number of steps.

What follows are good reasons to make more stuff visible at once.

- **It saves time**—For content, higher information density means the user doesn't have to scroll or navigate to see more information. Everything is visible at once, for quick reading and comparison. For controls, presenting all features up front as peers means everything that the technology can do is only one touch away. But this speed boost doesn't usually appear until the user has become comfortable with the interface and has learned how to navigate its attention-demanding layout. Until then, it's likely to be slower.

- **It's empowering**—More stuff at once eventually makes people feel expert and empowered. Once they get used to what your app offers and have deciphered the array of visible elements, they can develop a fast, smooth workflow that feels like playing the piano. Mastering an app that presents itself as a professional-grade tool makes certain types of people—such as nerds who write books about software—feel really cool.

- **It's reassuring**—Especially for people used to desktop interfaces, it's reassuring and educational. Some users haven't yet developed the sense of adventure that makes them feel comfortable poking around an interface and figuring out all it can do. If important features aren't brought to the surface, there is a good chance those folks will miss them. Whatever your opinion of App Store reviews, it's not uncommon to find people complaining that features don't exist in an app when they really do but are hidden behind a couple of taps. You could argue that it's the user's fault for not looking hard enough, but if enough users have the same impression, then it's probably the designer's fault after all.

- **And doggone it, it looks cool**—There is no denying that exposing features makes technology *look* more powerful. An appliance with lots of buttons seems more featureful than one with few buttons, even if the functionality is the same, and appliance makers have known this for decades. (Don Norman tells a famous anecdote about visiting Korea and being intrigued by how much more complicated-looking the appliances were, because consumers preferred them that way.) One way to market your product as powerful and full featured is to put those features on display. That doesn't mean you should artificially clutter your interface. But there may be a time when you're not sure whether a key competitive feature deserves to be brought one level closer to the surface; it might help to recognize that putting it up front would help people discover what your app can do.

UI Furniture

iOS has less user interface paraphernalia overall, compared with other platforms. Some designers call the various UI elements that populate a screen *chrome*, slightly pejoratively, because they seem extraneous. Most of the time you're not using them, so they *are* extraneous. Edward Tufte calls them *administrative debris*, somewhat more pejoratively, for the same reason. This book occasionally uses the term *UI furniture*. UI elements are necessary, sometimes, just like furniture is. You want to have furniture in a well-appointed room, but you tend to push it toward the walls and corners so that it's not in the way. And you certainly don't want so much of it that you can barely use the room.

Stacked in Time

Stacking usefulness in time on iOS generally means moving a feature elsewhere in the app, where the user must make an effort to get at it. It's not "hidden"; it just lives somewhere other than your current location. This practice removes elements from the main, more commonly used screens and puts them instead in temporary or less-visited locations.

The result is an experience characterized by choosing from few options, with a greater number of steps.

What follows are good reasons to make less stuff visible at once.

- **It looks simpler**—Hiding features gets you closer to the much-coveted "simple" look. The more you tuck away, the more elegant and svelte your app (and screenshots) will appear. With fewer elements visible, it's easier to make a screen look polished and "designy."

- **It's less distracting**—Having less visible on the screen means that a user can dedicate more of her attention budget to whatever it is she would prefer to look at. Most of the time, unless your app is *all about* pushing buttons, users almost certainly prefer to concentrate on the content and not the UI furniture.

- **It provides more chances for logical grouping**—You have more opportunities for conceptually grouping features. When all possibilities are in one big list, for example, you're limited in the ways you can group them. But when you can create subgroups that need to be navigated into, you can label them and separate them by purpose.

- **It gives you space**—Moving a feature to its own screen usually means you have more space for it. On a dedicated screen you can stretch out and give the feature the presentation and explanation it deserves.

Progressive Disclosure

A useful way of looking at the experience of your app is as a sort of **self-guided tour.** A guide-guided tour would be one of those "wizard" experiences that ask the user a linear series of questions—and quickly get patronizing.

But a self-guided tour is more like a trip to a good grocery store. If it's your first time there and you don't yet know your way around, you could just wander the aisles and see what's available. But you could also glance at the signage, quickly find the general section you need (dry beverages), narrow the category (coffee), go to the brand (Equal Exchange), and then go to the specific product (whole-bean Midnight Sun). Once you're familiar with the store, you can effortlessly take the steps you need to get to the result you want.

Software can be even more helpful by showing you *only* the choices for the level you've reached: you don't see what's inside a category or grouping until you open it (the folders in the iOS home screen, with their tiny preview icons inside, are a notable exception). That's **progressive disclosure:** a good balance between a flattened, everything-at-once presentation and a linear, wizardlike presentation.

Progressive disclosure quiets down each step, but it also means you must be good at labeling the choices so that people know what to expect inside each one. At each step of the way, a good progressive-disclosure experience is gently saying, "Here are some things we think would be reasonable for you to see next." Each of the options presented is roughly equivalent and stems logically from the preceding choice. Consider the steps you take for a process as mundane as changing your ringtone (see Figure 12.1).

- At the home screen, you see dozens of apps—24 of them on a full iPhone 5 home screen without folders. You choose the Settings app, knowing it lets you make general changes about how your iPhone works. (The mechanical-looking icon and the app name may help you decide if you didn't already know where to look.)

- At the top level of the Settings app, you see a screenful of system-level settings—10 table cells. Only a few of them—the ones you're most likely to want to change quickly (like Airplane Mode and Do Not Disturb)—are leaf nodes, meaning they don't contain anything. The rest are groupings that disclose another level. You tap Sounds, an obvious choice for dealing with ringtones.

- Scanning down the Sounds screen, among the 7 settings that are visible without scrolling (15 in all), you see the magic word you have been looking for: Ringtone. You tap it.

- Finally, but without very much cognitive burden or time investment, you've arrived at the list of 53 included ringtones, along with any you've installed. On only your fourth step, you've made your way through the thousands of destinations your iPhone makes possible, each time choosing from a limited number of equivalent alternatives, organized by both meaning and importance.

There are plenty of questionable information-architecture decisions in Settings (for example, General ▶ About ▶ Advertising ▶ Limit Ad Tracking), but this one makes good sense.

Figure 12.1   Progressive disclosure is the way of things on iOS. Here, a user begins at the home screen (left), the "top level" of iOS, and discloses one grouping after another until arriving at the leaf node she is looking for: the ringtone setting.

Group by Meaning, Arrange by Importance

When deciding where to place functionality in the geography of your app, you should consider both meaning and importance.

Meaning is the way people expect functionality and content to be grouped. That is, it's how you assemble chunks of stuff that should appear adjacent in space. The Sounds screen in Settings makes sense, because everything in it is related to the audio that comes out of the iPhone: ringtones, master volume, the behavior of the volume buttons, and so on (or the absence of sound, such as whether you want the phone to vibrate when in silent mode).

That seems obvious, but think about how important it is that such groupings are predictable and understandable. There are dozens or hundreds of possible paths through your app; people need good signposts to guide them along the way, helping them understand which next step will take them closer to the ultimate destination they have in mind.

When you're creating groupings, it's also important to keep in mind the user's understanding of the concepts involved. Although it would be logically defensible to put the ringtone setting under a grouping called Output or Signals or Notices or some other technical term, that wouldn't be very helpful to the tech-innocent user who just wants to change the annoying sound her phone makes to a more pleasant one.

Each grouping you create, whether it's a navigation controller node, a popover, a tab, or anything else, should be easily nameable and describable. The three popovers in Pages are clearly defined.

- **Style** is for changing the appearance of the selection.
- **Insert** is for adding new content to the document.
- **Tools** is for administrative tools dealing with the document itself.

If you have a hard time succinctly describing the purpose of an element or group, there's a good chance it won't be understood by users either. (You could even say that each grouping should define its own tiny "platform," just as apps need.) Usability testing—as simple as putting the layout in front of someone and asking him where he expects to find things—can give you an idea of whether your groupings make sense.

It's important to put a good label on your grouping. Some users were confused when the brightness slider in iBooks was moved into the View popover, signified by an *A* in both cases. They thought that button was obviously strictly for font controls and didn't even bother checking there when trying to figure out where the slider had gone.

After you establish groupings, **importance** helps you decide how prominent those groupings should be. You indicate importance by using promotion and demotion, as described in the next section.

Something to avoid is mixing up this principle, by grouping functionality based on its importance. Consider the Undo feature in iWork. It's an important and commonly used command. Promoting it to the very top by putting it by itself in the toolbar works great: it's prominent and reassuring to the user who just made a mistake.

But imagine if Undo were grouped along with other commonly used features such as, say, Find and Italic. The three have nothing to do with each other except that they're supposedly commonly used; one is about changes you just made, one is about locating certain words, and one is about styling. Even if a user understood that they were grouped because they're supposedly common commands, that distinction is a matter of opinion.

Furthermore, Undo is an important enough command that it needs to live on its own in a prominent and reassuring location. For the user who never uses Find, it'll be confusing and irritating that she needs to remember that Undo and Italic are in that one popover along with Find. The designer's notions about which features are most important shouldn't result in a design that pulls features out from where they actually belong: in recognizable and memorable locations.

Promotion and Demotion

In Chapters 1 and 2, you saw that much of app design can be seen as a hierarchical list or flow chart of features, distributed across screens. With most navigation schemes, certain screens are considered more "main" than others.

Your primary job in determining the quietness or forthcomingness of your app is to decide which features to promote and which to demote. This decision doesn't necessarily say anything about the worthiness or goodness of a feature; it's all about making sure everything is in the best place it can be for the sort of experience you're trying to create.

Promoting a feature means placing it closer to the surface of your app: the screens and the areas of the interface that get the biggest share of a user's attention. The more features you promote, the more stuff you'll have adjacent in space on your surface screens. Your app becomes more forthcoming. This practice is, naturally, also called **surfacing** a feature.

Demoting a feature means placing it deeper in the app, requiring more taps or scrolling or other user interaction to get from the surface to the place where the feature is visible. The more features you demote, the more stacked in time the whole experience gets. Your app gets quieter. This is also called **burying** a feature, not always pejoratively.

Screens like the following are closer to the surface and thus tend to be sensitive to presenting elements adjacent in space.

- The initial screen presented when the app is launched for the first time. (Subsequent launches are likely to pick up at whatever screen was last open.)
- The root of your app's navigation, the conceptual "top" of the app, such as the leftmost screen in a navigation controller hierarchy. (Often, but not always, it is the same as the initial screen.)

- Screens where the user spends most of his time getting something done, such as the document editing screen in a productivity app. Because of the amount of time spent here, these screens can feel closer to the surface than the previous examples.
- Wherever concentration is paramount and distractions would be especially intrusive, such as the reading screen of iBooks or Instapaper. Because of the way users expect to focus here, these can feel closer to the surface than the shelf view or the article list.

Screens such as the following are further from the surface and thus are where you can move features when you want to stack them in time:

- Deeper levels of hierarchy in the navigation scheme, requiring more taps to reach
- Temporary "screens" or screen states like popovers, modal views, action sheets, or alerts
- Screens that act as a segregated repository of administrative stuff and are populated with plenty of controls, such as your settings screen

Table 12.1 and Figure 12.2 show a few examples of hypothetical features for anonymous apps, each showing the contrast between a more-surfaced possibility and a more-buried possibility.

Table 12.1   **Promoted and Demoted Approaches to Presenting Features**

Feature	Promoted Approach	Demoted Approach
Three roughly equivalent general-purpose commands in a document editing screen (see Example A in Figure 12.2)	Three dedicated toolbar buttons	A single toolbar button that summons an action sheet with three buttons
Three related settings (see Example B in Figure 12.2)	A three-row group in the grouped table view of the settings screen	A single chevron row labeled with a descriptive name, which navigates to a dedicated screen for the three settings, possibly with extra explanatory text
A command that applies to the selected object on a canvas	A hovering button that appears immediately whenever the object is selected	A contextual menu command, available when the user touches and holds on the object
24 fields and controls for editing an object	One big, scrolling screen with all 24 fields and controls	A segmented control acting as tabs, each tab containing several of the fields and controls

Table 12.1   **Promoted and Demoted Approaches to Presenting Features (*Continued*)**

Feature	Promoted Approach	Demoted Approach
Display and editing of a row of data	Dedicated cells for each field, all editable in-place	One consolidated, condensed view of the data, which, when tapped, opens a modal view with dedicated cells for each field
Long swaths of text	Narrow margins and small text in order to fit more on the screen at once	Generous margins and larger text to keep an easily absorbed amount of text on-screen at once
A color picker with 64 options	An 8×8 matrix of all available colors visible at once	A spinning carousel that shows about 10 colors at once

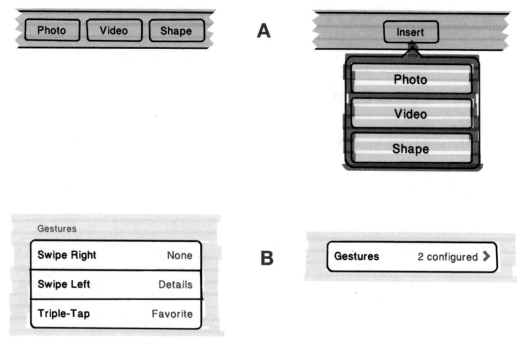

Figure 12.2   Two examples of promoted and demoted approaches to presenting three options. Example A consolidates three toolbar buttons into an action sheet. Example B gives three table cells their own screen, where the user needs to navigate to edit.

Splitting the Difference

Note that there is a range of overlapping possibilities for any given feature and not only a single forthcoming answer and a single quiet answer. There are a number of ways you can split the difference, techniques that demote a feature a bit without pushing it all the way to a different screen. The following are tips about the relative quieting power of demotion techniques.

- Requiring scrolling to reveal an element or content keeps it hidden from view initially but is lightweight. The obvious choice is to have the thing in question scrolled off the bottom of the viewport. But there's also precedent for having view-related features such as sorting and search scrolled off of the *top* of the viewport, as in Mail's message list and the iWork document picker.

- Pagination is not quite as lightweight as scrolling, but it's lighter than navigating to a different screen. Pagination feels lighter if only one layer of the screen moves, as when users move between messages in Mail; it's slightly less so if the entire screen moves, as when users move between locations in Weather.

- Temporary screens, subscreens, and elements such as popovers, action sheets, contextual menus, and modal views are lighter weight than navigating to a different screen, because they don't take the user out of the present context. See the next section for more about these heroic contextual elements.

iOS Loves Context

You have leeway within the quiet area that iOS inhabits. But if you try to build an app that's fully as forthcoming as a desktop app is, it's bound to feel a bit forced and out of place on iOS.

To see why, try using the web interface for a productivity app like Google Docs or OpenOffice on an iPad. At every moment, the typical desktop productivity app is proud to show off how capable it is and how many commands you could invoke at a moment's notice. On the desktop, that's fine. But iWork, the closest equivalent that is at home on iOS, would rather present you with step-by-step decisions, with only a few branches at each step, to arrive at those same commands. (See Figure 12.3.)

The main way iOS achieves its quieter overall design sensibility is by caring about context: what the user is doing right this second and what makes sense to offer based on that information.

Many of the standard iOS elements available to you as a designer are biased toward paying attention to context.

- A popover appears only when the user explicitly indicates that he wants to see it. It floats over the rest of the interface, indiscriminately covering up whatever happens to be beneath it, casting a broad drop shadow that says, "I'll just be here for a moment." Each screen in a popover can scroll. A single popover can contain multiple tabs, each with its own little navigation controller hierarchy. None

**Typical iOS
Experience**

**Typical Desktop
Experience**

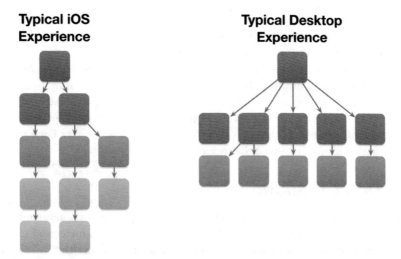

Figure 12.3   Idealized typical experiences on iOS and on the desktop.
iOS tends to have longer step-by-step interactions, whereas the desktop
tends to offer access to features with fewer clicks. This works because
relative to clicks, taps are cheap.

of that stuff in the popover need appear on the main screen that spawned it; the
stuff stays hidden until it's requested. It remains visible precisely as long as it's
needed and then disappears. Popovers that exist only to make a single choice are
automatically dismissed once the choice is made; most other popovers disappear
as soon as the user tries to interact with something else.

- An action sheet is even more aggressive about focusing on one decision. It asks
the user a direct (though usually implicit) question about what he wants to happen next. Look at the action sheet in Mail that appears when you try to close a
message in progress: the options are Save Draft, Delete Draft, and Cancel. (The
implicit question is, "Do you want to save this message as a draft?") This design
alleviates the need for some sort of clumsy Save Draft command that's always
available while users are composing a message. Instead, you aren't even made
aware of the concept of saving or deleting a draft unless you decide to close a
message; the interface keeps quiet about the possibility until the context calls
for it. (You could argue that new users wouldn't intentionally hit Cancel on a
message they intended to keep, and you'd be right. It takes times to discover the
drafts feature. It keeps the composition screen quieter in exchange for being hard
to discover at first.)

- A contextual menu does a good job of suggesting actions related to an object
without taking over the focus of the screen or the user's attention. It's small and
light enough to remain inconspicuous if it isn't what the user wants; that's why
apps tend to be liberal about when it should appear (often upon mere selection of

an object). But even so, a contextual menu doesn't appear until the app has good reason to believe that it might be needed, and then it appears right at the point of need, attached to the object it applies to.

- A modal view creates a dedicated space for pursuing a feature, where only the elements that directly serve the feature are present. In essence it offers a small, self-contained experience. This is in contrast to cramming a miniaturized version of the experience into a corner of the main screen. Many experiences that are presented in modal views on iOS would on the desktop have been free-floating windows, left up to the user to manage and maintain.

Hide, Don't Disable

There's a tradeoff between hiding controls that are inapplicable at the moment and disabling them. Hiding controls makes the interface cleaner and quieter and doesn't require the user to dig through stacks of dimmed elements to find the available ones. Disabling controls means that nothing will ever get lost and that it's easier to find out which features exist, even if you don't know how to make them available.

The desktop has traditionally taken the side of disabling controls. iOS has pretty firmly taken the side of hiding them. It recognizes the benefits and drawbacks and almost always opts to get rid of stuff that can't be used.

If it bothers you as a designer that switch B won't be discovered because it depends on switch A to be turned on first, you can almost always make it visible in some other way than by leaving grayed-out controls lying around, as in the following examples.

- Put explanatory text near switch A.
- Make it so that turning on switch B automatically turns on switch A.
- Make a three-way setting with the options "Off," "A," and "A & B."
- Consider whether A and B really need to be separate switches.
- Accept that users who don't ever turn on switch A probably don't need to know about switch B anyway.

As always, there are exceptions. iWork disables its Undo button instead of hiding it when there's nothing to undo, because that button is something users come to expect to see in a certain spot. The document editing screen is very close to the surface of the app, so it's more important that the screen remain stable. And it's a button that's reassuring to see.

Disappear

There is a logical but surprising outcome of paying attention to context and presenting only UI furniture that is needed at the moment: during some of those moments, no UI furniture is needed at all. So it makes perfect sense for the interface to simply disappear.

This is something that was barely thought about before, except in the case of watching videos and playing certain games. (*Myst* was a notable early entry in immersive, nearly UI-free games.) But once you start looking for it, you realize how demanding desktop interfaces are of your attention: menus, menu bar items, the Dock, toolbars, subtoolbars, status bars, and sidebars are all visible at once, and that's not even counting the arbitrary number of apps you can have open in the background. It all seems so self-important, as if it all thinks it deserves your attention. Compared with that, the iOS experience of one app, with a minimal interface, is really quiet. When that minimal interface fades away, it's as quiet as an app can get. (With the full-screen feature in Mac OS X, the desktop is also coming around to the value of focusing on one task at a time and keeping the chrome out of the way.)

So apps that present content or experiences that could benefit from total immersion should offer interfaces that disappear. In iBooks, the UI furniture disappears so that you can get lost in a good story. In Photos, it disappears so that you can proudly share the memories of your latest vacation as largely as possible. In iA Writer, it disappears so that you can agonize in peace over every word of your important manuscript. It is a confident step by software designers to admit that sometimes the content is important enough that their own work should go away entirely.

In fact, it's a worthwhile and humbling exercise to assume that for users, the content they put into your app could very well be the most important thing in the world—whether it's a draft of their revolutionary scientific theory or a video of their newborn child. Let's leave the user alone for once.

Another situation to consider is the desire of a user to hold up his iPad or iPhone to show it to someone else. He should be able to make his argument, illustrate his idea, make his interlocutor laugh, or otherwise get his point across without his audience having to see anything on the screen but the content.

So if you intend to present an immersive experience, you should consider a disappearing interface. But don't do it just to join in the trend; some experiences don't make a lot of sense in full-screen mode, and enshrining their content with an immersive view would feel like overkill.

There are generally two ways to invoke a full-screen mode on iOS.

- For consumption-oriented apps, where a single tap on a typical piece of content doesn't do anything, you can take that gesture to mean "go full-screen." It's great, when you think about it, that we have a platform where the most basic gesture possible, tapping the middle of the screen, makes the interface go away.

- For editing-oriented apps, where tapping in the middle of the screen is likely to already have a meaning, you can provide a full-screen button, typically on a toolbar in the corner of the screen. Once full-screen mode is on, you may need to leave a tiny bit of chrome behind: a subtle "exit full-screen" button, which, as an exception to the usual advice for strong contrast, should blend into the background.

Taps Are Cheap

All this progressive disclosure and waiting for the right context to display things might sound like a lot of work for the user, ergonomically and cognitively. Tap to open the popover, tap to switch tabs, tap to go down a level, tap tap tap tap. It's tempting to count taps and try to minimize them in all cases. But that's thinking like a desktop designer, for whom counting mouse clicks really is important.

As it turns out, taps are much easier than clicks for the hand and for the mind. The process is as simple as seeing the thing and then poking the thing. You're not shoving a hunk of plastic around on a desk to satisfy an abstraction that says this little flea on the screen called a cursor represents your finger. You just use your finger directly.

So, as David Barnard of App Cubby put it, taps are cheap. Here's a cheat sheet for the number of taps you should expect an interaction to take.

- For crucial or common commands, sure, go ahead and make them available with one tap. (This includes selection, the Undo button, the Back button, and so on.)
- For normal commands, you can easily require twice as many taps as the number of clicks you would have required on the desktop (for changing fonts, exporting data, changing view settings, etc.).
- For rarely used commands—ones that people are likely to use about zero or one time in their entire careers of using your app—go crazy. Don't be afraid to hide them (setting up an account, connecting to an external service, or changing set-and-forget settings) behind lots of taps.

When you start second-guessing a decision to put something a bit out of the way, making the rest of your interface quieter, remember that taps are cheap. (But also remember that unless you have a home button of some sort, every tap to delve down a level comes with another tap later to get back out.)

Loud and Clear

Remember from Chapter 9, The Gracious Interface, that text is one of the loudest ways your interface can communicate. It's made entirely of contrasty little lines and curves, and the brain has no choice except to look at it and decode it. At the same time, it's hard to misunderstand, so it can be a major help in getting a point across when it's difficult to do so with an icon. The closer to the surface of your app a piece of text is, the louder it will seem.

The same goes for the principles of visual weight from Chapters 4 and 5. Elements with more visual weight, whether it comes from size, styling, or contrast, speak loudly. When those elements are on a screen closer to the surface, they start to shout. It's a good idea to turn down the volume on your visual design just a bit as you work on screens closer to the surface.

Finally, the amount of information in an element affects how much noise it introduces. Compare a progress bar to an indeterminate progress indicator (or "spinny"). A progress bar visually conveys a ratio of completion to total time, offering more information but simultaneously demanding more of the user's cognitive effort to decipher it. A spinny, on the other hand, conveys one bit of information: the fact that work is in progress. For processes of reasonable length, that's usually all that matters. When you're choosing elements, think about whether the user really needs all the information you're feeding her or whether you could choose a quieter way of communicating.

Making SnackLog Quiet

The design for SnackLog, as it has been presented so far, is pretty quiet, as shown in the following descriptions of each screen and in Figure 12.4.

- **Capture screen**—Assuming we don't go ahead with the whole tagging feature, the only controls are the number pad, the Purchases button, and the price placeholder. The idea of including an Undo button was nixed to keep the design quieter. Without it, users will need to venture to the Purchases screen in order to take back a capture. Considering how rare we expect accidental captures to be, it seems safe to cut this control.

- **Capture screen during capture**—While the user is entering a price, the top toolbar is populated with the price being entered and a Cancel button. Nothing

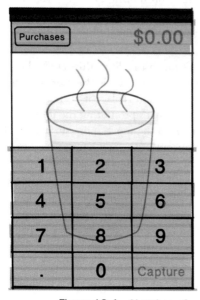
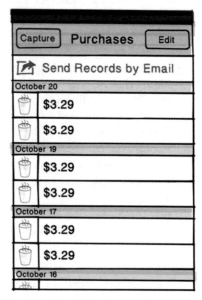

Figure 12.4   Sketches of a quiet approach to SnackLog's Capture and Purchases screens

to remove here. (We could go overboard on quiet and make tapping the price cancel the capture, but that's probably a bit too hard to discover.)

- **Purchases screen**—The top toolbar contains a Capture button for getting back to the Capture screen and an Edit button. Both are essential. In the purchases list, though, we have a choice of how to display each row. If we want to be especially quiet, we could show only the photo thumbnail and the price of each item; those two pieces of data are the only essential information about a purchase. If the user wants to see any further info, he'll need to delve into the item detail screen. Settings and Send are both relatively rare commands that can be safely buried. By moving the settings into the Settings app and incorporating the Send command into the table view, initially scrolled off the top, we eliminate the need for the bottom toolbar.

- **Item detail screen**—This screen is dedicated to showing as much information as there is to show, so quieting it down would not be very rewarding.

Making SnackLog Forthcoming

If you want to make SnackLog feel more professional, empowering, and informative, there are a few things you could do. Here is the screen-by-screen again, as illustrated in Figure 12.5.

- **Capture screen**—If you want to be extra-reassuring about the success of the capture process, you could add a partially transparent bar to the top of the camera view that summarizes the last purchase. That's promoting one item from the Purchases screen to the more surface-level Capture screen. At first, it seems to be almost certainly overkill, but, because recognition is much more reliable than recall, it might be a worthwhile feature.

- **Capture screen during capture**—There isn't much to add to this screen, but hiding the last-purchase indicator is probably a good idea while the user is in the middle of recording a new purchase. Perhaps you would replace it with a field for adding a title right at the moment of capture. That's promoting the item title feature all the way up from the item detail screen to the much more surface-level Capture screen. It gets away from the initial concept of the app being a no-fuss, quick-capture sort of experience, but it's helpful in its own way.

- **Purchases screen**—To be more informative, you could populate each row with as much data as possible: the photo thumbnail, title (or "Untitled Purchase" if a title hasn't been assigned), time, location, and price. You'd likely need to make each row bigger to promote all that information up from the detail screen. To go all out, you could even put a tiny map inside each row, centered on the location where the purchase happened.

- **Item detail screen**—This would remain unchanged, because its job is to show the full details of an item.

 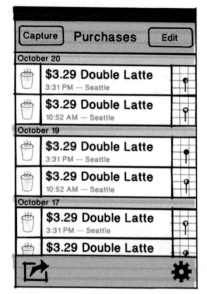

Figure 12.5   Sketches of a forthcoming approach to SnackLog's Capture and Purchases screens

Summary

The primary distinction between a quiet interface and a forthcoming interface is whether its functionality tends to be stacked in time or adjacent in space. iOS in general takes a progressive-disclosure approach, in which functionality is grouped by its meaning and then either promoted or demoted depending on its importance.

You can make an interface as quiet as possible by paying close attention to context. This means offering only what's immediately useful given the state of the app and the user's situation in it. Sometimes that means hiding some controls; sometimes it means hiding the interface entirely.

Exercises

Time to experiment with quiet and forthcomingness. Here are a couple of ways to explore the space between the two extremes.

1. Pick an Apple app or a well-designed third-party app. Walk through its interface, identifying the hierarchy of its experience. How does it progressively disclose its functionality? Can you put a clear label and description on each grouping?

2. Pick a feature (or a cluster of features) in your own app, and design the quietest and most forthcoming variants of it you can. The forthcoming variant will probably involve placing an awkward version of the feature on the surface screen of your app, and that will probably be terrible and hilarious. Do it anyway, just to see whether it inspires any unexpected insights.

13

Friction and Guidance

Now that you have a grasp of the ways an app can be simple or complex, it's time to get back to thinking about the interaction between the app and the user. This chapter is about how to influence the user's behavior toward or away from certain interactions and help her find her way through the app.

From a standpoint totally naïve to software design, it may seem as if you would want to make every interaction as easy as possible. Why should anything be more difficult than necessary? The "everything one or two clicks away" approach that the desktop took for years, as you saw in Chapter 12, takes that position.

The answer is that not all interactions a user can have with software are equally consequential. Part of the responsibility of a designer is to guide the behavior of the user by modulating the attractiveness of each interaction at each step.

The Difficulty Curve

The amount of cognitive and physical effort a task requires is sometimes called **friction.** A single tap on an obvious target—for instance, to launch an app—is probably the most frictionless interaction possible on iOS (although you could argue instead in favor of some accelerometer-based input like a tilt). In contrast, on the frictiony end, tasks like setting up a VPN (virtual private network) connection require a great many taps, a lot of scrolling around, and entering highly specific strings of text.

You can draw a curve that represents how complex a task is versus how much friction it incurs. On the desktop, the curve has traditionally been rather flat, with introductory tasks being moderately difficult, and the most involved tasks being only somewhat more difficult. A famous Alan Kay quotation, taken way out of context, seems to embody the desktop spirit: "Simple things should be simple; complex things should be possible."

iOS endeavors to tip that slope in favor of the most common tasks: the work that's been explicitly anticipated by the designers. In exchange, the complex stuff becomes not difficult, but impossible. That's a meaningful thing to realize: part of the reason iOS feels welcoming and easy to use is that a huge pile of stuff that the desktop has been keeping on the table as viable has now been swept off the table.

In Figure 13.1, the three shaded areas represent three tasks you might want to attempt using iOS or a desktop system.

- **Task A**—"I want to send an email to my cousin Steve." Not too taxing on a desktop system. And because it's a common, anticipated use of the system, it's dead simple on iOS.

- **Task B**—"I want to make a spreadsheet of my mortgage." Fairly difficult no matter where you attempt it. But because it's right within the recommended uses of Apple Numbers, your experience will be comparable on either platform.

- **Task C**—"I want to run a protein-folding simulation in the background and pipe the output to Twitter." You can actually do this on the desktop, given enough determination. On iOS, though, Apple has decided that it's OK for this sort of thing to be impossible.

Eliminating the ability to do esoteric, nerdy stuff is part of what has allowed the system to be approachable for the typical user. Generally speaking, iOS tends to prioritize the typical user's experience over the expert's. Some people argue that this approach does a disservice to people who like to experiment and tinker with technology, in the frontier spirit that characterized the first few decades of personal computers. But that view assumes everyone wants to and can tinker with their technology rather than just rely on it to work.

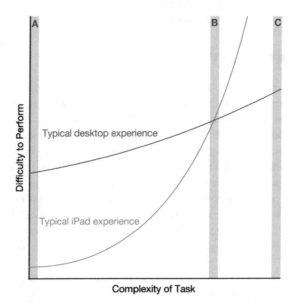

Figure 13.1 The slope of the difficulty curve is much steeper on iOS, leading to dead-simple interactions at the introductory end and impossible ones at the complex end.

The criticism aimed at iOS is that it's a walled garden, where the apps are supervised and where people aren't allowed to explore all of what's technically possible with the devices they own. That's true; unless you're a developer deploying your own code locally, everything that runs on an iOS device needs to come through the App Store.

But a locked-down system, where apps live in their own sandboxes and every bit of code has been centrally approved, makes the "It just works" reliability quite a bit more realistic. If you're a lawyer or a vintner or a bicycle mechanic or a zookeeper, chances are you want your iPad or iPhone to just be as reliable as possible and help you do your job, maybe providing some diversion and relaxation when you're finished. For tinkerers, there's always the desktop or the possibility of building their own iOS apps for personal use.

Experience Weight

All right, time to talk about how to control that curve yourself. Just as each element on the screen has visual weight, each interaction has **experience weight.** Lighter-weight tasks are smaller on the screen and quicker to perform, feel more casual, and seem to be sanctioned or expected by the designer as a mundane part of the typical workflow. Heavier-weight tasks are bigger and feel more momentous, but they don't necessarily feel as if they're straying outside the intent of the app. They communicate to users that something significant is happening and that they might want to pay attention.

Any interaction you design has natural built-in friction that's usually appropriate for the task. But in some cases, the amount of friction may not be in line with the consequences. A task might be tedious and tortured but yield almost no significant effect; or a command as simple as tapping the toolbar button right under your thumb might actually have very consequential results. You can adjust the amount of friction and guidance to add weight to an interaction or to make it feel less weighty.

In iBooks, for instance, it feels lightweight to place a bookmark. Tap the monochrome, flat bookmark button in the toolbar area, and it's replaced by a similar-looking red bookmark icon having texture and depth. Tap it again, and it goes away. There's almost nothing to it, and that's good, because placing a bookmark should be a casual and commonplace thing with little effect on your reading experience.

But switching from the library view to the store view (the two personalities of the app, as described in Chapter 3, Getting Familiar with iOS) is a fairly big deal. The entire interface of the app is swept up in a long, fancy animation to communicate that you're going to a different place, one filled with books you could buy rather than books you already own. That weighty transition feels right, because it signifies a shift in the entire purpose of the app.

Why Add Friction?

Sometimes, you need to add friction. Why would you want to make a task more difficult than it needs to be? It's because it could very well end in sadness. As happy as software can make people, it can make them equally unhappy when it fails or does something unintended. Now is another time to think about the worst-case scenario. Here are the main situations that justify adding a bit of extra safety.

- **Data destruction**—Whenever the user could lose work because of an action he's taking, that's a great time to add friction. Personal computers have been asking us for decades whether we really want to delete files, whether we really want to close without saving, and whether we really want to reformat the hard drive. (Unfortunately, we've become so accustomed to clicking through other, more frivolous confirmations that we often breeze through these without thinking, too.) It's good to make extra sure before destroying data. Note well that "data" is a broad term, encompassing anything the user has done that would take a significant amount of work to re-create—from documents all the way to the six-field form he just spent 90 seconds filling out.

- **Significant functionality changes**—Something like switching the cloud service you're syncing your documents to might not *destroy* any data, but it makes a big difference in how the app works. Making a change that big isn't suited to an innocuous little toggle in a toolbar. It deserves a dedicated screen with some *gravitas,* some icons for the various services, and probably some explanatory text about the ramifications of cavalierly changing sync services.

- **Annoying others**—Some apps, especially ones that are communication oriented or include social features, have the potential to bother not only the user but also other people in her life. Anything that could send data to other people, especially automatically, should require an appropriate amount of intent. (A breakdown of this sort is apparent in how easy it is in iOS to have a shared calendar automatically set as your default Siri reminders repository, thus causing all your coworkers to get "Remember to buy tickets for the Rush concert" alerts. Just as a totally hypothetical example.)

- **Embarrassing the user**—Accidentally sharing something you didn't mean to can be mortifying. A communication app that's all too eager to start a video chat because you simply tapped on a contact is one example. If you notice in time, you have to scramble to cancel the call before your colleague sees you in your bathrobe. A more subtle case occurs when an app allows the user to post to Twitter or Facebook about something he's viewing in the app but doesn't show the full text of the post before it's sent; there's often some sort of ad for the app itself included in the post. Showing the text of the tweet beforehand, and letting the user make the decision for himself, is the right thing to do.

How to Add Friction

In cases like those, it's great to have a bit of friction to slow down the user before something regrettable happens. As she undertakes a task, if it feels as if the process is resisting her a bit, she may second-guess whether she really wants to go through with it. Here are some things that add friction to an interaction, thus giving the user a bit of a speed bump and getting her to think for a moment about what she's doing.

- **Add more steps**—Forgiving accidental or exploratory taps by requiring confirmation is the classic source of intentional friction, described in the Forgiveness section of Chapter 9, The Gracious Interface. Tapping a toolbar button and then the action sheet that appears is one more step than simply tapping the button, and it gives users an extra moment to change their minds (or take back an accidental tap).

- **Bury it**—If it takes a few steps to even get to the feature, it of course feels further from the surface and thus less recommended as part of a normal workflow. Delving down a level in a navigation controller to a screen dedicated to the option makes it feel bigger, especially if that screen presents a single choice.

- **Require more-involved gestures**—The very first iPhone interaction Steve Jobs showed off was "slide to unlock"; here, the friction is literal. If there were a simple Unlock button, requiring only a simple tap, it would be too easy to invoke it accidentally. Instead, you have to really want to unlock the phone.

- **Make a big deal out of it visually**—This can work either way. Depending on the cues you use, drawing attention to a single element can make it more attractive, as discussed later. But using warning cues such as coloring a button red, using the trash can icon, or otherwise giving off a destructive or dangerous vibe usually makes the user think twice. "Make it look scary" is a common, if exaggerated, line among designers.

- **Put it among other visually weighty options**—Even if you don't use scary cues, because there's no data at risk, you can indicate significant functionality changes by giving all the choices additional visual weight. Anything that increases visual weight works, such as using colorful icons in addition to ordinary text labels. (See Chapter 5, The Mockups, and Chapter 15, Rich and Plain, for ways to control visual weight.) If all of several alternatives have a heavier presentation, as in the sync location setting described previously, the choice between them seems more significant (see Figure 13.2).

Unintended Friction

Keep an eye out for unnecessary friction in experiences that you're not trying to discourage users from taking lightly. Designers have become masterful at smoothing out processes by looking for steps that can be skipped and work that can be put off, especially up front when a user is getting familiar with an app.

For example, think of account setup: five years ago, any new web-based service you signed up for might require your name and email address, a username, a password, a password *confirmation,* and possibly payment info, before you could even start exploring.

Figure 13.2   A sketch of three approaches to the same screen. The first (left) is as simple as possible, with no indication of the gravity of the choice. The second (middle) adds more visual weight and explanation for each option, making the choice seem more significant. The third strongly emphasizes the importance of the decision using a unique layout with big, weighty icons and a textual explanation.

That's a lot of friction up front, and it certainly scared away plenty of potential users who didn't have the patience to wade through it just to try the thing out.

In a well-designed up-to-date web service, especially one that revolves around an iOS app, the sign-up can be as simple as an email address field. Designers have learned that for many services, none of that other stuff is necessary up front.

- Your email address probably works fine as a username. You can't forget it, and it's guaranteed to be unique. No separate username is needed.

- Your email is also likely to be among the more private ways of communicating with you. As long as you promptly hit the confirmation link in the email the site sends you, the sender knows it's yours. That means it can also automatically log you in the first time and send you an email with a link to set a password at your leisure. Two more annoying fields gone. (There are, of course, lots of security implications to consider before choosing a signup process for a service; this is only an idealized example.)

- A name, address, or any other personal information doesn't have much to do with setting up your account, so it can be entered later if it becomes necessary. Some services might let you browse and participate with only an email address but require a full name before you start posting content yourself. There go the rest of the fields.

- Some services can even use your Facebook or Twitter account as your credentials, so as long as you trust them enough to link your account, you don't need to enter any information at all. The app simply hands you off to a confirmation screen, where you can choose to allow or deny access.

This trend isn't only about designers getting better at what they do. It's also that designers are being given more say in how systems are built. In this way, they can influence the entire user experience design, rather than apply a thin film of user interface design to a technical system that's already been built.

You might not be setting up a fancy web service with an account setup process to polish. But you can see how the typical signup experience has become smoother over the years and has captured casual users who would have given up on a more demanding process. When you're dealing with a crucial, central experience like that, and it must be as painless as possible, think about whether you can do some extra design and development work to make things easier for the user.

Don't Expose Underlying Mechanisms

Avoid interfaces that simply expose the underlying mechanisms of the software. It's easy to take the engineer's understanding of a beautifully crafted hunk of code and simply reproduce it in the form of controls laid out on a screen. (Especially if you're the engineer!) But you need to strike a balance between presenting (a) a representation of the system that's accurate enough to be predictable and (b) one that your audience can develop a mental model of. That's why, for example, email clients provide sensible, understandable layouts with conveniences like address book lookup and conversation threading, rather than simply tossing a list of messages on the screen, with all the raw headers on each message.

In short, users often benefit most from an idealized portrayal of reality that's accurate enough for their needs. It's like what a subway map does, abstracting away a lot of irrelevant geographical minutiae to help you get to your station with minimal fuss.

So go back to your outlines (or make new ones) to review the goals of each feature and identify how you can serve them with your design. You can't ignore the technical implementation that's going on behind the scenes, of course, because it affects what's realistic for the design. But you should put it out of your mind enough to start from an ideal, implementation-naïve design and then work toward a realistic compromise. Aim to tell a consistent, understandable story that gives users the information and options that are actually interesting and useful to them, omitting the information and options that aren't.

Streamline Input

When you can, reduce the amount of input you require. Usually, you wouldn't add unnecessary input to a workflow, but if it's there, you should know that it's usually a significant source of friction in the user's mind.

Notice that even in Notes, an app whose whole point is entering and manipulating text, users aren't required to type a title for each note. Instead, the first line of a note is appropriated as its title. If users care to name it, they can type a title there on the first line. If they'd rather get to the point of the note, then whatever text the note happens to start with will become its title. That gives people who want titles the opportunity to create them, but without a need for a separate field.

Similarly, lots of times you can automatically log metadata like time and location to help people organize items later. That's why you can view your photos in so many different ways in iPhoto (events, places, faces) without ever doing any manual data input or organization.

Guidance

The counterpart to putting friction between the user and a possibly undesirable outcome is to guide the user toward a happy outcome. There are ways to lay down grooves in your app that guide people toward a certain destination without necessarily forcing them there. Really great guidance can help a user who doesn't understand or care about the vision of an app to bumble through anyway and get it to do its thing. *Assume incorrect usage,* and create an experience that works anyway.

Zero Options

Before iOS, software had a habit of requiring users to make important, data-imperiling decisions but keeping them secret until the last second. You'd create a document, work on it for several hours, and then, when you were ready to call it a night, try to quit the app. All this time, the system had been unsure whether you actually wanted to save your work and had been putting off asking you. When you quit, it finally asked, Save or Cancel? At this moment, you were one click away from discarding everything you did all evening.

On iOS, there is no decision. The system makes the totally sane assumption that when you create a document, you intend to keep it. If that's the case, then you can at your own leisure decide to give the document a name. If not, you're free to delete it. (See Figure 13.3)

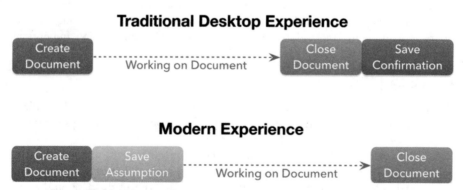

Figure 13.3   iOS and the modern Mac OS X no longer defer the question of whether to save your work until the last minute. Instead, they remove the question and assume you always want to save your work.

That's a powerful lesson. When the situation is that clear, take the opportunity to eliminate the choice. Rather than ask the user to make a decision one way or the other, the system simply makes the safer assumption. Then it allows the user to take an explicit action if she actually intended otherwise. The result is a non-option that requires zero input, and thus there is no incorrect choice.

Manual Autosave

The state of document management on the desktop got people into the habit of ritualistically hitting Command-S every time they made the slightest change to their document, just in case. Make a change, ⌘-S. Make another change, ⌘-S. I call this "manual autosave."

Whenever anyone lost work, it seemed it was his own fault for not saving often enough, as if it should be the user's job to remember to mechanically poke that key combination every 30 seconds or so. But, in fact, when software encourages such automatic behavior on the part of the user, it's a sign that the software is failing to do part of its job. Automatic and repetitive actions are exactly what computers excel at. Look for such automatic behaviors as opportunities for your app to take pressure off the user.

The pitfall for apps that automatically take care of maintenance tasks like saving or syncing is when users miss doing it manually. If people start asking for a button to hit, it could be a sign that they don't trust the automatic process. Maybe it has failed them once or twice, and unreliable automation feels worse than no automation at all. Then it may be time to improve the automatic process until it's rock solid and provide persistently visible feedback (such as an inelegant but reassuring last-saved timestamp) that the process is working—or to give up and add the button.

One Option

When there's only one sensible next step, it often makes sense to go ahead and choose it automatically. If you're navigating to a screen that consists mainly of a big text field, go ahead and have the keyboard already up when you get there. If the first action after creating a document is always to add an item and start editing it, have the item already there and in editing mode when the document is created. And so on.

There's an exception to this guideline. When you prefer to educate the user a bit about a step, because it's not always the only option, then you shouldn't take that step automatically. And when the step is actually kind of fun, you might not want to deprive the user of it.

Diet Coda, the iPad web editor from Panic, contains a perfect example, on both the education and the fun counts. The very first time you launch Diet Coda, the only thing on the screen is the big, inviting Add Site button (see Figure 13.4). The designers could have dropped you right into the site setup form sheet, but instead they give you the satisfaction of making that first monumental tap and watching the cute

Figure 13.4   Diet Coda's initial state is as simple and understated as can be. This experience elegantly guides you straight to the one option available.

animation as the button curls toward you and becomes the sheet. They've also taught you how the site browser works, so that when the time comes you can confidently set up your *second* site.

Guidance among More Options

Occasionally, there are several legitimate options, but you want to gently nudge the user toward one. Without guidance, software can feel to users like a series of intimidating, or at least tiresome, decision points. When they step through the screens of your app, users need to consider all the branches at each step, at least momentarily. The buttons on an action sheet or alert, the chevron-bearing cells of a table view, the tabs in a popover—all of them ask the user to make a decision about where to head next. But people should be able to rely on software to have a decent idea of what comes next rather than constantly ask them to choose between several equivalent-looking options.

Here's a guideline for how to treat each option at a decision point depending on how likely it is to be the right choice.

- **75% or more**—An option this common deserves to be preferred somehow. See the next bulleted list for ways to guide users toward it.

- **10–75%**—A "normal" option, which can be treated normally.

- **10% or less**—At around 10%, you should start considering axing the option. If it's rarely chosen but still crucial, you can probably bury it elsewhere rather than require users to step around it every time. See Chapter 12 for information about demoting less-important elements.

Here are ways you can guide people to what's likely the right choice.

- Make a big deal out of it visually. Earlier you saw how to use warning cues to guide users away from a choice or make all the options of a choice seem equally significant. But you can also use inviting cues to guide them toward a single option: people are eager to hit big, shiny, vividly colored (especially blue or green) controls, with positive labels like "Connect," "Go," or "Done." (The converse is that people love to hit "Cancel" as an all-purpose get-out-of-trouble button, but you should not make it too easy to hit Cancel accidentally.)

- Make it easily accessible. People are more inclined to mash controls that fall within the thumb field (described in Chapter 8, The Graceful Interface) or toward the bottom of screens or views in general. When users step rightward through a procession of screens, buttons that appear on the right or that seem to suggest rightward motion (as with an arrow) are more attractive.

- Pick a sensible default. In a lot of cases, rather than ask, you can simply pick the recommended option and allow the user a chance to change it. In the Photos app on iPad, when you use the Share button to send a photo app via email, it automatically chooses a size for you; you can then tap the size indicator if you care to choose a different size. (See more about the way of the sensible default later in this chapter.)

- Skip steps. If users tend to take a certain fixed path through the experience, you can make them happy by promoting that common choice upward to a more surface level. The classic, delightful example of this is the famous "Use Last Photo Taken" button (see Figure 13.5). One day Neven Mrgan (a designer at Panic) noticed that whenever he attached a photo to a tweet, it was almost always the last one he took. So why don't Twitter clients offer "Use Last Photo Taken" alongside the "Take Photo or Video" and "Choose from Library" buttons on the action sheet? The folks at Tapbots promptly recognized the good sense of the idea and did just that in their next version of Tweetbot. It makes the action sheet slightly noisier, but in exchange it saves a brain-taxing couple of steps almost every time you attach a photo. This is a triumph of recognizing the way humans actually use a piece of technology, rather than sternly insisting on a strictly logical system.

Figure 13.5   Tweetbot's Use Last Photo Taken button is a triumph of recognizing how people actually use technology.

Sensible Defaults

It used to be that you could get away with shipping the *ability* to create something cool but not going out of your way to make it particularly easy. For example, consider desktop presentation software. When Apple Keynote first came out, part of its appeal was the tastefulness and good design sense of its included templates. You could conceivably have made nearly identical-looking presentations in Microsoft PowerPoint if you really knew what you were doing, but the point was that with Keynote, you didn't have to. You could focus on developing the content of your presentation rather than on getting it to look professional and attractive. That's a boon to people who don't fancy themselves designers or who don't want to have to act as designers all the time. (Yves Peters of The FontFeed calls those people who have good taste but who don't obsess over details "office users.")

PowerPoint was famous instead for giving people bad guidance: easy access to all manner of ill-advised design decisions like overwrought animations, sound effects, and clip art, thus making their presentations worse than if there were no defaults at all.

Division of Labor: An Anthropological Interlude

For centuries, the division of labor has been recognized as one of the positive feedback loops that make civilization possible. (Jared Diamond compellingly lays out the mechanisms of civilization in *Guns, Germs, and Steel,* if you're interested.) The hyper-simplified explanation goes like this.

Everyone living in a hunter-gatherer band must develop a broad mix of skills to survive. But in a settled society, work can be split up. If you're a blacksmith and you can count on the farmers to farm and the potters to make pottery, then you have more time to get better at smithing. Everyone benefits most when each person has the maximum time and energy to devote to a craft that he then shares with everyone else. You can go DIY and take up pottery as a hobby if you like, and some people may even develop a new skill to a professional level, but chances are that the pots you get from the life-long potter will be better. The point is that you shouldn't *have* to set aside your anvil and study the craft of pottery in order to have a nice bowl.

The division of labor has quite a lot to do with the philosophy of software design. Consider how much time and energy you as a designer have put into figuring out how your software should work and what kind of content it can create. It's possible but unlikely that a random user will know, or care, as much as you do. A few users will care quite a lot and will consider learning the intricacies of your app, and the domain that your app deals in, to be part of their job or a compelling hobby. But for the rest, they shouldn't have to invest as much as you have in order to benefit from your product. Part of your job is to build your expertise into the app, in the form of the guidance and sensible defaults described in this chapter.

The Blank Slate

The first level of sensible defaults is the basic initial state of your app and whatever content it creates. If your app has preferences, what are their initial settings? If your app creates documents, what does a freshly created blank document look like? The goal here should be to come up with a set of defaults that provides the most reasonable experience for the most people.

The Holy Grail is defaults that work well enough that most users will never need to adjust them or even to know they exist. But then when people do find themselves wishing the app worked slightly differently, they should be able to pop open and peruse the various options and make the adjustment they need.

It's easy to put together your own data during your beta period and forget about that blank slate experience. Here are ways to make sure you're paying attention to your blank slate.

- Take the time to set up a dedicated device (or at least the iOS Simulator) that you can wipe clean regularly and test the first-run experience.

- For any state you think should be easily achievable (such as your basic use cases from your outlines and your common and interesting use cases from Chapter 11, Focused and Versatile), walk through the process necessary to get there from the blank slate. Could a typical user get there from here by following a series of reasonable, obvious steps? Or do some of the steps count on your special knowledge as a designer? If you can't realistically imagine a user getting there on her own, you probably need to build more guidance into the app.

- If you find yourself constantly turning on certain settings or walking through certain steps every time you start from a blank slate, consider whether they should be the default settings in the first place. Or at least explore whether you can make the steps more obvious and easier to take.

- The "blank" template counts. There isn't such thing as a blank template; when you create a new document and start drawing or typing, *something* has to appear there, and you have to decide what that something will look like. What is the default font? What are the size and shape of the default paintbrush, shape tool, or whatever other content-creation tool you provide? You should pay extra attention to what people get when they say they don't want any prefabricated content, because the characteristics you decide on there define the neutral state of the content your app creates.

Templates

Almost any app that creates content can benefit from templates. The Keynote templates previously mentioned have evolved over time to continue offering brand-new users and experts alike a set of tasteful, modern, versatile starting points for their work (see Figure 13.6). The other iWork apps do the same: Pages and Numbers both ask you every time you create a new document whether you'd like to start from a blank document or use a template. That premade content is an excellent way to cram some of your own hard-earned knowledge and expertise about the app's problem domain into a format that benefits users.

Your templates and sample data work both as starting points for real documents and as exhibits of what the app can do. You should put the same amount of visual design and information design care into them as you would into the most important marketing materials your organization publishes. Self-aware placeholder data ("Some Name" or "$0.00") tends to look lazy, so put in the effort to create realistic data (like Apple's famous "Johnny Appleseed" and "$3.29"). Some apps, such as Pages, even go to the trouble of identifying placeholder data and highlighting the entirety of a paragraph of it for easy replacing.

Presets

When you walk into a paint store, they don't just have a little form that you fill out with numbers and then hand over to have your paint mixed. They have walls and walls of cards printed with carefully balanced and paired color swatches, each with an evocative and memorable name. They have booklets of color scheme ideas. They have bits of trim exhibiting the various sheen levels so that you can see what the heck "eggshell" really looks like.

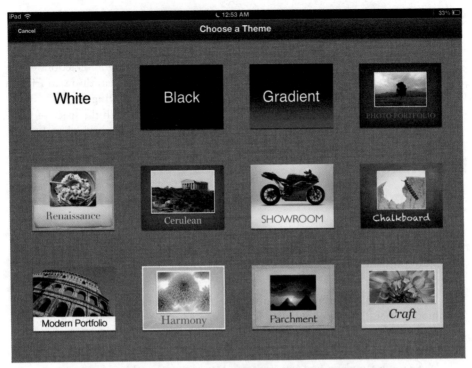

Figure 13.6   Keynote's templates are a key part of its success, because
people love being able to create professional-looking content without
needing to become professional designers first.

Presets are great because people love having something they can point to and say, "That's kinda what I want," rather than having to build it themselves. From there, either they can decide that the preset is close enough, or they can customize it further. It's especially helpful to provide content presets that work well together: it can be intimidating to build color schemes, font ensembles, and audio tracks from scratch, but it's great fun to assemble them from carefully curated suggestions. When left on their own with the vast space of possibilities, people often get frustrated at having so much power and so little guidance.

The better the presets you provide, the more likely it is you can get away with providing only presets. Pages happily offers 24 flat colors, 6 gradients, 6 textures, and 5 grays as the only choices for object fills. This limits possibilities and keeps users focused on their text, at the price of a bit of a letdown when they want a fill that's not included. Other apps compete on versatility by including full-on color sliders in addition to their presets. Finding a balance between full control and assured simplicity is part of your design job.

Summary

For each interaction in your app, find the right degree of ease, which isn't necessarily "as easy as possible." You have several tools at your disposal to make interactions easier or harder, and to make them seem heavier or lighter-weight. You can throw in friction to slow users taking a potentially dangerous step, meanwhile removing friction from common and safe actions. You can help users find their way through the space of possibilities that your app offers by giving them expert guidance and sensible defaults.

Exercises

Try these exercises to practice modulating the amount of friction and guidance in a real app.

1. Pick an interaction in an existing app that you think might benefit from a bit of extra friction. (Wouldn't it be nice if it were a little harder to accidentally send an unfinished text message or email?) Sketch out how you would slow users down.

2. Do the same thing in the other direction: find an interaction that's slower and more difficult than it should be. Sketch some ways you could smooth it out. Can you think of any good reasons it's designed as frictiony as it is? Or is your smoother approach actually better?

3. Make some templates and some presets. If you're not working on a content-creation app yourself, pick an existing one. Build some impressive documents and some top-notch modular bits of content that people could use as starting points for realizing their own ideas.

14

Consistency and Specialization

In *The Elements of Typographic Style,* Robert Bringhurst lays down decades' worth of definitive, authoritative advice on the topic of typography. But before launching into his catalog of the rules and commandments every designer must know, he offers this encouragement: "By all means leave the road when you wish. That is precisely the use of a road: to reach individually chosen points of departure." As it is with type, so it is with software. Much of your quest as a designer will be to find the right times to stick to the road, and the right times to step off it.

No app is an island. An app exists within a landscape of Apple apps and third-party apps, each of which has its own ideas about how to get things done. However useful someone finds your app, she'll probably spend most of her time in other people's apps. Whatever decisions you make about your own design need to coexist with the decisions of hundreds of other designers you've never met. It's kind of a miracle that it all works out, but for the most part, it does.

How It All Works Out

It all works out because designers pursue **consistency** by following guidelines, conventions, and trends. App design is not a wild frontier where everyone fends for himself, each inventing his own design methods independently. We learn from each other. The layers of consistency on which we learn from each other form a sort of milieu (see Figure 14.1).

The basic guidelines document that you're expected to be familiar with is, of course, Apple's *iOS Human Interface Guidelines.* Everyone is presumed to be starting from that common ground, and each of us can decide when and how to diverge from it.

Next, conventions have existed for some time in the desktop and web worlds and often make good sense to follow on iOS. Such conventions aren't necessarily explicitly delineated by the HIG, but there's a common understanding of how they work. This layer includes everything from the common practice of touching and holding an item to "lift" it up, to the entire concept of selection.

Figure 14.1 The zeitgeist of design can be seen as a pyramid, with each layer's relative size representing roughly how much weight it should carry in your decisions. The guidelines form the foundation; conventions build on top of the guidelines; trends build on top of the conventions; and specialization hovers above it all as something to use in moderation when the situation warrants it.

Finally, there are more or less well accepted trends that emerge as individual iOS designs hit upon patterns that work well, and others adopt them. Sometimes, competing patterns exist, and you need to decide which of them suits your app best. This decision can be as minor as using a gear to represent settings or as major as putting a toolbar along the left edge rather than the top or bottom.

All these sources of inspiration and precedent are the reason you need to devour as much design as you can: the more inspiration you expose yourself to, the better you'll understand, and make use of, the zeitgeist. The better you know the platform, the more ideas you'll have to draw on and the more you'll understand how well each one fits among the other apps out there. People who care about their own apps are known to buy whole home-screens' worth of apps without any intention of using them, just to see how other designers are solving problems.

On the other side of the slider from consistency is **specialization:** the innovations you bring to your app that are unique, or at least distinctive, from other apps. Your specialized designs may solve problems that no one else has yet run into, thus making you the first designer to ship a solution. Or they may consciously run counter to the existing solutions because you genuinely think your idea is better.

Getting the Most Out of the HIG

Chapter 3, Getting Familiar with iOS, enjoins you to study the *iOS Human Interface Guidelines,* known affectionately among designers as "the HIG." It's essential to be familiar with the HIG, to understand its recommendations and rules, and to refer to it often. But one thing you shouldn't do is follow it like scripture.

There's a good reason they're called guidelines. Apple recognizes, possibly better than anyone, that software design is not a process you can succeed at by following strict rules. Every situation is different. Every app is unique. The work of design requires a balance between adventurousness and adherence. So Apple couldn't possibly put together a document that would definitively describe a watertight process to turn requirements into an app. (Neither can this book.)

Much of your skill as a designer comes in the form of understanding when to stick to the guidelines and when to diverge from them. Sometimes it makes sense to eschew more general guidelines such as "Restrain your information hierarchy" if the app you're working on benefits from a more detailed hierarchy. But it never, ever makes sense to ignore the specific rules such as how to make standard controls behave predictably; don't abuse those switches, date pickers, and segmented controls. You also need to either interpret the more abstract guidelines (such as "Enable collaboration and connectedness") in a way that's meaningful for your app, or recognize them as not applicable to your app.

And don't worry too much about committing a dreadful solecism. Some might complain that you used a horizontal swipe for something other than deletion. But that's like complaining about ending a sentence with a preposition. The practice doesn't actually do any harm; it's only a bit of rules folklore that people like to perpetuate.

Apple Agrees

At Apple's Worldwide Developers Conference, you can reserve a time at the User Interface Design Labs to discuss your UI with an Apple designer. It's an invaluable chance to get your app in front of someone from the mother ship who's as well equipped as almost anyone on the planet to give you good design advice. In 2008, the year the App Store launched, some colleagues and I brought our first iPhone app to the lab for feedback.

As we explained our decisions so far and asked our questions, we kept referring to the HIG. "We thought about laying out this screen like this, but the HIG said..." and, "We did this because the HIG recommended it..."—the HIG this and the HIG that. After a while the Apple designer stopped us and said, "Hey, why do you care so much about the HIG? The HIG is for when you don't know what you're doing. *You guys* don't need to worry about it so much."

That was a bit of a wake-up call for us to stop trusting the guidelines more than we trusted our own instincts. When in doubt, turn to the HIG. But hopefully you're not *always* in doubt.

The Consistent Design

Consistency has long been one of the most fundamental goals of software design. The default understanding is that a user approaching a new piece of software should be able to trust that it will look and behave more or less like other software he has encountered on the same platform. (See Figure 14.2 for a counterexample.) Layouts that look similar should communicate similar information, controls should work uniformly wherever they appear, and movement around the app should be internally sensible. Here are examples.

- Table cells are always self-contained and are almost always interactive in some way. It would be bizarre to see a table in which each cell was used to display a line of explanatory text.

- Standard iOS switches always have two states: on and off. If you were to create a switch that looked just like the standard one but included a third position in the middle, users would be surprised indeed. If you need a three-position setting and if a segmented control or three-cell table view with checkmarks won't do, the control you design should look different enough from the standard switch that people don't mistake it for one.

- A link, indicated by a different font style with an underline, is a way of taking a portion of ordinarily untappable text (such as explanatory labels or web views) and making it tappable. Links have no place in interactable controls like table cells.

- You know well that navigation controllers always put more-general screens to the left and show more-specific screens as you move rightward; and when a single screen has more information than can fit on the display, it scrolls vertically. An app that for some reason mirrored that architecture, moving from right to left, would feel alien. So would an app that put the more-general screens at the top and disclosed more detail as you move downward (unless it had a good reason to do so, with a well-thought-out and convincing visual presentation).

Figure 14.2   This mockup breaks every example listed in the text. Hopefully, you can see how wrong it feels to have text spanning between table cells, to have a link in a table cell, to use a switch as if it were a slider, and to have a back button pointing to the right.

If people needed to relearn from scratch how to use their devices every time they installed a new app, the result would be chaos, frustration, and abandonment. It's true that part of the appeal of iOS is that each app turns the entire iPhone or iPad into a device specifically for one task. But each of those virtual devices needs to feel that it draws on a coherent design philosophy.

Precedents, Motifs, Patterns, Shorthands

Contrary to the image that some people have of it, most software design isn't a matter of dreaming up innovative, utterly new experiences. Instead, it's finding the right precedents that exist in other apps, in the operating system, and occasionally even on web sites or other platforms. About 19 times out of 20, there is already a good solution out there for the design challenge in front of you.

Browsing documents, listing options, navigating hierarchies, moving objects around, enabling and disabling settings—all these things have been done in iOS itself or in official Apple apps. Other interactions have been done especially well in third-party apps; occasionally, Apple itself even appropriates those good ideas. This isn't stealing. It's good sense.

In general, it's smart to conform to precedents, especially those set by Apple. The iWork document browser in Figure 14.3 is an excellent example. If you're creating a

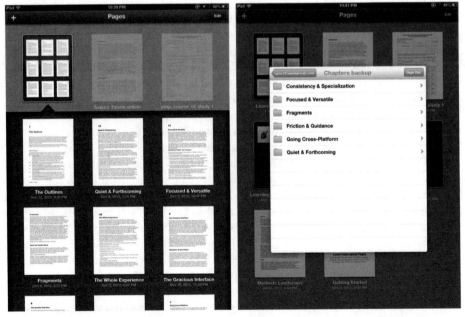

Figure 14.3   iWork has provided an excellent precedent for browsing local documents (on the left) and remote documents (on the right). Your app would need to be especially unique to diverge very far from its example.

productivity app that creates visually interesting documents, you would need to have a marvelously mind-blowing new design for file browsing to justify doing anything other than mimicking iWork's document browser. The reason is twofold.

First, when you follow precedents you save your users time and effort. Every inter-action in your app that looks familiar because they've already seen it in Mail, Settings, or iWork is an interaction they don't need to learn anew. Instead, they just jump in and use it. If instead you create your own unique way of doing the same task, then not only do people need to learn how to use it, but also they need to switch back and forth between the different ways as they move between your app and more conventional apps. As shown by the psychology concept of task-switching, adapting to a system that works differently from what you are used to incurs a cognitive cost.

One caveat: if the original interaction changes, you'll need to update yours to match. The iWork document browser started as a carousel that displayed one docu-ment at a time; later, Apple replaced it with a matrix of documents that made more efficient use of the screen real estate. For a while, all the apps that imitated the origi-nal design looked old-fashioned until they had a chance to catch up.

Second, when you follow precedents you save yourself time and effort. Getting a design right takes a lot out of you. If you recognize those 19 out of 20 times that there is a good precedent, you can spend that much more of your resources on the things that your app is uniquely *about,* the things that no one else has figured out before.

Believe this: you will have no shortage of new and interesting decisions to make as you work on your own product. You don't need to spend a lot of time second-guessing the ones that have already been made. If you focus on your own problem space, you'll get a better return on your investment of resources, and you'll make a better product.

While thinking about or discussing design ideas, you can use those precedents as shorthand for the sort of thing you're aiming to do. "We'll have a Mailesque sidebar over here," "This pane will act like the Wi-Fi setup in Settings," "This bar appears while you're editing, like the Favorites in Safari," and so on. There's no shame in Frankensteining bits of existing apps together, smoothing out the seams, and then finding ways to differentiate yourself, as a way to kick-start your creativity—especially if the core usefulness of your app is something that none of those original apps does.

Even if you follow a precedent, you're bound to find little ways that you can tailor it to your app's needs or make it a touch more convenient. Excellent! If you think you may have come up with an improvement, take time to ponder why the original design didn't include your idea in the first place. Take the other side, and try to find reasons your change might not work. Sometimes, a seemingly obvious convenience is not as clear a win as it seems. Other times, it's only a matter of taste, and yours might differ a bit from the original developer's. If it still seems like a good idea, then go for it.

In rare cases, you might have a revolutionary new solution for an existing prob-lem. Maybe you think you've come up with a dramatically better way to do, say, file browsing. Maybe it's so much better than what's out there that it's unequivocally worth the drawbacks listed here. Don't let this book stop you. If you're right, Apple might end up copying *you.*

Avoiding Cargo Cult Design

Of course, there's another side to following precedents, which is getting caught up in **cargo cult design.** In anthropology, a "cargo cult" is a primitive culture that has come into contact with a modern culture and has become preoccupied with imitating its trappings. The interesting part is that they do this without any understanding of how the modern culture actually works. It happened in World War II, when Allied forces occupied the land of native Pacific island folk who'd never made contact with outsiders before. After the soldiers left, some natives built faux military paraphernalia from wood and grass and reenacted the behavior of the soldiers in an attempt to summon back their materiel-rich friends.

Cargo cult design means imitating popular designs without understanding why they're successful. The quintessential example of cargo cult design is pull-to-refresh. Tweetie was the premier Twitter client for iPhone, developed by Atebits and introduced in 2008. One of Tweetie's signature innovations was that as you scrolled upward chronologically through tweets, when you hit the end you could attempt to drag upward past the newest tweet at the top of the timeline. A charming little animation indicated that dragging a certain distance beyond the top would trigger a refresh, loading newer tweets. It made use of the apparent intention to scroll beyond the topmost item: scrolling into the future. It's a brilliant, delightful design that exploits a gesture you would have naturally stumbled upon anyway, thus eliminating the need for a dedicated refresh button.

It rightfully got a lot of praise, and then the imitations began. For a while it seemed as if every app that had a refresh function adopted the pull-to-refresh gesture. But wait—they did it even if it wasn't the sort of refresh that loaded more items at the top of a list. Web browsers used it to reload a page, even though scrolling past the top of a web page to reload it seems unintelligible. Or they snapped the view back to its previous position, whether or not new content was loaded, requiring you to scroll *again* in order to see it. Eventually, pull-to-refresh started getting used for things other than refreshing. It no longer had anything to do with scrolling past the top of a list and was only a cute and trendy gesture that everyone wanted in on.

Apps that used the gesture without understanding why it was so clever in the first place? They were practicing cargo cult design. Don't do that. If you imitate, understand why you're imitating. If a cool design isn't appropriate for your app, resist the temptation to adopt it.

On Copycats

A lovely thing about the iOS development community is that when one of us hits upon a brilliant design idea, it's shared and celebrated. It's imitated, emulated, and built upon, and not reserved for exclusive use by its inventor. If your app's only competitive advantage is a list of interactions that you made up and that you insist no one else can use, it's unlikely to be a great app. Your pride should be invested in the *whole* of the app, possibly with clever new ideas woven organically into it. Your pride shouldn't lie in patented gimmicks that, if implemented verbatim by someone else, would eliminate the appeal of your app.

Steve Jobs was fond of an old quotation: "Good artists borrow; great artists steal." If you're merely good, you'll take something that someone else came up with and use it for your own purposes. But if you're truly great, you'll recognize the best ideas and *make them your own* by building them up to their true potential, far beyond what their originators imagined. Having your ideas borrowed is nothing to worry about.

But maybe someone really will try to "borrow" the entirety of your app, and not only an idea here and there. It's happened to an app that this author worked on, and I can tell you it's surreal to look upon an app that attempts to replicate your own work, to imagine some poor designer slaving away just to reproduce, as closely as possible, something you made. But in the end, a copy of a good app is not a good app. If the people who copied it were talented enough to accurately reproduce every graphic, implement the nuances of every interaction, and deal gracefully with every edge case, they wouldn't be borrowing. They'd be putting their talents toward *stealing* your ideas, adding their own genius, and turning them toward something great that could hold its own in the App Store. The competitors who do that are the competitors you should be contending with.

The Specialized Design

In the mid-2000s, the Mac was enjoying a huge surge in popularity among the general public, in large part because of the superb customer experience of the Apple Store, the cool image projected by Apple advertising, the compelling industrial design of the hardware, and the appealing visual design of the software. The Mac was the place to be for hip designers and developers looking to create something fresh and fashionable.

A wave of "shiny," hyped-up Mac apps appeared, combining the freeform creativity of web design with the richer, more expressive possibilities of native software. These apps were dubbed the "Delicious Generation" by Paul Kafasis of Rogue Amoeba, after the trendsetting app Delicious Library. They went beyond (or eschewed entirely) the interface design conventions of the Mac platform in favor of a more stylish presentation. Some of it was great fun; some of it was eye-rollingly pretentious at the expense of functionality or reliability. But even Apple itself began to stray a bit from the traditional Mac experience by experimenting with the interfaces in its iLife suite of apps, and especially with iTunes. Its own divergence from the guidelines seemed to be tacit approval of exploration beyond the expected.

When iOS arrived, the stage was set for it to be a platform that embraced a degree of distinctiveness and whimsy. The original set of official Apple apps included with iPhone covered a wide range of design ideas that start from a central theory but then set off in their own directions. From the inception of the App Store, iOS has welcomed and encouraged experimentation in the design of third-party apps. So some measure of new ideas is unsurprising in an iOS app, but the onus is on the designer to make sure the new ideas smartly fit the spirit of the platform.

Harmless Distinctiveness

At the surface level, there's a lot of purely stylistic customization you can do to an interface without harming its understandability or its congruence with iOS. For instance, certain elements like toolbars and navigation bars have always accepted a tint color, which is algorithmically applied to give them a distinctive flavor. Starting with iOS 5, most standard controls can also have a tint applied. Many can even have images swapped in to change their appearance without affecting their functionality.

An app like Find My Friends is a specimen of the way you can "skin" (an especially appropriate term in this case) standard controls with a unique style while maintaining their layout and behavior (see Figure 14.4). You have a lot of work to do to follow good visual-design principles such as maintaining proper contrast and tastefully making use of color and value, and your variants should still be recognizable as the original control. If you do a good job, this sort of customization is harmless and can give your app quite a lot of character without damaging its usability. (But as the reception of Find My Friends has shown, you run a higher risk of turning off users who find the whole thing too twee; see Chapter 15, Rich and Plain.)

Appearance customization is also useful for practical purposes. Imagery like the icons on the ends of a slider can communicate the purpose of a control (see Chapter 9, The Gracious Interface). Cues like color and texture can gently guide users toward or away from the control (see Chapter 13, Friction and Guidance).

Conscientious Divergence

Below the surface level, thinking about functional divergence is trickier. All other things being equal, it's a good idea to follow convention. That's because, in the absence of a unique situation, people like consistent experiences. But unique situations exist; there are times when the needs of your users call for behavior that diverges from the norm.

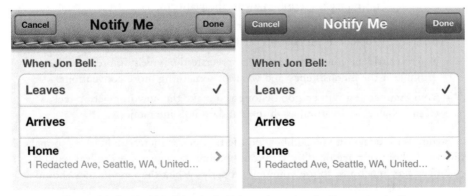

Figure 14.4   Find My Friends (left) is a showcase for the customization of standard controls. At right is a mockup of what the app would look like without any customization.

Messages is a prime example. The HIG unambiguously states, "Restore the state of the app to that in use when the user last stopped using the application." But what does Messages do when you launch it? If you've got a new text message, it takes you to that conversation rather than the last one you had open when you left it. The chances are excellent that you're more interested in reading the new message that came in ten minutes ago than in continuing the conversation you left last night. It's a clear case of the purpose of the app (semisynchronous, never-ending conversations with lots of people at once) overriding the usual tendency of people picking up where they left off. The beautiful thing is that most users never notice this inconsistency, because it serves their needs perfectly.

Other times, you have no choice except to break from convention. Although the HIG strongly recommends keeping settings separate from your app proper by putting them in the Settings app, it's not always possible to do so. The Settings app allows only a static list of standard controls and can't, for instance, show and hide controls based on the situation nor execute any code. If your app requires anything much more sophisticated than a column of dumb switches and text fields, you'll have to put your settings in the app. (And find a way to keep the settings button from making your interface too noisy.)

One Free Novel Interaction

Chapter 8 recommends sticking to the six reliable gestures (tap, drag/swipe, touch and hold, double-tap, pinch/unpinch, and rotate) and using exotic, undiscoverable gestures only as shortcuts. And Chapter 3 advises that it's always best to stick to either the standard controls, or custom controls that are closely modeled on them. Although each app requires unique solutions, you usually create them by slightly tweaking standard solutions.

All that advice still stands, but you can probably get away with introducing about one truly novel interaction per app. If all of the following are true, you may be in the right position to introduce something new to the platform.

- You believe it's the best way to solve the problem at hand, and not just a gimmick that people will smile at on the first run and scowl at by the tenth run.

- You're confident your audience will appreciate the novelty more than they grumble at the inconsistency and wish for something more conventional.

- Your engineering will be good enough to make the new interaction feel as clean, reliable, and natural as all the standard iOS interactions.

Each novel interaction you add beyond the first one is increasingly likely to make your app feel out of place on iOS. It's presumptuous to expect users to learn and remember very much just to use your app properly. When they use it, they shouldn't have to set aside the iOS knowledge they've gained from other apps. The more novelty you add, the more scrutiny your design will be subject to, and the more responsibility you have to make sure it's all impeccably conceived and implemented. See the next section about the dangers of going novel.

Here are some famously novel interactions from successful apps.

- Convertbot became famous for its custom dial control, which was unlike anything else on the system. Rather than pick from lists, you spin a dial to choose your conversion type and units. The resulting experience isn't necessarily more efficient or more accurate than poking buttons or table cells, but it's certainly more fun. Convertbot is specialized because it prioritizes novelty and delight. (Fun is a feature. Whether it is worth the extra effort to learn it is up to the individual user; some will prefer it, and others will look past it for something more conventional.)

- Paper, a sketching app, is known for its "rewind" gesture for undo. Because the personality of the app is so defined by its quiet interface (see Chapter 12, Quiet and Forthcoming) and by the speed of gesture-based input, there is no Undo button. Instead, the app asks that you learn one special gesture: put two fingers on the screen and move them in a circle counterclockwise, as if you are turning back time. To redo, you go clockwise instead. Paper is specialized to prioritize quiet and speed.

- Instapaper, an article-reading app, introduced a "tilt-to-scroll" mode. In this mode you don't even need to touch the screen in order to scroll; you just tip the device forward or backward, and the content gently scrolls in that direction. The idea is that tilting the device is less physically and mentally demanding than dragging on the screen, so you can pay more attention to the article you're reading. Because Instapaper is built around the concept of making reading as comfortable, effortless, and focused as possible, users welcome any slight improvement in ease. Instapaper is specialized to prioritize immersion.

- 1Password, an app for managing logins and other secure data, has a unique bottom bar. In one mode it's a tab bar, and in another mode it's a toolbar. Each mode has a horizontally draggable handle that you can slide to switch between the two modes. There is even a subtle animation of the screen toward or away from the user to emphasize that the horizontal movement is not the normal delving movement of a navigation controller. This scheme allows two faces of the app to coexist, with a quick way to switch between them. 1Password is specialized to prioritize speed.

- And of course, Tweetie gave us pull-to-refresh, described earlier. This decision combines several goals: it makes the UI quieter by removing the need for a reload button, it's efficient because it doesn't make you switch from scrolling to button-tapping when you hit the top of the timeline, and it's just a fun interaction. Tweetie was specialized for several complementary priorities.

All these interactions were unconventional when introduced, but adventurous users who were willing to learn found them pleasant and useful. But don't forget the many people who were inevitably turned off by them. Every decision attracts some people and deters others.

Novelty Is Hard

You can point to famous and successful apps that introduced their own novel ideas, and you can claim them as excuses to introduce lots of novelty into your own app. But it's easy to forget that those apps are the exception to the rule; most of us aren't as experienced, capable, and lucky as the designers and developers who pulled off those unique ideas. It's rare to hit upon a new idea that actually works wonderfully and that no one else has yet implemented to its full potential. (If it weren't, we'd have a new Beatles, a new Pink Floyd, or a new Nirvana every year.)

This isn't to say that you should never take a leap of faith on an original design idea that you believe in. But it is to say that succeeding with those original designs takes quite a lot more effort and luck than does a disciplined, standard design that solves an original *problem*.

Time for another irresponsibly oversimplified graph. Figure 14.5 shows the typical level of "output," meaning quality and success, you can expect to get from a given level of "input," meaning design resources, effort, and expertise.

As you can see, taking the standardized, predictable, consistent route yields a decent result even if your resources are scarce or your skills are fledgling. An app that correctly uses table views, switches, desaturated-blue toolbars, and navigation controllers to get its job done is hard to complain about. As your input gets better, your output steadily gets better, too. Consistency is safe; it's unlikely to offend anyone (although, yes, it's also unlikely to inspire anyone).

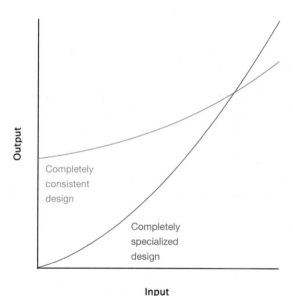

Figure 14.5   For a specialized design to be worthwhile, you need to put in a lot more effort and talent. Otherwise, it'll only hurt you.

The specialized route, on the other hand, is risky. Specialized apps with the lowest level of input are the worst apps on the platform. An app that tries to diverge from the prescribed, expected design practices but doesn't have a prodigious amount of work and talent behind it is doomed. As described in the following list, the field of specialized apps that fail to justify their specialization is vast and varied.

- The use of standard interface elements for purposes and behaviors that are odd or frankly wrong.
- Custom controls that don't work anything like any standard control, don't behave reliably, break the suspension of disbelief (as described in Chapter 8), or otherwise don't live up to the expectations users have of iOS controls.
- Custom-drawn interfaces that fall far short of the top-notch visual-design standards set by Apple and expected by users.
- Apps that are really web apps with a veneer of faux-iOS styling but that still look and perform just like poorly optimized web sites.
- Apps designed and built with cross-platform libraries that promise to let developers deploy on a multitude of platforms with minimal effort, and thus generate lowest-common-denominator experiences that don't feel right on *any* platform. (Getting the feel of iOS's distinctive inertial scrolling wrong, for one example, is a dead giveaway.)

Mediocre specialized apps are still not nearly as good as mediocre consistent apps. The quality of output for specialized apps doesn't catch up with that of totally consistent apps until the quality of input is quite high. If you want to go very specialized, you must nail it. Your custom controls should be so well realized that no one would ever guess they didn't come built into the OS. If your app is secretly a web view, it should be so painstakingly crafted in both appearance and behavior that no one can tell the difference.

Of course, the graph shows only the most specialized and the most iOS-consistent approaches. In reality, almost any app will be somewhere in the middle, using some number of unique ideas while resting on a standardized foundation. The slope of the output curve for an in-between app depends on how much uniqueness you inject into its design. As long as you reserve novelty for situations where it's warranted and avoid using it so much that your app stops feeling at home on iOS, you can keep it from upsetting your overall balance and quality.

Summary

Design is all about finding equilibrium. Possibly the most important balance to aim for is that between consistency with other apps on the platform and specialization for the particular needs of your app. When you decide to stick to the precedents set by other apps, it should be for a good reason: that the needs of your app match the needs of those apps that came before. When you decide to diverge from the precedents, it should also be for a good reason: that your app's needs are unique or because you've genuinely found a better way.

Sticking to the expected is safer than setting out into new territory; the further you diverge, the more mastery will be expected of you. But doing something novel can, at times, be just the flourish you need to set your app apart from the others. Consistency is not an end in itself, only a means to an end.

Exercises

Here are some ways to think about where apps choose to stay consistent and where they choose to specialize.

1. Pick a general guideline from the HIG and try to imagine a situation where you think it would be justified to diverge from it. Or find an existing app that successfully diverges from the HIG, and think about why it succeeds.

2. Look around in Apple apps for precedents that seem modular enough that you could use them as a starting point for your own app. For each one you find, list the ways you could tweak it to be better for your own purposes. (And think about whether there's a good reason it's not that way already.)

3. Pick a well-regarded third-party app and try to find its roots. Which of its screens and interactions seem inspired by an Apple app or another third-party app? Which trends does it follow? Which parts are original?

15

Rich and Plain

I've saved the most conspicuous and controversial topic of software design for last: looks, appearance, aesthetics—how the pixels come together to create an image. Whether or not people recognize all the other work that has gone into the design of an app, almost anyone can glance at a screen and decide whether she likes the way it looks.

The overall aesthetic of an app is the most immediately apparent contributor to its personality. Just looking at what's built in to iOS, on one hand you have Mail, Safari, and other standard-looking, understated apps. On the other, you have Calendar, Contacts, and other bold, adventurous apps. What makes them different? Why would Apple choose one style or the other?

You can measure apps along a continuum from rich to plain, which can be roughly broken down into the contributions of three dimensions.

- **Color versus monochrome**—The greater the variety of hues in your interface and the brighter and more saturated the individual colors, the richer it seems.

- **Depth versus flatness**—The more your interface uses light and shadow effects to create an illusion of depth beyond the flat screen of the device, the richer it seems.

- **Realism versus digitality**—Emulating real-world objects and practices tends to have a richer feeling than creating an artificial, idealized experience.

Of course, no combination of these factors is inherently right or wrong. This chapter helps you decide which path through the jungle of possibilities you prefer, both for your app as a whole and from screen to screen within your app. The decisions you make about your app's appearance will affect its potential audience just as much as the decisions you make about its feature set. You should make these decisions definitively. The app you end up with should always feel internally consistent, no matter where you choose to fit in among other apps.

Personal tastes come into play strongly here. Decide to make your app's interface dark and subdued? Bam! You've attracted a huge swath of people who like a professional, serious app, and you've scared off those who prefer a fun-looking app. Decide to use textured surfaces and realistically rendered objects? Boom! You've earned the interest of people who browse for slick UIs on Dribbble and have earned the derision of people who laugh at slick UIs on Skeu It.

If you're a pessimist, it may seem you just can't win. But cheer up. It's liberating to think that no matter what you do, someone will dislike it, so you may as well do what you like best. If someone doesn't like the path you choose, let her take on the job of finding another path through the jungle. Don't ignore complaints, because some of them can help you figure out where you're falling short of your vision. But don't worry about the people who are just upset that your vision is different from theirs.

Color versus Monochrome

Chapter 5, The Mockups, introduces some color theory and the HSB (hue, saturation, brightness) color model. HSB works great for design, because each of its dimensions maps to an effect on human perception.

Using Hue

Some hues tend to be associated at least loosely with a feeling, based on both instinct and culture. For most people in the Western world, at least, blue and green seem relatively safe and encouraging; red and amber elicit caution; brown and beige feel organic; blacks and grays feel industrial and cold, and so on. This is a vague and slippery effect, so you can't count on it as communication, but you should have it in mind as you choose colors so that you can give hints and avoid misuse.

The more hues that are visible on the screen, the richer and noisier the interface seems. Many apps stick to a handful of hues across their entire interface, often with one main hue for each screen; the exceptions tend to be a few important color cues in temporary areas such as popovers, modal views, and action sheets. The more content focused an app is, the more likely its interface is to stay out of the way by being neutral and monochromatic.

For large swaths of color like backgrounds and bars, ordinary elements that don't need special attention drawn to them, or color choices that for whatever reason need to stay innocuous, your best bet is to stick with the following safe hues.

- Blue, at around 215° on your HSB color picker, is a typical theme color throughout iOS. It appears in the standard toolbar, the pinstripe background, the common blue text (as in autocorrect suggestions and table cell labels), the standard popover frame, and numerous other places. It's usually desaturated in most places where it appears, from 1% on keyboard buttons up to 50% at the bottom of a standard toolbar. It's hard to go wrong with a nice desaturated blue.

- The hueless black, white, and gray are also safe, although the more you use them the colder and less friendly your interface becomes. It's hard to find completely desaturated grayscale anywhere in standard iOS interfaces, apart from content such as the black-on-pale-gray of a standard table cell. Surfaces that appear gray, such as the keyboard or the common linen texture, are often actually gently saturated 215° blue. It's also uncommon to find pure black pixels in iOS, apart from text, because it too is an unrealistic color. Most of what seems black around us is actually reflecting a tiny bit of light.

- Brown and beige are commonly considered "neutral," at least in art and interior design; in HSB they're actually variants of red, orange, or yellow. These are the warm counterparts to the typical blue. You can get away with using these colors as a theme for your app without its feeling overwhelming, because humans are used to wood- and earth-colored surfaces, objects, and spaces. Brown and beige will give your app an organic, natural, traditional feeling—think iBooks—rather than the cool, technological feeling of blues and grays.

The bigger the area covered by a color, the more its hue takes over the atmosphere of the screen. That's generally fine for blue or brown, the hues that users expect to see everywhere in iOS. But even the faintest pink or pale green can make a potent difference in the feeling of an app if it covers the entire background. Thus, hues other than the safe ones are usually used sparingly to draw special attention to something, such as a logo, a weighty interaction (see Chapter 13, Friction and Guidance), or an abnormal status.

Occasionally an organization whose branding relies heavily on a vivid color like bright red tries to saturate its official app with its "identity": bright red toolbars, bright red text, bright red controls. The result is tense and irritating (see Figure 15.1).

Figure 15.1   If the branding you're working with is based on a vivid color, you don't have to go totally unbranded to stay tasteful. Avoid obnoxiously bright and saturated colors, and be selective in the places you apply them. The "decent" example here uses a custom white Done button to avoid clashing between strong red and blue, and a desaturated, darker variant of red in its toolbar and in part of its detail text.

Designers who understand branding know that vivid identity colors are more effective when they're reserved for a logo and a few flourishes here and there, and not smeared across an entire app (or catalog or store). If you want to use a certain hue for branding reasons, you may need to adjust its saturation or brightness to keep it from looking garish. When it's subdued, red can be a perfectly pleasant theme color.

Using Saturation

Very saturated colors are rare in iOS interfaces. Usually, there is content that deserves more attention than the UI furniture, so the interface elements need to avoid being too prominent.

Furthermore, intensely saturated colors almost never appear in the real world anyway. If you take a sample from a photograph of an object you consider to have vivid color—a leaf, a flower, a book cover—you'll rarely find a saturation greater than 80%. Even the most saturated of iOS control styles—such as the blue of a Done button in a toolbar or the red of a Delete button in an action sheet—top out at 78% and 88% saturation, respectively. Real life has a lot of gray mixed into it, so iOS doesn't need to get saturated to achieve its trademark slightly hyperrealistic look.

It's easy to toss in 100%-saturated, totally pure colors, but unless you have a great reason for it, you shouldn't ever ship something that saturated. Avoid it like a retina-scorching plague. Because it's quick to code up these colors in RGB just to get something onto the screen for testing purposes, this book affectionately calls them "programmer's colors."

- **Pure red**—#FF0000 or rgb(255, 0, 0). Not even stop signs are this red, but you commonly see it used in software for warnings, or even as a text color.
- **Pure green**—#00FF00 or rgb(0, 255, 0). This color is especially intense because humans are so sensitive to green. Almost nothing in reality is nearly this saturated, so its presence in a design is a dead giveaway to your brain that you're looking at something fake, thus breaking the suspension of disbelief necessary to get immersed in a software experience. Not to mention that it almost hurts to look at.
- **Pure blue**—#0000FF or rgb(0, 0, 255). This is the least offensive of the programmer's colors, because blue is a dark hue anyway. But it still tends to look odd and uncanny when it appears among realistic colors.
- **Pure yellow**—#FFFF00 or rgb(255, 255, 0).
- **Pure magenta**—#FF00FF or rgb(255, 0, 255).
- **Pure cyan**—#00FFFF or rgb(0, 255, 255).

Figure 15.2 is only an approximation, because these colors can't be reproduced in print. They're possible on screen because the display is shooting photons into your eye, whereas a printed page is merely reflecting the available light.

Figure 15.2   The best approximation that can be made in print of the hypervivid "programmer's colors." If these colors ship in an app, something has gone wrong.

Using Brightness

In Chapter 5, you learned that the brightness of individual elements and their component parts is important for determining their value so that you can create good contrast. But you also need to consider the overall brightness of each screen.

Very dark interfaces tend to feel techy, stereotypically cool, and possibly intimidating. Bright backgrounds give you the best opportunity for high contrast, because people are used to reading black-on-white text. But it can be fatiguing to stare at overly bright screens in most lighting situations except for direct sunlight, so you should consider how you imagine people using your app. And elements with too much contrast between them can lose their coherence as part of a single layer: a standard grouped table cell is not really white but 97%-brightness gray, to blend in better with its subdued pinstripe background.

Bright elements can also steal focus away from content. For apps dedicated to content, especially reading, it's best to use a scheme that balances strong contrast with a brightness that's tuned for comfort. iBooks serves as a good example of smart approaches to brightness. It offers three themes to choose from, and each for a good reason (see Figure 15.3).

- The original White theme is black-on-white (actually 97%-brightness gray again, because pure white is too intense), for a reading experience that looks like a book in daylight.

- The Sepia theme is brown-on-beige (a hue of about 45°). The slightly dimmer, warmer colors are much easier on users' eyes when they're reading in a room with artificial light, which is important for human health. That's because when your brain sees pure white light, it interprets it as sunlight and keeps you awake. Thus, staring at computer screens at night can cause sleep problems. The orange-colored light of typical light bulbs and of the Sepia theme is more like fire,

Figure 15.3   iBooks' White, Sepia, and Black themes are carefully tuned to combine with the brightness adjustment to provide comfortable reading in any surroundings.

which humans have spent hundreds of thousands of years getting used to seeing at night.

- The Night theme is designed for times when you don't have any other light on in the room at all. In that case, when your pupils are dilated as wide as they can get, even the Sepia theme at minimum brightness would be much too bright (although even the black areas glow a bit, until we have OLED iPads). Not to mention that it benefits the person right next to you in bed, who's trying to sleep while you're turning page after page of the latest from George R.R. Martin.

These themes, plus the in-app brightness slider, make it easy to adjust the appearance of the screen to match what a real page would look like given your current lighting conditions. (If you have a white iPad, you can even use its border as a reference.) For most apps, you should of course choose a single theme that makes sense for the typical use (possibly one inspired by these three). But Apple recognized that people are likely to spend hours and hours in iBooks, so it paid attention to its brightness needs (and hue needs) accordingly.

Depth versus Flatness

Depth is a powerful cue. Whether you plan for it or not, every element you present has some degree of apparent depth: either its visual effects cause the eye to read it as protruding or receding from the screen, or it appears as flat. If you pay attention, you can take advantage of the perception of depth to send hints about the various elements of each screen.

If you look carefully around iOS, you'll realize that almost everything has at least some tiny amount of depth: the drop shadow on the clock digits of the lock screen, the inner shadow of a search field, the underhighlight of a grouped table, the gradient of a toolbar. Depth is everywhere.

It's not just for fun. Carefully tuned depth styling helps the user in several ways.

- It subtly hints at the layer structure of an app, such as which parts are controls and which are content. Most of the depth effects in a good iOS app are quiet enough to work at a subconscious level until you look for them. In that way, they subtly help your brain make sense of the layers present.

- Many effects help the legibility of elements, especially text. A slight white underhighlight on dark text, for instance, helps define the contour of each character and create good contrast against a medium background. Overzealous effects, though, detract from legibility. Lay off the stark black shadows and bright white highlights; instead, use transparency to blend into the background.

- And, yes, it looks cool. On iOS, just splatting some flat text or a flat shape onto a background tends to look cheap and unfinished. Taking the time to think about how the element relates to the surface it's on—whether it's resting on top, etched, or inset—shows the kind of polish people have come to expect from high-quality iOS apps.

Generally speaking, elements with some depth appear more permanent and seem to belong to the app itself: controls, labels, explanatory text, and so on. Text etched into a background seems to be an integral part of the background, and not simply printed on top of it. A flat treatment, on the other hand, tends to evoke printedness, like text on paper. Flat elements seem more like content and thus seem more mutable: data that the user can edit, values that can be swapped out for other values, stuff pulled from the Internet, and the like.

Consider Mail. The cells that appear in the message list in Mail come and go all day long as emails arrive and are filed away; they're little chunks of content. The user expects to see different stuff in the list every time he visits. The controls surrounding the content, though, clearly exist in a distinct, permanent layer (See Chapter 4, The Wireframes). Their depth cues, including their nearly invisible little drop shadows, clearly separate them from the flat stuff in the middle. The result is a sense that the navigation bar and toolbar belong to the app, whereas the messages belong to the user. Likewise, in Settings, the immutable sections listed in the sidebar are presented as beveled cells bearing etched text, whereas the editable options are presented as flat white cells with flat black text.

Lighting

The way your eyes recognize depth in the real world is by taking advantage of binocular vision and by recognizing how light is reflected from surfaces. Binocular vision doesn't do you any good on a completely flat display that sends the same image to both eyes, so software designers need to suggest depth by relying on lighting effects alone.

In reality, objects reflect light to your eyes from a source, and the relationship between the source, the object, and you determines how your brain processes the resulting image. Highlights appear on the edge closest to the light, shadows appear on the opposite side from the light, and the surfaces between tend to have a gradation of light from one side to the other. Of course, objects on the screen can't react realistically to the lighting conditions of the space around the device. (Not yet, anyway. The volume knob in the Music app on iPhone subtly shifts its lighting effect as you tilt the phone around, possibly portending the environment-aware interfaces of the future.) Any light actually reflected by the display is overpowered by the light being emitted from within it. So the device needs to bring its own light source, as it were, and simulate lighting effects based on assumptions about the kind of light each screen should pretend to be reflecting.

Here's a rule that should not be broken: everything in iOS is lit from directly above. Everything. (OK, sure, games are exempt.) You can picture an imaginary light fixed above the display, moving with it and sending the same uniform flood of photons from the same direction, no matter what's on the screen. For each element you style, you need to recognize where the light is coming from and establish an illusion of reality. Here are the most common lighting effects you'll need (see Figure 15.4 for examples).

- **Drop shadow**—This is a slightly blurred area of darkness that appears directly below the element and conforms to its shape, to suggest that the element is blocking some of the light source. This effect sends the message that the element is protruding from the background. Drop shadows don't need to be very strong; too broad a shadow makes the element seem to be protruding or hovering unnecessarily far toward the viewer; too dark or too sharp a shadow makes the light source seem harsh.

- **Inner bevel**—This is a highlight on the element's top, often accompanied by a shadowed area on its bottom. It makes the element appear to have a rounded or chamfered edge, as most real-world objects do (perfectly sharp 90° angles are difficult to find in reality).

- **Underhighlight**—Basically, this is a drop shadow that's light instead of dark. Rather than represent an absence of light caused by a protruding element, it represents the light source bouncing off a bevel or chamfer surrounding an element. The eye reads the element as either flush with or recessed into the background.

- **Reverse drop shadow**—This drop shadow appears above the element rather than below it. On iOS, it exists almost exclusively to give light-valued text a recessed look, because an underhighlight would muddy its contour.

- **Inner shadow**—This slightly blurred area of darkness appears *inside* the element, conforming to its top. It makes the element appear to be recessed from the background.

- **Gradient**—This is a gradual change in value across the surface of an element. A moderate gradient that starts out light at the top and becomes darker toward the bottom is standard for most flat surfaces; it reads as the light subtly shifting as it hits different parts of the surface, and the result looks more realistic. It doesn't take a very strong gradient to get the point across; most people never notice the gentle gradient that's applied to the standard pinstripe background, but it's there, and it helps the screen seem real. A stronger light-to-dark gradient makes an element appear convex, which matches well with drop shadows and inner bevels; the opposite makes an element appear concave, which matches well with under-highlights and inner shadows.

Users expect some depth, and thus some lighting, on anything that appears in certain areas of the interface: pinstripe backgrounds, toolbars and navigation bars, buttons, and almost anything else that's not pure content (such as the flat, black-on-white contents of a typical table view). If you leave your text or graphics completely flat and devoid of lighting effects in those areas, they're bound to look unfinished (unless you're going for an intentionally flat design, as described next.)

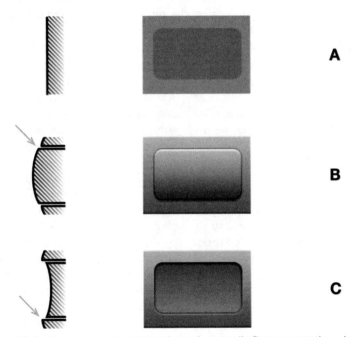

A

B

C

Figure 15.4   Some typical styling recipes. A, a totally flat presentation, doesn't look interactive at all. The toolbar and button in B look convex because of their light-to-dark gradient. The button in B seems to protrude because of its inner bevel and its drop shadow. The button in C seems to be recessed and concave because of its inner shadow, underhighlight, and reverse gradient. The orange arrow shows the edges where the light source creates highlights.

Extremes of Flatness and Depth

Occasionally, a designer decides to intentionally push her app toward a flatter or a deeper presentation than what's typically seen on iOS. She knows that a normal app is a few millimeters deep, but her vision is more extreme. These apps are not necessarily wrong, but it's a lot harder to get them right. When a developer decides to diverge from the norm, the burden is on her to justify it.

Here are examples of apps that decided to diverge and pulled it off successfully (see Figure 15.5).

- **Letterpress** is a word game with a unique visual presentation. Unlike most other word games at the App Store, Letterpress doesn't simulate a real-world board game by representing the letters as wooden or plastic tiles. Instead, it uses an almost completely flattened style. Elements are drawn without gradients or lighting effects, and the only hint of depth is temporary: when a player lifts a piece and moves it around, it gains a drop shadow to illustrate that it's moving in front of the rest of the board. The flattened world of Letterpress works well for several reasons. Nearly everything is interactable, so there isn't much need to differentiate controls from content; the animation is lively and believable, preserving the user's sense of being in a consistent world with reliable rules; and the finesse of its color, typography, and layout makes it lovely to look at.

- **Track 8** is a music app that adopts Microsoft's design language for Windows Phone (formerly known as "Metro"). This exceptionally flattened style is a famous response to the depth and faux tactility of iOS. Unlike most iOS competitors, the Windows Phone team commendably decided to run in the opposite direction from what Apple was doing. Instead of attempting to simulate realistic surfaces, Track 8 takes its inspiration from typography and print design: it relies on solid fields of color with crisp edges, makes judicious use of spacing and alignment, and uses the metaphor of navigating around a single huge landscape of content rather than moving from screen to screen. Microsoft calls this approach "authentically digital" because it takes pride in living in the idealized world of the screen, rather than emulating reality. The from-scratch reimplementation of the Microsoft experience on iOS without the benefit of the Windows Phone API is impressive, and it's the closest thing you'll get to seeing what it's like to be a Windows Phone user without actually buying a WP device. It's also proof of how the design language of a different platform can succeed on iOS as long as it's executed flawlessly. The app isn't for everyone, but it is a delight for those who recognize it as a fun experiment and who don't mind visiting a foreign interaction scheme from time to time.

- **GarageBand** seems to be Apple's playground for especially realistic interfaces. It makes sense, given how much people in the music equipment industry have already developed their own visual language in the form of specialized hardware like instruments, effects pedals, amplifiers, and mixing boards. Rather than try

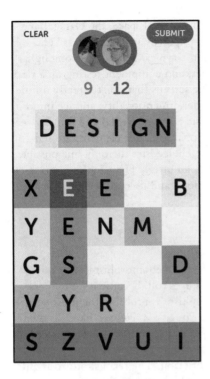

Figure 15.5   Letterpress (top left) succeeds at inventing its own simple, flattened aesthetic. Track 8 (top right) adopts the print-inspired Windows Phone aesthetic. GarageBand (bottom) is notoriously aggressive in its use of depth.

to reinvent the experience of making music in a virtual space, the GarageBand designers embraced the rich imagery of real equipment and ran with it. The result is an app that has much more depth than a typical app, with strong lighting effects, richly rendered knobs and switches, and equipment resting on a floor that recedes far into the background. Even the screens that don't directly mimic a real piece of equipment still draw on the style, dimensionality, and feeling of real equipment. It works because making music is experimental and fun anyway, and of course because all the unconventional interface elements are reliably implemented. Note well that this stylistic choice isn't the only one possible. It's entirely possible that someone could create an utterly plain-looking music app that did all the same things GarageBand does, and it could well be just as successful.

Realism versus Digitality

You've made it this far without encountering the term "skeuomorphism," but no longer. Just mentioning the word can make people's eyes roll, because it's often misused or assigned a purely pejorative tone. Skeuomorphism is probably the most volatile topic in iOS design at the moment, and anyone you ask is likely to have his own strongly held view. It's a mine field. But it's an important idea that can't be ignored. Let's do this.

In case you haven't bumped into it yet, here's a briefing. The term **skeuomorphic** comes from archaeology and anthropology; it originally described the way some artifacts exhibit features emulating artifacts of an older or more prestigious kind. Pottery was made to look like baskets, or architectural features of wooden buildings were reproduced on stone buildings where they no longer had any function. So a skeuomorph is a vestige of one technology that's used on another technology where it isn't necessary.

Around the dawn of the iOS era, the term also came to be used to describe the way some software interfaces emulate real-world objects. It's an academic-sounding, know-it-all kind of word, often applied derisively and with an air of superiority, in that way people seem to have of labeling what you're doing to indicate it's no good. "Oh, you're going *skeuomorphic,* huh? I thought good designers had outgrown that." But in reality, the various design techniques that get labeled this way are neither always good nor always bad; as with everything, you need to exercise good taste and sensible reasoning to make a decision for each situation.

Almost as intense as the debate about the merits of skeuomorphic design is the debate about the strict definition of the word "skeuomorphic" itself as it applies to software. Some people insist that the word can apply only to unintended, spontaneously emergent features and not to consciously designed ones. Others start crying, "Skeu!" as soon as they see a gradient or a drop shadow. For the purposes of this book, I break it into a few dimensions rather than take it as a binary descriptor that can be definitively identified for a given design. What follows is a tour of the various characteristics that have been called out as skeuomorphic, along with advice on their merits and hazards. These categories are fuzzy. They overlap and blend together, but it's helpful to have the vocabulary and theory to think and talk about decisions about realism and digitality.

Texture and Tactility

The most innocent way to base a design on real objects is to borrow materials. The toolbar in Pages looks like leather (as if from a desk blotter), and the ruler looks like wood; but that's only styling. Those elements needed to have some kind of surface, so the designers decided that they might as well choose those materials and hark back to high-quality writing supplies of yore. It's not really a metaphor, because the user doesn't need to have ever met a leather blotter or a wooden ruler to grasp what these elements are about. The result adds a bit of charm, character, and tradition to the app without harming its usability.

It may even help usability a bit. Those textures suggest permanence and invite interaction, differentiating them from the content. And choosing distinctive materials gives each app a unique feeling, thus gently helping people to recognize which app they're in and recall how to use it.

If the designers had decided not to call upon real-world materials, the app would still function the same, but with different styling choices. One could argue that even the shelf view in iBooks is laid out no differently than it would have been if it had an "authentically digital" presentation. Arranging cover art in a grid makes a lot of sense, whether or not it's against the backdrop of a virtual wooden bookshelf.

Metaphor

For as long as consumer software has existed, designers have been using metaphor to help users make sense of how software works. The desktop metaphor—with its documents, folders, and trash cans—made the original Macintosh interface well loved and successful. In fact, several of the "desk accessories" (or "desk ornaments" as they were called at first) in the original Macintosh operating system in 1984 featured designs that directly mimicked real objects in appearance and behavior. (See Figure 15.6.)

But those metaphors were invented to ease the learning of people who had never interacted with a computer before and thus needed extra help making sense of it. Now there is less and less need to refer to office supplies in order to make a piece of software understandable. In fact, many members of the younger generation using technology today have never seen a manila folder (or plenty of other objects that designers often want to refer to). Accordingly, "folders" on the iOS home screen and in the iWork document browser don't actually look anything like folders; instead, they use an abstract style that helps you preview what's inside.

The question is whether it helps to use a real-world metaphor to explain the behavior of objects in your software. Almost every time you're tempted to use one, try it without the metaphor and see if it still works. Do the projects in your task management app need to look like lined index cards, arrayed haphazardly on a corkboard?

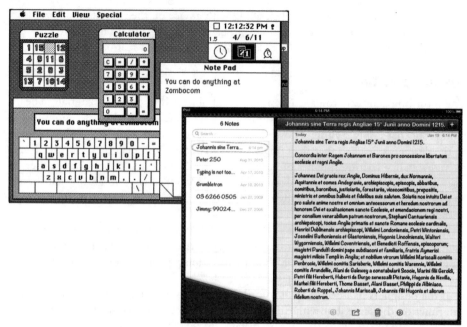

Figure 15.6 The use of office supply metaphors goes all the way back to 1984. This sort of metaphor can be cute and comforting, but it also limits you and can be seen as tacky.

Or could they just as well be anonymous, tactile-looking rectangles tidily arranged on a beautiful, textured background? Just because Apple recommends designing apps to have physicality and realism doesn't mean you should necessarily also design them to be nostalgic.

Sometimes, you may decide that the metaphor really does help. That's fine, as long as you've honestly considered the alternatives. Built-in apps like Notes and Calendar replicate office supplies as best they can. But those apps don't do much more than their real-world counterparts. They're very focused (see Chapter 11, Focused and Versatile), so they can more or less get away with their cute, retro presentations, conforming to the limitations of the objects they're recalling (as with Calendar showing one month per "page," rather than letting you scroll between them). For users who don't care for it, an App Store full of minimally designed alternatives (such as Elements and Calvetica) awaits. For designers who don't care for it, a business opportunity may exist in creating elegant, inventive alternatives to twee, backward-looking apps.

Ornamentation

Some designs go out of their way to add decoration. They not only choose a real-world object as inspiration for styling the essential UI elements that were present in the wireframe, but also they add nonfunctional trappings from a real-world object at the visual-design phase.

The top bar in Find My Friends doesn't just bear a leather texture; it also consumes an extra 10 points of vertical space to make room for stitching. Some users may find this charming; others may resent those 10 points. The situations in which an extra 10 points' worth of content would have made a difference are probably rare. But on principle, encroaching on content for functionless embellishment is enough to make some people shake their heads. (Not to mention the apparent impossibility of the content area, which the toolbar is apparently stitched on to, scrolling freely.)

In the debate about ornamentation in Apple interfaces, perhaps the most emblematic snippet of screen is the area just below the toolbar in the Calendar app for iPad (see Figure 15.7). In keeping with the conceit that the app is a reincarnation of a desktop calendar, there are shreds of torn-off paper sticking to a strip of adhesive. Some people never notice them. Some see them, smile at the touch of realism, and then carry on.

But for a person preoccupied with order and tidiness, those shreds of paper are a constant irritation. "Isn't technology supposed to be *less* messy than reality? On a real calendar I wouldn't be able to relax until I pulled off those shreds, but here they'll never, ever go away." And so on. Again, it's the principle that the designers went out of their way to make the software look imperfect, just to show off, thus inducing anxiety in certain people every time they open the app. It would be trivial to remove the shreds, but now Apple's pride is on the line; if it ever makes the change, it'll be an admission that its cute little joke was a bad idea. (In fact, Apple eventually offered a setting to turn off the superfluous page edges in iBooks after enduring a lot of ridicule.)

As Robert Bringhurst said of overly dramatic typography and book design, "The script of Macbeth does not need to be bloodstained and spattered with tears; it needs to be legible." If you haven't got it yet, the point of this section is that fanciful ornamentation may be impressive or endearing, but it's just as likely to provoke the pet peeves of some subset of your audience. Whether the decoration is worth the risk of bothering some users is a decision only you can make.

Simulation

At a certain point, imitating a real-world object goes beyond metaphor and enters the realm of simulation. You're not just using a familiar experience to help the user understand the original constructs of your app. Instead, the entire purpose of such an app

Figure 15.7 The divisive adhesive strip in Calendar for iPad and its vexatious torn paper.

is to re-create an experience as faithfully as possible in digital form, albeit likely with some conveniences that are possible only in software.

Much of GarageBand is simulation: the drums, piano keyboard, and guitars. The modes that both look like a guitar and behave like a guitar are delightful for anyone to play with. Simulation works best when the system can faithfully re-create the experience of using the real thing.

The simplified, remapped modes that look like a guitar but behave very differently, on the other hand, can feel wrong to a lifelong guitarist. Rather than simulation, those modes are more accurately described as new experiences with a highly stylized, guitar-like veneer. Their similarity in appearance to the simulation mode and to real-world guitars is uncanny and even mildly disturbing (see Figure 15.8).

The lesson of GarageBand is that the more faithfully your interface resembles a familiar object, especially one that the user has a strong, emotional relationship with, the more it will be expected to work like that object. Some users can, of course, come to terms with a disconnection between the design and the functionality, but some may

Figure 15.8   The guitar simulation breaks down. A guitar fretboard with no frets, hovering in front of the body of the same guitar. A tiny replica of the guitar itself, a couple of tiny effects pedals, and a couple of controls that have no place on a real guitar. The mind of a guitarist finds this tableau unnerving.

never get over the weirdness of it. You need to weigh the benefits of the resemblance against the ways your implementation falls short of the real thing.

Take It Easy

Although they can be harmless or even helpful when used carefully, the various practices that get labeled as skeuomorphism can get you into trouble if you go overboard. An app that fanatically replaces every interface element with hyperrealistic, richly styled metal and wood and leather and fabric is likely to feel much too dramatic compared with other apps on the system. Especially if the app fulfills a mundane, modest purpose, users are likely to wonder what the big deal is and perhaps grow skeptical of the merits of your app.

Any shortcoming is likely to make people wonder why you put so much effort into the visuals but didn't bother to make the thing work right. Put another way, if you're selling a platinum-plated, ruby-encrusted can opener, you have a lot of work to do to justify its apparent pretentiousness. Not to mention that developing and maintaining such extravagant styling is certain to eat into the time and resources you have for more worthy pursuits, such as all the design work that takes place outside Photoshop.

Furthermore, think about the future. Once you've designed your precise replica of whatever device or tool your app emulates so that it perfectly fills the screen space, where will you put the new features? As other apps get revisions to the standard controls along with the rest of the OS for free, will you be all right sticking with the same old custom design you've always had? Will you be ready to rethink the whole thing to accommodate future versions? You *are* planning for future versions, right? What happens when you add a feature that doesn't fit into the metaphor you've spent so much time investing in? The last thing you want is to be seen as yet another Photoshop-skills showcase app that sells itself on gorgeous screenshots but includes fatal bugs, has no customer support, and never gets updated. A clean, standard, modular, straightforward design will be worlds easier to iterate on and update well into the future.

Summary

A huge share of the personality of your app comes from how rich or plain its presentation is. A richer interface can be more memorable, more distinctive, and more fun to make and to look at, but it's also more distracting and has the potential to become tiresome. The plainer your interface is, the safer you will be from irritating individual tastes (if that is important to you) and the easier it will be to work on into the future.

Richness can also communicate. Color is a powerful cue for setting an atmosphere or guiding a user toward or away from a certain action. Depth helps you define your app's layers and identify which elements are interactive controls; flatness helps identify content that belongs to the user. Realism and the mimicry of physical objects can be a charming and informative way to approach your app's design, but it can also easily lead to a divisive app that's hard to maintain.

Exercises

Here are ways you can develop your talent for making a screen work within a given set of styling constraints.

1. Try mocking up a screen for an app that successfully incorporates a brand identity. Get the identity colors in there in a way that doesn't overwhelm the rest of the interface or feel ostentatious compared with other iOS apps.

2. From any standard-looking app, pick a screen containing a healthy amount of both content and controls, and create a totally flat version. This is hard. Without lighting to rely on, the only tools you have to work with are your layout (alignment, whitespace, and typography) and the contrast between flat fields of color.

3. Take a screen from an app that tries to imitate reality (Calendar is a good choice) and mock up a less nostalgic variant. Pretend you're following the same wireframe by keeping all the elements in the same place and obeying the same navigation scheme, but present the elements in a minimal and idealized way: the smooth glass, plastic, and metal of an app like Safari.

Index

Scope bar, as standard control, 50
Scope, choosing app, 224–225
Screens
    elements adjacent in space on single, 238–239
    elements as building blocks of. *See* Elements
    manual undo and, 189
    mockup assembly and, 106–107
    navigating. *See* Navigation
    for paper prototypes, 113–114
    tab bar dominance on, 36
    thinking in terms of, 55–57
    for Wizard of Oz prototypes, 114–115
    workflow sketches of paths between, 26–29
Screenshot Journal app, 60
Screenshots, 81–82, 204
Scrolling, 74–75, 79
Search bar, as standard control, 50
Section headers, plain table view, 44
Security, respecting user data, 216
Segmented controls, 50
Segmented-controls-as-tabs, 36–37
Selection, as visible status, 178–179
Self-guided tour, of your app, 240–241
Semiotic engineering, 169
The Semiotic Engineering of Human-Computer Interaction (de Souza), 169
Sensible defaults, 265–269
Sepia theme, iBooks, 289–290
Service, customer, 211
Settings app
    gear imagery for, 171
    grouped table view in, 44, 66
    subtitle cell style for Notifications screen of, 45
    value 1 cells for, 45
Settings-like split view navigation, 33–34
Shading, 58–59, 62–63
Shake to Undo gesture, 188
Shape layer, creating custom buttons, 101–102
Shine effect, app icons, 202
Shortcuts, 27–29, 154
Shorthand, using precedents, 276
Signatures, Mac Mail, 132
Signup experience, reducing friction in, 260–261
Silence, in failed feedback, 147
Similarity, layout principle of, 64
Simulation, of real-world objects, 299–301
Single-taps, 148
Size, visual weight and, 64–65
Sketching
    creating paper prototypes, 114
    creating versatile app, 233–235
    creating Wizard of Oz prototypes, 114–115
    exercises, 29
    exploring design ideas with, 15
    interactions, 24–26

interfaces, 22–24
    playing devil's advocate using, 22
    rubber ducking and, 17–18
    situations for, 20–21
    sketchiness of, 19–20
    summary review, 29
    thinking by, 15–16
    through conversation, 16–18
    tools for, 18–19
    using precedents, 21–22
    wireframes vs., 55–56
    workflows, 26–29
Sketching User Experiences (Buxton), xxvii, 15
Skeuomorphic design
    metaphors, 297–298
    ornamentation, 298–299
    overview of, 301
    simulation, 299–301
    taking it easy, 301
    texture and tactility, 297
Skeuomorphism, 301
Skinner, B.F., 183
Skinning standard controls, harmless distinctiveness, 279
Slicy app, 106–107, 202–203
Slide to unlock, adding friction with, 259
Slider, as standard control, 51
SnackLog sample app
    Five Whys and, 197–198
    as focused app, 228–230
    introduction to, 8–9
    making forthcoming, 252–253
    making graceful, 163–164
    making gracious, 191–193
    making quiet, 251–252
Specialized design
    conscientious divergence in, 279–280
    consistency vs., 271–272
    difficulty of novelty, 282–283
    exercises, 284
    getting the most of HIG, 272–273
    harmless distinctiveness in, 279
    how it all works out, 271–272
    one novel interaction per app, 280–281
    overview of, 278
Spinning indicator
    progress indicators vs. quietness of, 251
    pull-to-refresh in Mail using, 158
    for response of more than three seconds, 148
    threshold for, 148
Split view
    as content view, 43
    current context modal view in, 38
    presenting navigation with, 34–35
Stacked in time, 237, 239–240

FREE
Online Edition

Your purchase of *Learning iOS Design* includes access to a free online edition for 45 days through the **Safari Books Online** subscription service. Nearly every Addison-Wesley Professional book is available online through **Safari Books Online**, along with over thousands of books and videos from publishers such as Cisco Press, Exam Cram, IBM Press, O'Reilly Media, Prentice Hall, Que, Sams, and VMware Press.

Safari Books Online is a digital library providing searchable, on-demand access to thousands of technology, digital media, and professional development books and videos from leading publishers. With one monthly or yearly subscription price, you get unlimited access to learning tools and information on topics including mobile app and software development, tips and tricks on using your favorite gadgets, networking, project management, graphic design, and much more.

Activate your FREE Online Edition at
informit.com/safarifree

STEP 1: Enter the coupon code: VSPQXAA.

STEP 2: New Safari users, complete the brief registration form. Safari subscribers, just log in.

If you have difficulty registering on Safari or accessing the online edition, please e-mail customer-service@safaribooksonline.com

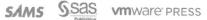